# OPERATION HURRICANE

The story of Britain's first atomic test
in Australia and the legacy that remains

## PAUL GRACE

*To B & T*

hachette
AUSTRALIA

Published in Australia and New Zealand in 2023
by Hachette Australia
(an imprint of Hachette Australia Pty Limited)
Gadigal Country, Level 17, 207 Kent Street, Sydney, NSW 2000
www.hachette.com.au

Hachette Australia acknowledges and pays our respects to the past, present and future Traditional Owners and Custodians of Country throughout Australia and recognises the continuation of cultural, spiritual and educational practices of Aboriginal and Torres Strait Islander peoples. Our head office is located on the lands of the Gadigal people of the Eora Nation.

 A catalogue record for this
work is available from the
National Library of Australia

ISBN: 978 0 7336 5054 3 (paperback)

Cover design by Luke Causby
Cover photographs courtesy of Australian War Memorial P00131.046 (plane) and P00444.045 (blast), and © West Australian Newspapers Limited (islands)
Map by MAPgraphics
Typeset in Adobe Sabon LT Std by Kirby Jones
Printed and bound in Australia by McPherson's Printing Group

MIX
Paper | Supporting
responsible forestry
FSC
www.fsc.org   FSC® C001695

The paper this book is printed on is certified against the Forest Stewardship Council® Standards. McPherson's Printing Group holds FSC® chain of custody certification SA-COC-005379. FSC® promotes environmentally responsible, socially beneficial and economically viable management of the world's forests.

# CONTENTS

# ABBREVIATIONS

| | |
|---|---|
| 2ACS | No 2 Airfield Construction Squadron RAAF |
| 5ACS | No 5 Airfield Construction Squadron RAAF |
| AERE | Atomic Energy Research Establishment (UK) |
| ARD | Armament Research Department (UK) |
| ASIO | Australian Security Intelligence Organisation |
| AWRE | Atomic Weapons Research Establishment (UK) |
| BCOF | British Commonwealth Occupation Force |
| DCA | Department of Civil Aviation |
| HER | High Explosives Research (UK) |
| Hurrex | Hurricane Executive (UK) |
| LCA | Landing Craft Assault |
| LCM | Landing Craft Mechanised |
| LST | Landing Ship Tank |
| NAAFI | Navy Army and Air Force Institutes (UK) |
| NOIC | Naval Officer in Charge |
| PMG | Postmaster-General's Department |
| RAAF | Royal Australian Air Force |
| RAE | Royal Australian Engineers |
| RAF | Royal Air Force |
| RAN | Royal Australian Navy |
| RANR | Royal Australian Naval Reserve |
| RANVR | Royal Australian Naval Volunteer Reserve |
| RE | Royal Engineers |
| RFA | Royal Fleet Auxiliary |
| RM | Royal Marines |
| RN | Royal Navy |

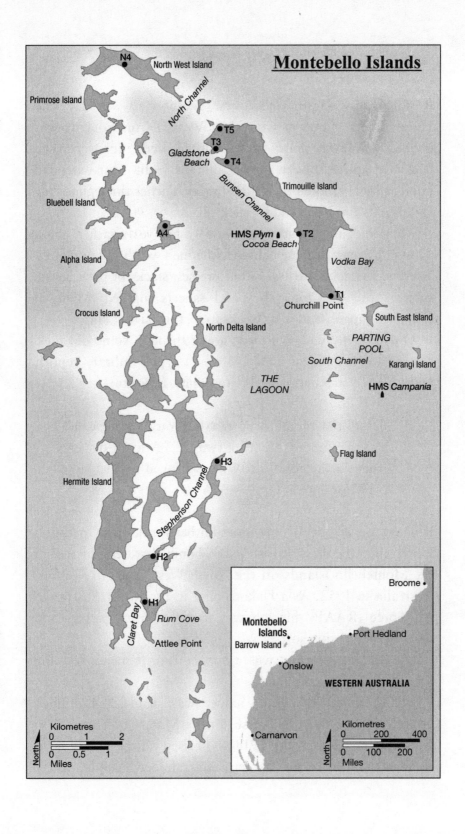

# Montebello Islands

N4
North West Island

Primrose Island

*North Channel*

T5

T3

*Gladstone Beach*

T4

Bluebell Island

*Bunsen Channel*

Trimouille Island

A4

Alpha Island

HMS *Plym*
*Cocoa Beach*

T2

*Vodka Bay*

Crocus Island

North Delta Island

T1
Churchill Point

South East Island

*PARTING POOL*

*South Channel*

Karangi Island

*THE LAGOON*

HMS *Campania*

Flag Island

H3

Hermite Island

*Stephenson Channel*

H2

H1

*Rum Cove*

*Claret Bay*

Attlee Point

Kilometres
0    1    2
0  0.5  1
Miles

North

Broome

Montebello
Islands

Port Hedland

Barrow Island

Onslow

WESTERN AUSTRALIA

Carnarvon

Kilometres
0    200    400
0  100  200
Miles

North

# AUTHOR'S NOTE

In 2016, my family made the decision to sell my late grandparents' home in Cottesloe, Western Australia. It was a rundown 1960s house with multiple sheds, an overgrown backyard and a sunken garden out the front. Our extended family often gathered there for Sunday lunches throughout my childhood, and I was sad to see it go.

My grandparents had passed away a few years earlier, about 12 months apart, leaving behind a lifetime's worth of belongings. There were cupboards full of old dresses, stacks of paperbacks, cabinets full of China cups and saucers marked 'Made in Occupied Japan'. It took us weeks to sort through it all.

One day, my dad, who was going through some old files, handed me a piece of paper. It was a typed military report, with short, sharp, numbered paragraphs. It began:

1) Before the Monte Bello test (Operation Hurricane) I was the Captain of one of two DC3 Aircraft detached from 36 Squadron 86 Wing stationed at Richmond, NSW for duty at Onslow, WA ...

It went on to detail my grandfather's role in Operation Hurricane, the first British atom-bomb test, conducted in the Montebello Islands off the North West Coast of Western Australia in 1952. As a Dakota pilot in the Royal Australian Air Force (RAAF), his job was to fly security patrols and 'coastal monitoring sorties'.

'Coastal monitoring' was a euphemism. It meant looking for fallout on the mainland.

My grandfather's full name was Ronald Campbell Grace. He was born in Nurse Jones's Maternity Hospital in Cottesloe on 26 October 1918 and raised on the family farm in Wyalkatchem in the Western Australian wheatbelt, where he studied to become a mechanic by correspondence. When the Second World War broke out, he tried to enlist in the RAAF as ground crew, but was rejected on medical grounds owing to a badly healed hernia operation. He joined the Army instead. While most of his mates shipped out to Singapore, only to become prisoners of war when Britain's 'impregnable fortress' fell to the Japanese, he was sent to Palestine as a driver mechanic with 2/3 Field Regiment, Royal Australian Artillery (RAA). In early 1942, the regiment was called back to Australia, and Ron, desperate for action, stuck his hand up for the Empire Air Training Scheme. This time he was accepted into the RAAF as aircrew.

Ron had a fascinating flying career. He qualified as a Halifax bomber pilot just in time to fly some of the very last missions over Germany with No 10 Squadron RAF. He stayed in the Air Force after the war, converting to Mustang fighters, which he flew on patrol out of Iwakuni, Japan, as part of the British Commonwealth Occupation Force (BCOF). After a couple of years on 'Civvy Street', he came off the Reserve list to serve in Korea, flying Dakota transports, with passengers including prime ministers and generals. For two years, he was mostly employed as a second pilot (co-pilot), and was pretty cranky about it, feeling that the job was beneath him. When he complained, he was given his own aircraft and sent to Onslow, Western Australia, to go looking for radioactive fallout. It was a case of be careful what you wish for.

I had always known that my grandfather was involved in a nuclear test, but never knew the details. When I was young, I found him to be an intimidating figure, and it did not seem like something I could ask about. Once, my Aunt Jill found a shot of an aircraft working on Operation Hurricane in a collection of old newspaper photographs. The plane was swooping low over a tent – very low. Just as a joke, I asked my grandfather, 'Is that you?'

He glanced at the photo and said, 'Yep, that was me.'

My eyes widened. 'How can you tell?' I asked.

'Well, there were only two of us up there, and the other bloke wouldn't fly that low', he growled. It was great hardboiled dialogue, but no more information was forthcoming.

So reading this report, in which my grandfather described his role in detail, was electrifying. It gave me an insight into his life and personality that I felt I did not have when he was alive. It also connected me, through him, to a fascinating moment in world history. Operation Hurricane made Britain the world's third nuclear power, and shifted the balance of power in the Cold War. It also marked the beginning of a long-term testing programme that would ultimately see 12 atom bombs detonated on Australian soil, with long-term ramifications for the environment and the health and wellbeing of Commonwealth servicemen and civilians, especially First Nations peoples.

The report also left me with a lot of questions. What the hell was going on up there? Why did the British Government feel the need to conduct its own atomic tests? And why on Earth did the Australian Government let them do it here?

I began reading. I found a few great books on the atomic testing programme, but none that covered the roles of the Australian services in Operation Hurricane in the level of detail I craved. Eventually it became clear that if I wanted to read a full history of the operation from an Australian perspective, I would have to write it myself.

At this time I was working in customer service for an educational organisation. I had a Bachelor of Arts (Honours) in English from Curtin University, majoring in Film and Television (ask me about the films of Akira Kurosawa sometime). Since graduating, I had spent most of my time working as a bookseller and film critic – talking about other people's work. I felt it was time to actually *do* something.

I also felt increasingly guilty about my lack of military service. My grandfather was not the only member of my family to serve this country. It's kind of the family business. Four of my great-great uncles fought in the First World War (two were killed in action). My maternal grandfather also joined the RAAF during the Second World War and worked as ground crew in New Guinea. My dad was sent to Vietnam as a National Serviceman and spent many years in the Special Forces. My brother drove an armoured personnel carrier in East Timor, then changed specialty and went to Afghanistan as a medic. My mother was a big wheel in the SAS Women's Auxiliary. Numerous uncles, aunts, cousins and sisters-in-law have served in all three services in both war and peacetime.

As a young man, I was more interested in movies and music than the military, but as I got older my feelings changed. I wanted to contribute in some way. Unfortunately, I was pushing 40, my back was stuffed, and I was genuinely alarmed by the prospect of doing sit-ups. Perhaps I could contribute in another way, though, by telling some of my family's stories.

So in 2018 I quit my job and began researching the nuclear tests fulltime. Over the next five years, I spent thousands of hours digging through archives, both physical and digital. I also interviewed some of the few remaining nuclear veterans and their wives, widows and descendants.

At first, I thought that establishing the facts and laying them out in order would be relatively simple, but I soon realised that everything about the nuclear tests is contested. British and Australian commentators tell markedly different narratives about the safety of the test programme. Nuclear veterans and Indigenous peoples dispute the official record, alleging that officers and scientists falsified reports to cover up mistakes and oversights. They also disagree with each other over what happened where and when, because of the passage of time and the fallibility of human memory. In retrospect, it was naïve of me to expect such a monumental task to be so straightforward.

In general, I have prioritised detailed contemporaneous reports over vague recollections made 70 years after the fact, unless there is a specific reason to suspect the veracity of a report. When an important document is missing, or redacted to the point of unintelligibility, I have leant more on the memories of the participants (with the appropriate caveats).

I had to make some tough judgement calls while weighing up all this evidence. Inevitably some people will disagree with some of my conclusions. I am sorry about that, but it would have been impossible to write this book otherwise. All I can say is that I have tried to be as fair and objective as possible, and have explained my reasoning and cited my sources.

I am conscious of the personal bias I bring to this endeavour. To be honest, I started out assuming I would take the side of the Australian servicemen in just about every argument with the British scientists, but that is not what happened in the end. The British boffins were not stupid – they were quite brilliant in many ways – and they got a lot right. But they did not get *everything* right. They made lots of mistakes here and there, and being rather arrogant and obsessed with security, they responded by covering them up. As a result, no one in Australia really trusts a word they say on the matter – especially the nuclear veterans, their families and the Indigenous communities who were inevitably affected.

A couple of notes on style: to evoke something of the feel of the era, I have used imperial measurements throughout. On the other hand, to avoid confusion, I opted for the standard two-word spelling for the Montebello Islands rather than the three-word variation that was common in the 1950s (i.e. 'the Monte Bello Islands').

# PROLOGUE

On the morning of Sunday 6 April 1952, two hulking Royal Navy ships arrived at the Cocos Islands, a tiny archipelago in the Indian Ocean. HM Ships *Zeebrugge* and *Narvik* were 2250-ton landing ships tank (LSTs) of the type that had carried out amphibious landings in Normandy, the Mediterranean and the Pacific during the Second World War. They were long and squat, with flat bottoms, huge bow doors and retractable ramps that allowed them to deploy tanks and troops on a captured beachhead. Both ships had been laid down too late to see action in the war but had since been given vital roles in the Cold War. Together, they comprised the 4th Landing Ship Squadron, the vanguard of an expedition to test the first British atom bomb at an undisclosed location somewhere in Australia.

Lining the decks of both ships, desperately craning their necks for a glimpse of the tropical islands, were some 480 officers, ratings and other ranks of the Royal Navy, Royal Marines, Royal Engineers and Royal Electrical and Mechanical Engineers. They had been at sea for six weeks, travelling from Portsmouth in England, via Gibraltar, Malta, Suez and Colombo, at the slow and steady rate of 12 knots, in ships so crowded that the marines, who were always hard done by, were forced to sleep in their landing craft for want of room elsewhere. The mission's secrecy had prevented shore leave at the earlier stops, and it had become clear to Captain George Colville, OBE, the 48-year-old Commanding Officer of HMS *Zeebrugge* and Senior Officer of the 4th Landing Ship Squadron, that his men needed to stretch their legs. He sent a message to the Royal Australian Air Force unit based at Cocos, asking for permission to stop by for a visit.

For the men of the Landing Squadron, the Cocos Islands, with their palm trees, white sands and turquoise waters, were a sight for sore eyes. Officially, the islands were administered by the British Colony of Singapore, but unofficially they were the personal fiefdom of the hereditary 'King of Cocos', John Clunies-Ross, a slim young Eurasian man who lorded over the colony of Malayan copra plantation workers on Cocos's Home Island in the manner of a benevolent patriarch. For strategic reasons, the islands were due to be transferred from Singapore to Australia, but negotiations were dragging on because of the difficulties created by the White Australia policy, which would render the Cocos Malays second-class citizens in their new home. In the meantime, the Australian Government had taken over an old wartime airstrip on Cocos's West Island with the intention of developing it into a civil airport and reserve airfield in times of war. The job of building it went to No 2 Airfield Construction Squadron RAAF (2ACS).

The Commanding Officer of 2ACS was Wing Commander PG 'Nobby' Lings, an experienced 45-year-old engineer from Perth, Western Australia. Lings's squadron consisted of 500-odd hardened construction workers and two nursing sisters. The airmen of 2ACS were used to living and working in remote locations: their last job had been at Woomera Rocket Range in South Australia, where they had spent four years building airfields in the middle of the desert. Their reward for finishing was to be sent straight to Cocos to do it all over again.

The squadron moved from Woomera to Cocos by sea in multiple stages from November 1951 to January 1952, transporting almost 4000 tons of equipment and supplies in the process. Owing to the shallow waters and dangerous reefs around Cocos, the heavy machinery had to be unloaded onto barges in a big swell 5 miles offshore. The airmen worked in three shifts, 24 hours a day, seven days a week, clearing trees, ripping up the old mesh airstrip, and mining the nearby coral reef for aggregate before commencing work on the airfield, where they went on to build a runway, control tower, roads and all the other buildings and facilities required in a modern airport.

Despite the idyllic surroundings, conditions were far from ideal. The airmen lived in tents, and were frequently assailed by centipedes, scorpions and giant crabs. Just before the main force arrived, the refrigeration units broke down, forcing the catering section to leave behind thousands of pounds of fresh meat and fish on the transport ship. Resupplies were delayed by protesting waterfront workers in Australia, and at one point the increasingly desperate cooks were forced to serve up boiled rice, barley and pawpaw, to the disgust of the airmen. The situation became a minor scandal when news of the deprivations reached the mainland press, leading to indignant denials from the RAAF and the Commonwealth Government.

The situation improved dramatically with the arrival of Wing Commander Lings and the rear guard with fresh supplies early in the new year. By the time the Landing Squadron arrived, work on the airport was proceeding apace, and morale had improved out of sight. The base now boasted excellent cricket and tennis facilities, a recreation hut with games and a radio, an open-air cinema, and an airmen's mess (wet) with a location to rival any pub in Australia. Situated on the seaward shore of West Island, the mess featured a marquee with 'a bar equivalent in size to the best in Kalgoorlie' and an open-air beer garden surrounded by palm trees.[1] Seated on four-gallon drums, off-duty airmen enjoyed a stunning view of the surf crashing on the nearby reef.

In response to Captain Colville's request, Wing Commander Lings gave the Landing Squadron permission to come ashore under one condition: no swimming. All along the western shoreline, a shallow coral shelf extended out to a reef some 200 yards offshore, where the ocean floor suddenly dropped away to a depth of 1500 feet, causing a thunderous break and a dangerous undertow. Accordingly, swimming in this area was strictly forbidden. Lings personally informed Colville of the standing order, and Colville passed on the information to his officers.

The LSTs anchored off West Island just after noon. Over the next few hours, hundreds of British servicemen swarmed ashore in boats, to be greeted by cheerful Aussie airmen. Various sporting competitions had been planned, but since an early-morning rainstorm had rendered most of the grounds unplayable, the day was spent socialising instead.

The British officers were entertained in the RAAF officers' mess, where they were delighted to find two real live females: nursing sisters Vivienne Boswell and Ethel 'Maggie' Morgan. The nurses were the only two women on West Island, and according to Lings they 'had a remarkable effect on the morale of the troops'.[2] They had a similar effect on the British officers too.

Down at the airmen's mess, the catering section laid on a top-notch barbecue for the British ratings and other ranks. Talk about the Landing Squadron's secret mission was strictly forbidden, but rumours still circulated, and word was that it had something to do with the atom bomb.

Unfortunately, despite the official ban, and further warnings from their hosts, five British sailors could not resist the lure of the sea and went for a swim. They were soon in trouble.

The alarm went up when some of the men on shore noticed the sailors struggling in the heavy surf out on the reef. Muttering under their breaths, a handful of Aussie airmen with lifesaving experience stripped off and charged into the water. Corporal John Kelly from Cottesloe, Western Australia, was the first to reach the reef, but by the time he got there the sailors had been swept further away from shore. Kelly shouted for the men to swim out further still, pointing away from the crashing surf, before being dumped back on the jagged reef by 15-foot waves.

Leading Aircraftman Bob Stewart and Leading Aircraftman Michael Rowan were next to arrive on the scene. The battered and bruised Kelly, their superior, told them not to proceed as it was too dangerous. They did not obey. Instead, both men plunged into the massive surf. By now, the British sailors had been battling to stay above water for half an hour. Stewart, a strapping 24-year-old lifesaver from the Gold Coast, Queensland, told one of the men to hang onto his neck and relax. He hauled the sailor through the surf until he was able to push him onto the crest of a wave, hurtling him forward onto the relative safety of the reef. Stewart then turned around and went straight back out.

Leading Aircraftman EJ Black and Leading Aircraftman RK Higgins had also joined the effort by this stage. Black was able to help another sailor onto the top of a wave, propelling him to safety. Higgins went to the aid of Rowan, who was in trouble, when a huge wave came crashing down, engulfing everyone. Rowan was torn from Higgins's grasp, and disappeared. Black and Higgins, both shattered, made it back to the reef before being helped ashore. Somewhere amidst all the confusion, a third British sailor made it in (according to some versions of the story, this was also Stewart's doing).

Back on base, Leading Aircraftman Ian 'Hambone' Hamilton, a tractor operator, had just gotten out of the shower and was heading to the mess, looking forward to a quiet beer, when he noticed all the fuss on the beach and went to investigate. As soon as he was told what was going on,

Hamilton stripped off, stuck his beer tickets in his boots, and grabbed a lifeline.

'I went in (barefoot and naked) to about 75 yds to this "channel rip" we knew, pulling this rope,' he would later recount. 'I went straight through this "channel rip" looking at what seemed "mountains of waves" ... The bloody waves were mountains and as they hit the edge of the Coral Reef they "dumped" ... still I managed to break through to the (greener) deeper water, and then had to swim UP the bloody waves.

'I clearly recall when surfacing from being dumped, I would scream "God oh God". I do think this clearing the air out of my lungs helped me to survive.

'At last (I do not know how many dumpers I survived) I broke through to comparatively calm water. Who do you think I saw? My mate Kevin Mason (Heavy Plant welder and ex Queenscliff surf club), Bob Stewart Cpl (I don't remember his mustering) and a bloody Pom.

'I said to the Pom "What the 'F' are you doing in this surf" and he said "We know all about surf we have swum in the Mediterranean."'[3]

Hamilton had in fact slipped the rope in order to assist Leading Aircraftman Mason, who was struggling. Too exhausted to face the breakers yet again, Stewart, Mason and Hamilton decided to look for a safer way in further down the coast, taking the English sailor along with them.

Meanwhile, a second lifeline was deployed from the beach. This time, Squadron Leader SR Scott, Leading Aircraftman Craddock, Leading Aircraftman DH Lorman and Aircraftman Peter Eccleston all went out, but by the time they broke through the surf the fifth and final member of the original swimming party, Able Seaman John Atkinson, was nowhere to be seen. Once it became clear that there was nothing more to do, Squadron Leader Scott signalled for the linesmen to haul them back in, but unfortunately the line had become caught in a crevice in the reef, severing the rope. In the maelstrom of the surf, it was a crucial quarter of an hour before the men in the water realised they were not being reeled in. By this time, they were completely worn out. Eccleston was particularly struggling. Before his mates could tie the rope around his waist to save him, he sank beneath the waves. The three other men managed to haul themselves onto the reef, but Craddock was so spent that yet another airman, Leading Aircraftman LD Sorenson, swam out to assist him until they could all be pulled to safety.

Stewart, Mason, Hamilton and the English sailor were now about half a mile offshore, swimming along the coast, doing breaststroke, and looking for a safe place to land. Stewart led the way, keeping everyone's spirits up by cracking jokes and conducting a singalong.

'We all sang (all we could remember) "I was born to wonder [sic], I was born to roam", nobody recalled the next line', Hamilton later wrote.

'By this time it was drizzling rain and getting dark.

'Remember this was 600 fathoms on the Navy Charts, Noah's (sharks) everywhere. At last "Maso" said "I've had it, I'm going for the shore."

'Rounding a small point we decided to have a go and go in. We pushed the Pom onto the first wave and I followed, after a few dumpers I put my feet on solid coral.'

By now it was dark. The four men had been in the water for over two hours, swimming 3½ miles. They were dragged out by relieved mates who had tracked their progress down the coast. They were not in good shape: half drowned, covered in lacerations, and suffering from hypothermia. Kevin Mason collapsed in exhaustion, and despite his own fatigue, Bob Stewart insisted on personally applying mouth-to-mouth resuscitation.

The survivors were wrapped up in rubber gas capes to keep them warm and driven back to camp in Jeeps. Hamilton rode with the CO.

'"Nobby" [Lings] asked me had I seen anything of Eccleston or Rowan. I said "No Sir." (Nobby was crying at this time, could have been the rain running down his face!!)'

The survivors were taken to the sick bay, where Hamilton was cared for by Sister Boswell. After two hours in the water, his genitals had disappeared into his abdomen, and had to be massaged down via immersion in warm water. He remembered Sister Boswell as 'an angel' for the rest of his days.

The next day, Hamilton went down to the beach and found his boots and beer tickets. 'I remember after the swim, asking for a beer at the Airman's Mess [sic], only to be told, "None left."'

Despite the efforts of rescue vessels scanning the water with searchlights throughout the night, nothing was ever found of Leading Aircraftman Michael Paul Rowan, Aircraftman Peter James Eccleston, and Able Seaman John Emery Atkinson, RN.

Later on, 2ACS erected a memorial to the three drowned men near the mess overlooking the beach. The airmen were justifiably proud of the rescuers, especially Bob Stewart, whose actions became the stuff of Air Force legend. When the story finally reached Australia, the *Courier-Mail* sent a reporter to interview his family in Brisbane. 'Bob's not the type to "blow", even to us', said his father, an old Digger and former POW. 'Bob's only reference in his letters to the "show" was to say he had been in a "mishap". His mates told me the story.'[4]

For his heroic efforts that day, Bob Stewart was awarded the George Medal, one of the British Empire's highest awards for acts of bravery. John Kelly was awarded the British Empire Medal and Michael Rowan and Peter Eccleston were posthumously awarded the Queen's Commendation for Brave Conduct. Ian Hamilton and the other rescuers all received letters of commendation. The airmen's efforts were similarly recognised by the Royal Surf Life Saving Association of Australia.

A few days after the incident, a bittersweet farewell bash was held in cramped quarters on board the *Zeebrugge* and the *Narvik*, after which the LSTs weighed anchor and proceeded for Fremantle, Western Australia, their last port of call before the top-secret test site. Only the Landing Squadron's officers knew their final destination was another obscure group of islands off the North West Coast of Australia: the Montebello Islands.

The Cocos incident marked the first meeting between British and Australian units since the beginning of Operation Hurricane, Britain's desperate attempt to join the exclusive club of nuclear powers, then comprising only the United States of America and the Union of Soviet Socialist Republics, and decisively shift the balance of world power back to the West. With the enthusiastic assistance of the Australian Government, led by Prime Minister Robert Menzies, the UK Government would conduct 12 major atomic tests and hundreds of so-called 'minor trials' at three Australian sites over the next 12 years. The atomic programme would displace Aboriginal peoples, expose thousands of servicemen and civilians to radiation, contaminate the Outback, and spread fallout right across the continent – and it all started with a dozen brave Australian airmen risking their own lives to rescue five British sailors from the surf, saving all but one, but losing two of their own in the process.

In other words, it was not a good omen.

# A BLOODY UNION JACK FLYING ON TOP OF IT

UK Prime Minister Clement Attlee had been wrestling with the question of the atom bomb since the beginning of his term in office.

Balding, with a clipped moustache and a pipe always at the ready, the 67-year-old Attlee was an unassuming man who was often underestimated. An Oxford-educated barrister turned social worker, he had served as an Army officer during the First World War before entering parliament as Member for Limehouse, a working-class borough in the East End of London. Never the most dynamic politician, he was competent and surprisingly progressive, enthusiastically advocating the introduction of the National Health Service and the creation of the modern welfare state. In 1935, he was elected Labour leader ahead of several more highly fancied contenders. During the Second World War, he served as deputy prime minister in the wartime coalition led by his conservative friend and rival, Winston Churchill, but after Germany surrendered the coalition collapsed. To the astonishment of all, modest, humble, self-effacing Clem Attlee led Labour to a thumping victory over Churchill's Tories in the ensuing election.

When Attlee moved into 10 Downing Street in July 1945, London was in ruins, the United Kingdom was virtually bankrupt, and the war in the Pacific raged on. To many, it seemed as though Japan would never surrender, but that soon changed with the bombings of Hiroshima and Nagasaki. On 15 August 1945, Japan surrendered unconditionally.

The world had entered the atomic age.

Like many others, Attlee was shocked by the effects of the bomb and uneasy about Britain's role in its development. Before the war, British scientists at the Cavendish Laboratory at Cambridge, under the direction of New Zealand's Sir Ernest Rutherford, had made a series of incredible advances in the field of nuclear physics, including the discovery of the neutron and the first successful attempt to 'split the atom'. One of 'Rutherford's boys', Australia's Mark Oliphant, had gone on to head up the Physics Department at Birmingham University where, in 1940, two Jewish refugees, Otto Frisch and Rudolf Peierls, had written a groundbreaking paper demonstrating that a uranium-powered atom bomb was theoretically possible. The Frisch–Peierls memorandum led to the creation of the MAUD Committee, which was formed to investigate the feasibility of producing such a weapon.[1] The MAUD Committee included some of Britain's greatest scientific minds, including Cavendish alumni Mark Oliphant, James Chadwick (who discovered the neutron) and John Cockcroft (who, along with Ernest Walton, split the atom). When the MAUD committee found that the production of an atom bomb was indeed plausible, Winston Churchill approved the creation of Britain's first atom-bomb programme. Established on 30 August 1941, Tube Alloys predated America's Manhattan Project by some six weeks. US President Franklin D Roosevelt initially offered to join forces with the British Government as equal partners in an Anglo-American atomic programme, but Churchill's response was strangely unenthusiastic and noncommittal.[2] Instead, the two programmes proceeded independently, and the Manhattan Project, with all its advantages in money, manpower and materiel, came to dwarf Tube Alloys. Churchill soon saw the error of his ways and tried to resuscitate the deal, but he had missed his chance for a 50/50 split. In August 1943, Churchill and Roosevelt signed the Quebec Agreement, committing to the 'full and effective' exchange of information on atomic research and development, but on terms which allowed the US Government to maintain control over postwar civil use of atomic power, which was expected to be extremely lucrative.[3] The Manhattan Project promptly swallowed Tube Alloys, and Britain's top scientists crossed the Atlantic to work for Uncle Sam.

Given Britain's role in developing the bomb, Attlee believed his country had a moral imperative to ensure that the world did not destroy itself in a fit of atomic madness. In August 1945, just weeks after the bombings of Hiroshima and Nagasaki, he wrote:

> The only course which seems to me to be feasible and to offer a reasonable hope of staving off imminent disaster for the world is joint action by the USA, UK and Russia based upon stark reality.
>
> We should declare that this invention has made it essential to end wars. The new World Order must start now …
>
> While steps must be taken to prevent the development of this weapon in any country, this will be futile unless the whole conception of war is banished from people's minds and from the calculations of governments.[4]

Needless to say, that's not what happened.

•

The Cold War began in earnest at 8.00 p.m. on 5 September 1945, when Russian cypher clerk and military intelligence (GRU) officer Lieutenant Igor Gouzenko walked out of the Soviet embassy in Ottawa, Canada, with a briefcase full of stolen documents. Gouzenko was planning to defect, and as evidence of his goodwill, he had amassed a cache of documents proving that the Soviet Union was operating an extensive spy network in North America.

Unfortunately, Gouzenko was not given asylum straightaway, but instead was referred from one department to another by polite but implacable Canadian bureaucrats, forcing him to spend two sleepless nights out in the cold with his wife and young son. On the second night, the Gouzenkos narrowly avoided capture with the help of brave neighbours who hid them while men from the NKVD (forerunner of the KGB) ransacked their apartment. They were finally rescued by the Ottawa Police and put under the protection of the Mounties.

During his debriefing, Gouzenko warned that officials at the Soviet embassy were openly preparing for a third world war. Communist Party members, he said, particularly hoped for it 'as a necessity in the setting up of Communism throughout the world'.[5] He also issued a chilling warning to Western governments about the threat of Communist Party members in their own countries: 'To many Soviet people here abroad, it is clear that the Communist Party in democratic countries has changed long ago from a political party into an agency net of the Soviet Government, into a fifth column in these countries to meet a war, into an instrument in the hands of the Soviet Government for creating artificial unrest, provocation, etc.'[6]

Gouzenko's defection, coming just weeks after the end of the war in the Pacific, sent shockwaves through the Allies. Among the stolen documents were lists of Soviet agents operating in Canada and the US, including some with close ties to the Manhattan Project, proving conclusively that the

Soviets were targeting scientists with access to top-secret information on the atom bomb.

That changed everything.

The West's alliance with the USSR had always been an uneasy one, forged in service of war against a common enemy – Germany. The Soviet leader, Joseph Stalin, was a ruthless, paranoid mass murderer who had killed millions of his own people in purges and famines engineered for political reasons. His foreign policy was just as belligerent: by the end of the Second World War, the Red Army occupied most of Eastern Europe, with no intention of going home. The Iron Curtain had been drawn across the continent.

The knowledge that Stalin was pursuing the atom bomb struck fear into the hearts of officials in Washington, DC, and London. To Attlee and his advisers, a Russian bomb clearly represented a threat to British security. In an era before NATO, there was no guarantee that the US would come to Britain's aid in the event of an attack. In fact, there were worrying signs that the Americans were returning to the policy of isolationism that had held sway until Pearl Harbor. That meant there would be nothing to deter Stalin from bombing London. Only a British bomb, and the threat of a retaliatory strike on Moscow, could do that.

From that point on, British and American atomic policy developed along two separate and contradictory lines. Officially, both nations were in favour of international control of atomic weapons under the auspices of the newly established United Nations Atomic Energy Commission, but behind closed doors they continued developing atomic weapons to defend themselves from the Soviets, while the Soviets developed atomic weapons to defend themselves from the West.

And so the nuclear arms race began.

•

Defence was the main reason the UK Government wanted the bomb, but it was not the only one – British prestige was also at stake.

For the past two centuries, the British Empire had been the dominant world power, but now that empire was crumbling. The war effort had bankrupted the UK, and independence movements were springing up in colonies all around the world. The new superpowers, the USA and USSR, had overtaken the old empire in leaps and bounds, but the bigwigs in London were not yet ready to admit it. To maintain Britain's status as a world power, they knew they could not afford to fall behind in the nuclear arms race. In the postwar world, the atom bomb was the ultimate symbol of power and prestige.

UK Foreign Secretary Ernest Bevin summed up the situation in a Cabinet committee meeting in 1946. Following a humiliating conversation with US Secretary of State James F Byrnes, Bevin arrived to find several colleagues arguing against a British bomb on the basis of cost. He blew up:

> That won't do at all, we've got to have this ... I don't mind for myself, but I don't want any other Foreign Secretary of this country to be talked at, or to, by the secretary of the United States as I have just had, in my discussions with Mr Byrnes. We've got to have this thing over here whatever it costs ... We've got to have a bloody Union Jack flying on top of it.[7]

Bevin won the argument.

Attlee and his ministers still hoped and believed that American cooperation would help make the British bomb a reality. According to the terms of the Quebec Agreement, both nations were committed to the 'full and effective' exchange of information on atomic research and development. But ever since the end of the war, the Americans had been strangely reluctant to share atomic secrets. Churchill and Roosevelt had been great friends and allies – it was with them that the storied 'special relationship' began – but now both men were gone. Roosevelt was dead, and Churchill was stuck in opposition. Their successors, Harry Truman and Clement Attlee, did not have a close relationship, and many in Washington either did not know or did not care about Britain's contribution to the Manhattan Project. Keen to maintain their atomic monopoly, the Americans dragged their feet on British requests for information and assistance.

Attlee was determined to rekindle the relationship, but his efforts were continually undermined by a series of spy scandals, beginning with the arrest of Dr Alan Nunn May in 1946. A nondescript-looking physicist from Birmingham, England, Nunn May had worked on a series of top-secret war projects, including radar, Tube Alloys and the Manhattan Project. From 1943 to 1945 he was based in Canada, specialising in heavy water reactor research at the Montreal Laboratory and routinely visiting other facilities in Canada and the US, including the Chalk River Pile and the Argonne Laboratory in Chicago. Unfortunately, he was also a Communist, having been radicalised at Cambridge in the 1930s. Before leaving England, while working on Tube Alloys, Nunn May had leaked a confidential report about the German nuclear programme to the Soviets, apparently out of genuine concern for the safety of Britain's wartime allies. Consequently, the Soviets had logged him as an asset.

One night in Montreal, a GRU officer named Lieutenant Angelov appeared unannounced at Nunn May's home and strongarmed him into writing an extensive two-part report on the theory of the atom bomb and the organisational structure of the Manhattan Project. Initially a reluctant spy, Nunn May (codename Alek) soon warmed to the espionage game and eventually stole several important documents and two samples of uranium for Angelov, who rewarded him with gifts of $700 cash and two bottles of whiskey. In true bureaucratic fashion, the GRU kept receipts for the gifts. These would prove to be Nunn May's downfall.

When Lieutenant Gouzenko defected to Canada in September 1945, his briefcase contained Alek's receipts from Montreal and plans for a clandestine meeting with an agent of the same name in London in October 1945. Nunn May never showed up at that meeting – he was, apparently, tipped off – but it was not hard for MI5 to put two and two together and deduce Alek's identity. Following months of surveillance, Nunn May was arrested on 4 March 1946. He was eventually sentenced to ten years hard labour, serving six.

News of Nunn May's treachery shocked the British public and outraged the Americans, bringing Anglo-American cooperation on atomic research and development to a shuddering halt. In August 1946, US Congress passed the McMahon Bill, which became the *Atomic Energy Act*, effectively tearing up the Quebec Agreement and restricting access to atomic information by all foreign countries, including the UK.

The Brits now had no choice but to go it alone. On 8 January 1947, a Cabinet committee convened by Attlee made the official decision to proceed with the independent development of atomic weapons. The Ministry of Supply would run the programme under the cover name 'Basic High Explosive Research', soon shortened to 'High Explosive Research' (HER). Unofficially, the decision had been in the works for some time. Attlee had already established the Atomic Energy Research Establishment (AERE) at Harwell, Oxfordshire, to study civil and military applications of atomic power, and commissioned two atomic piles at Sellafield, Cumberland, to produce large amounts of weapons-grade plutonium. Both facilities had been established with an eye to producing atomic weapons.

The man chosen to head up HER was Dr William Penney, a brilliant mathematician and physicist with doctorates from Cambridge and London universities. Bespectacled and tousle-haired, with a solid build and a gap-toothed grin, Penney was universally liked for his cheerful, unpretentious demeanour. The son of a sergeant major in the Royal Army Ordnance Corps, he followed in his father's footsteps by specialising in explosives, albeit on a much grander scale. Early in the war, he studied the blast effects of aerial bombing for the Home Office and underwater blast waves for the Royal Navy. While at the Admiralty, he helped design Bombardons – the floating breakwaters that helped protect the portable Mulberry Harbours during the D-Day landings.

By the time the Allies invaded Normandy, Penney had already been drafted into Tube Alloys and the Manhattan Project and sent to Los Alamos, New Mexico. There, in the high desert, the Americans were developing two separate bomb designs. One was a 'gun-type' device, codenamed Thin Man, which was triggered by firing one subcritical lump of plutonium at another. The other was an implosion device, codenamed Fat Man, which was triggered by sending an explosive shockwave inwards onto a plutonium core. Owing to problems with the Thin Man design, the director of the Manhattan Project, J Robert Oppenheimer, eventually restructured the project around Fat Man and a uranium-powered variation of Thin Man, codenamed Little Boy.

On arrival, Penney was sent to work for the Theoretical Division (T Division), calculating the effects of shockwaves created by hypothetical atom bombs. In one memorable lecture, he cheerfully described the horrific effect of German bombs on London during the Blitz, grinning all the while, earning him the nickname 'the smiling killer'.[8] The new nickname would soon seem bitterly ironic. In 1944, while Penney was in the US, a German V-1 rocket struck his home in London. His wife, Adele, survived the initial blast, but never recovered from the trauma and died in April 1945. The Penneys' two young sons were left in the care of a nurse named Joan Quennell, whom Penney later married.

The tragedy did not stop Penney from working. Even the cocky Yanks could see how sharp the humble British professor was, and he was soon put to work on the implosion device in addition to his T Division duties. 'I spent about half of my time working on some of the scientific phenomena going inwards into the bomb and the other half on scientific phenomena going outwards', he later explained, with characteristic simplicity.[9] Penney became so valuable that when the Target Committee met in Washington in April 1945, with the intention of deciding which Japanese cities to bomb, he was the only British scientist in the room.

Events moved quickly after that. On 16 July, the Fat Man device was successfully tested at Alamogordo, New Mexico, in a trial codenamed Trinity. Three weeks later, Little Boy was dropped on Hiroshima. Three days after that, Fat Man was detonated over Nagasaki.

Penney witnessed the bombing of Nagasaki from a US Army Air Forces B-29 high over Japan. Later that night, at the air base on Tinian Island, near Guam, he and his fellow observers talked about what they had seen:

> All of us were in a state of emotional shock. We realised that a new age had begun and that possibly we had all made some contribution to raising a monster that would consume us all. None of us could sleep. We argued well into the night, and in our talks were raised the same tremendous issues that have been debated ever since.[10]

Of course, that did not stop him building more bombs.

After the Japanese surrender, Penney was sent to Hiroshima

and Nagasaki with some American colleagues to calculate the size of the blasts from the rubble on the ground. The British scientist now had no choice but to contemplate the devastation he had wrought. After wandering around for a while with no idea what to do, he started looking at bent flagpoles, crumpled petrol tins and other items measurably impacted by the blast. While cautioning that his estimates could be out by as much as a third, he calculated that the Hiroshima blast was equivalent to about 10,000 tons of TNT, and the Nagasaki blast possibly as much as 30,000 tons. Given the materials he had to work with, these were pretty good estimates: today the accepted yields are about 15 and 21 kilotons respectively.[11]

Penney used a similar trick the following year, at Bikini Atoll in the Pacific Ocean, during the first postwar American test series, Operation Crossroads. Before the tests, Penney sailed around the atoll, depositing 1000 jerry cans full of seawater on various islands. The Americans thought he was mad, but when the first bomb was dropped off target, most of their expensive chrome-plated gadgets were wiped out. It was Penney who saved the day by estimating the size of the blast from the state of the damaged jerry cans.

After the war, Penney was keen to spend more time with his family and return to the quiet life of academia, but duty called once again. His Majesty's Government had decided that Britain needed a bomb of its own, and clearly there was only one man for the job. Reluctantly, Penney accepted the role of Chief Superintendent of Armament Research (CSAR, pronounced 'Caesar') at the Armament Research Department (ARD) at Fort Halstead, Kent.

Building an atom bomb was hard enough with the seemingly unlimited resources of the US Government at your disposal, but in the postwar Britain of austerity measures and petrol rations, Penney was expected to produce the same results with a fraction of the budget. He also had a deadline. It was now 1947, and the military intelligence chaps estimated that the Soviet Union would have an atomic arsenal big enough to destroy the UK within ten years. In order to function effectively as a deterrent, Britain's arsenal had to be online by 1957. Factoring in the time required to manufacture the weapons in sufficient quantities, that gave Penney five years to come up with a working prototype. His deadline was 1952.

To make life easier for himself, Penney decided to copy the Fat Man device. This was the weapon with which he was most familiar from his time at Los Alamos; it had also proven to be more powerful and efficient than Little Boy. Unfortunately, because of Washington's decision to tear up the Quebec Agreement, Penney had no access to Fat Man's blueprints, and the compartmentalised nature of the Manhattan Project meant that he only knew bits and pieces of the design. Even for a man with Penney's brains, the problems were daunting.

In an implosion device like Fat Man, two hemispheres of subcritical plutonium are held face to face. When crushed together into a single mass, the plutonium becomes supercritical and a chain reaction occurs, leading to a nuclear explosion. But for the chain reaction to occur, the inward force compressing the core needs to be evenly applied. To achieve this, a layer of conventional explosives is used, with multiple detonators spaced out evenly around the surface of the sphere. Once detonated, the explosives send a series of powerful pressure waves inwards via a layer of slow-burning explosive lenses which combine and shape the waves into a single, spherical, implosive pressure wave. Another layer of explosive known as the 'supercharge' accelerates the pressure wave, which is further intensified by a thin layer of uranium called the 'tamper', which fits around the plutonium core. At the heart of the core is the initiator, a tiny polonium-powered device which produces a burst of neutrons, initiating the chain reaction.[12] For the weapon to work, each step of the process must be calculated precisely, each component designed and refined to perfection. A tiny mathematical error here or a manufacturing flaw there could render the whole thing a fizzer.

Work on HER began in June 1947 at Fort Halstead and the Royal Arsenal in Woolwich. It was slow going at first, with Penney fighting tooth and nail for every penny from the bean counters at the Ministry of Supply, but eventually the programme took shape, and within a few years it had grown so large that it could no longer remain under the umbrella of Armament Research. In 1950, the decision was made to separate the two organisations, and HER was given dedicated facilities at an old RAF base in Aldermaston, Berkshire. Penney was now known as Chief Superintendent of High Explosive Research (CSHER).

Meanwhile, the Cold War was heating up. In 1948, the Russians blockaded Berlin, forcing the Western Allies to organise the Berlin Airlift to keep West Berlin supplied with food and other essentials. One year later, the Chinese Red Army, led by Mao Tse-tung, marched into Peking and declared the People's Republic of China. Worse still, on 29 August 1949, the USSR detonated its first atom bomb in the Kazakh Steppe. There was no announcement. American scientists learnt about the bomb (which they dubbed Joe-1) when a mysterious radioactive cloud was detected drifting east across North America from the Pacific to the Atlantic. Subsequent analysis showed that it could only have come from a Soviet atom bomb.

Stalin had the bomb.

This was a catastrophe for the West, and yet another blow to British pride. Attlee and his officials had believed they were years ahead of the Soviet Union, comfortably in second place in the nuclear arms race. Now they were relegated to third at best. No one could understand how the Soviets had beaten them to the punch. The answer, when it came, was another humiliation for MI5.

Klaus Fuchs was one of Britain's top nuclear physicists. A German refugee who had fled the Nazis in 1933, Fuchs worked on both Tube Alloys and the Manhattan Project before being named head of theoretical physics at the AERE in Harwell. Small and intense, with round glasses and a high forehead, he was one of few outside experts to visit HER to advise on the implosion device. Fuchs undoubtedly made a major contribution to the British atom-bomb programme. Unfortunately, he also made a major contribution to the Soviet atom-bomb programme. For, like Alan Nunn May, Klaus Fuchs was a Soviet agent.

Fuchs's association with Communism dated back to his student days at Kiel University, where he joined the German Communist Party in 1932. He never officially joined the British Communist Party, but when his friend and mentor Rudolf Peierls recruited him to join Tube Alloys, he immediately contacted the Soviets and began leaking atomic secrets. At Los Alamos, where he worked in T Division with Penney, he smuggled out a treasure trove of technical information on bomb design. It was a spectacular intelligence coup for the Soviets, and one that probably changed the course of history.

After the war, Fuchs took up his post at Harwell, but continued passing on secrets to the Russians in clandestine meetings arranged in dingy pubs and Underground stations. Meanwhile, American codebreakers working on the Venona Project deciphered wartime intercepts revealing that a Los Alamos scientist codenamed Rest or Charles had leaked atomic secrets to the Soviet Union. The list of suspects was quickly narrowed to Fuchs, whose name also popped up in the address book of a suspect in the Canadian spy ring exposed by Gouzenko. Following a series of interrogations by MI5, Fuchs confessed to espionage in January 1950. He was convicted on four counts of breaking the *Official Secrets Act*, and eventually served nine years in prison. Fuchs's arrest infuriated the Americans all over again, putting paid to Britain's latest attempts to rekindle the special relationship.

•

By 1950, the British bomb was nearing completion, and Penney had begun planning a trial. The two main questions confronting him were how and where. The Americans had blown up bombs on towers, dropped them from B-29s, and detonated them 90 feet underwater, in far-flung locations like the desert of New Mexico and the middle of the Pacific Ocean. Penney had to decide whether to copy them or try something new, and he had to find a safe place to do it.

In July 1950, Penney was attending a meeting of the Sub-Committee on the Strategic Aspects of Atomic Energy, which included senior representatives from the services and all relevant government departments, when several committee members began discussing the possibility of a merchant ship smuggling an atom bomb into a British port. This gave Penney an idea: *Why don't we blow up a ship?* By detonating the weapon in the hold of a surplus warship, HER could test the bomb's functionality *and* measure the effects of the blast on the surrounding environment. The extra data would be extremely useful for civil defence purposes, and might even be of interest to the Americans.

The method of detonation was ultimately contingent upon the availability of an appropriate site, however. To make the 1952 deadline, Penney had to find one fast. Great Britain and its surrounding islands were ruled out for obvious reasons: too small, too densely populated and, frankly, too close to home. Instead, Penney and his colleagues looked overseas, identifying three main candidates among friendly nations: the USA, Canada and Australia. Penney's first preference was to use an established American site like Eniwetok Atoll in the Pacific Ocean, thereby saving time and money, but the poor state of the special relationship made American agreement seem unlikely. Nevertheless, a request was sent to Washington. The reply: deafening silence.

With no firm answer either way, Penney began looking for backup options in Canada and Australia. His second choice was Canada, a huge British dominion with wide-open plains and acres of frozen tundra. As a junior partner in Tube Alloys and the Manhattan Project, Canada was already a member of the atomic club, with a seat on the Combined Policy Committee which controlled access to the Allied uranium stockpile. Canada would be seen as a safe choice in both Washington and London.

Then there was Australia, a remote British dominion, far off in the southern hemisphere, with a vast red centre and thousands of miles of empty coastline. The current prime minister, Robert Menzies, was a loyal Anglophile who was likely to agree to any reasonable request from London, but there were question marks over some of his countrymen. A few years earlier, Venona intercepts had uncovered a Soviet spy ring operating in Australia, implicating members of the previous Labor Government. As a result of the revelations, the US and UK had ceased sharing intelligence with Australia, forcing then Prime Minister Ben Chifley to establish the Australian Security Intelligence Organisation (ASIO) to hunt Communist spies.

All in all, Canada seemed like the way to go, so in August 1950 Penney flew to Ottawa for a feasibility study. Ideally, he was hoping to find a permanent testing ground where Britain could return time and again to develop bombs of greater power and efficiency. Accompanied by Dr OM Solandt, Chairman of the Canadian Defence Research Board, Penney investigated seven sites around Canada. His top pick was Fort Churchill, Manitoba, a remote outpost on the west coast of Hudson Bay. It was almost ideal, except that the water was too shallow for ships to come close inshore. Penney certainly wasn't worried about contaminating the surrounding tundra, which he described as 'valueless'; today, Churchill is best known as the 'Polar Bear Capital of the World'.[13] Its human population is mostly Indigenous.

While Penney was in Canada, Royal Navy staff officers at the Admiralty in London were busy poring over dusty charts of the Australian coastline, looking for back-up test sites. They considered Groote Eylandt in the Gulf of Carpentaria and the Houtman Abrolhos Islands off the coast of Western Australia, but eliminated them for climatic reasons.

The staff officers also examined the Montebello Islands (often referred to as the Monte Bello Islands) off Western Australia's remote North West Coast. Situated about 50 miles offshore, the Montebellos were isolated, uninhabited and rarely visited. The nearest mainland town was Onslow, a small port 85 miles south which – crucially – was upwind of the proposed test site. The surrounding area was sparsely populated, so if anything went wrong only a handful of natives and colonials would be affected.

From the Navy's point of view, the Montebellos were perfect. The Admiralty put forward the suggestion to the Chiefs of Staff, who recommended the site to Prime Minister Attlee in September 1950. With still no word from the Americans, the British leader decided to sound out his Australian counterpart. In his office at 10 Downing Street, Attlee began drafting a cable to Menzies.

## 2.

# DEFENCE CALL
# TO THE NATION

On Tuesday 19 September 1950, Prime Minister Robert Menzies was in his Melbourne office at Treasury Place, putting the final touches on a speech to be delivered the following evening. It was the first of a three-part series entitled 'Defence Call to the Nation', designed to launch a major recruiting drive for the armed services. The speeches would be broadcast on the ABC and commercial radio stations all around Australia, each focussing on one of the three services and its role in the defence of Australia. Menzies insisted on drafting the speeches himself, writing them out in elegant longhand, as he did all his public remarks.

With the Second World War still fresh in everyone's minds, Australia found itself in dire need of troops once again. For the past two years, Malayan Communists had been waging a guerrilla war against British colonists. In June, the Australian Government had sent the Lincoln bombers of No 1 Squadron RAAF and Dakota transports of No 38 Squadron RAAF to Singapore to help crush the insurgency. At almost the exact same time, North Korean tanks crossed the 38th parallel and invaded South Korea. As part of a UN response, Australia redeployed elements of the British Commonwealth Occupation

Force (BCOF) from Japan to Korea, including destroyer HMAS *Bataan*, frigate HMAS *Shoalhaven* and the Mustang fighters of No 77 Squadron RAAF.

To Menzies and other Western leaders, it seemed as though these conflicts were the opening skirmishes in a new world war: a great clash of arms and ideologies between East and West, good and evil, democracy and totalitarianism. It was a war that, thanks to the atom bomb, could literally mean the end of life on Earth.

At 56 years of age, Robert Gordon Menzies was in the first year of his second stint as prime minister. With his silver hair, black eyebrows, imposing height and patrician demeanour, Menzies was the personification of 1950s Australian conservatism. The son of a country shopkeeper turned politician, he practised as a barrister in Melbourne before following his father into state politics. In 1934, he was elected federal member for Kooyong in Melbourne's leafy eastern suburbs, representing the now defunct United Australia Party (UAP).

A lifelong Anglophile, Menzies famously called himself 'British to the bootstraps', but despite supporting conscription he did not feel compelled to join the Australian Imperial Force and serve overseas during the First World War.[1] Instead, he joined the Melbourne University Rifles, a part-time militia unit that spent the war marching around parade grounds in Melbourne. This was apparently a family decision. Menzies had two elder brothers who were already at the front, and his only sister had eloped – scandalously – with a lowly private. At a family conference, it was decided that young Bob would stay home to finish his studies and look after his ageing parents. The decision would haunt him throughout his life, with rivals on both sides of politics questioning his integrity and insulting his honour. Labor MP Eddie Ward famously quipped that Menzies 'had a brilliant military career cut short by the outbreak of war'.[2] Menzies did not always do himself any favours with tone-deaf self-justifications such as 'the path of duty does not always lead to the recruiting depot', which made him sound like a hypocrite.[3]

Menzies's first term in office began with a leadership ballot following the death of Prime Minister Joseph Lyons in April 1939. Five months later, when Britain declared war on Germany, Menzies announced:

> Fellow Australians, it is my melancholy duty to inform you that in consequence of Germany's invasion of Poland, Great Britain has declared war upon her, and as a result Australia is also at war.[4]

To Menzies, and indeed most Australians at that time, it went without saying that if Britain was at war, then so was Australia. The British Empire was still very much a going concern, with Canada, Australia, New Zealand and all the other dominions largely deferring to the Crown and taking their orders from the Mother Country.

In 1941, during the dark days of the war, Menzies spent four months overseas, including ten weeks in London. The ill-advised trip was intended to demonstrate leadership and give Australia a seat at the table with Churchill's War Cabinet. It failed on both counts. While Menzies lobbied unsuccessfully for better defences in Singapore, detractors at home whispered that he was scheming for a permanent role in London. When he finally returned to Australia, he was unceremoniously dumped as prime minister in favour of Arthur Fadden, leader of the UAP's coalition partner, the Country Party. It was a personal humiliation for Menzies and a case of shuffling deckchairs on the *Titanic* for the Coalition. Following a historic no-confidence motion, they were turfed out of office and replaced by the Australian Labor Party, led by John Curtin. It would be eight long years before Menzies made a triumphant return to power as leader of the newly formed Liberal Party.

Like most conservative political leaders of the Cold War era, Menzies was a staunch anti-Communist. He framed the 1949 election as a 'referendum on socialism', intentionally conflating the socialist policies of Labor, now led by Ben Chifley, with the totalitarian state socialism of the Soviet Union.[5] In one memorable speech, he labelled his opponents 'Communists', 'Socialists' and 'Fascists' intent on establishing an 'economic dictatorship'.[6]

It was a cunning strategy. With the Communist-led Miners' Federation on strike in New South Wales, causing widespread disruption to power and transport around the nation, and Communist forces on the march overseas, anti-Communist sentiment was at an all-time high. The Coalition took the lower house in December and tabled a 'Communist Party Dissolution Bill' in January. The bill not only banned the Communist Party of Australia, it also gave the government the power to ban other organisations suspected of being fronts for the Communist Party, prosecute individuals for knowingly belonging to such organisations, and blacklist individuals with alleged Communist associations from working in the public service or holding office in any unions or industries 'vital to the security and defence of Australia'.[7] This was McCarthyism, Australian style. When Labor attempted to amend the bill in the Senate, Menzies promptly withdrew it, announcing that he would reintroduce the bill 'in the precise form in which it left the House of Representatives on the last occasion'.[8] Menzies was playing hardball. 'I do not think my opponents want an election', he said, threatening Labor with a double dissolution on the issue of Communism.

Menzies made that statement on Friday 15 September. Four days later, he was in Melbourne preparing for the following night's broadcast when he received a visit from Deputy UK

High Commissioner WJ Garnett. A lifelong civil servant, Garnett had been in Australia for almost 20 years, in various roles usually concerned with migration. In the absence of the High Commissioner, he had been sent to deliver a top-secret cable to Menzies. The cable had arrived with a cover letter under the codeword EPICURE. The subject was so sensitive that all relevant communication through the UK High Commission was to be copied, cyphered and handled by Garnett personally. In exquisitely diplomatic terms, Garnett suggested that Mr Menzies might like to make similar security arrangements on his side. Then he handed over the cable.

The contents, conveyed in Prime Minister Attlee's plain, matter-of-fact style, were explosive by any standard:

TOP SECRET AND PERSONAL
MESSAGE FROM MR ATTLEE FOR MR MENZIES
During recent months we have been considering the arrangements which will be necessary for testing our own atomic weapon when it is ready. Among the most important of the various decisions which must be taken is the choice of a suitable testing range. We asked the United States authorities earlier in the year whether they would let us use their own testing site at ENIWETOK but so far we have had no firm reply and it is not clear when one may be expected. Meanwhile it is clearly advisable if only as a precaution to consider possible alternative sites in British Commonwealth territory and to carry out a reconnaissance in the selected area. This would not of course necessarily involve a firm decision to hold the test there. One possible site which has been suggested by our experts is the MONTE BELLO ISLANDS off the north-west coast of Australia. I am telegraphing to you now to ask first whether the Australian government would be prepared in principle to agree that the first United Kingdom

atomic weapon should be tested in Australian territory and secondly, if so, whether they would agree to our experts making a detailed reconnaissance of the MONTE BELLO ISLANDS so that a firm decision can be taken on their suitability. It will clearly take some little time for the survey to be organised and for its results to be studied, and if reconnaissance is to be really useful and effective we should like it to be put in hand at once. If you agree that the survey may be made we can then work out with your authorities the detailed arrangements for it; these would include special arrangements for safeguarding secrecy.

We are instructing the United Kingdom High Commissioner in Canberra, who will give you this message, to take special precautions in his office for handling this and all future communications between us on the subject and it may be that the most convenient arrangement would be for all future such communications to he channelled through him.

We are arranging to let your Resident Minister know personally and on a TOP SECRET basis about this message.

Sept. 16th, 1950.[9]

Menzies had recently returned from talks in London, and may have been advised that a request like this was in the offing. He certainly did not act as though he were surprised in any way. According to Garnett's subsequent report of the meeting, he was positively enthusiastic about the idea:

On reading Mr Attlee's message Mr Menzies at once said that any special facilities which Aust [sic] might possess for this or similar purposes would of course be made available. He called the Acting Minister for Defence [Philip McBride] into consultation and said that at this stage no one else would be informed except [Defence Secretary Sir Frederick] Shedden.[10]

This was a remarkably quick decision on a matter of such import. Attlee had formed a Cabinet committee to decide whether to build the bomb, but Garnett's account makes it clear that Menzies's mind was made up before his two most senior Defence officials had even entered the room. It was the same logic he had used to declare war on Germany in 1939: if Britain was in a Cold War with the Soviet Union, then so was Australia. As loyal subjects, Australians were duty-bound to pitch in. If that meant sacrificing a few supposedly useless, uninhabited rocks off the coast of Western Australia, so be it. Better than sacrificing thousands of British lives in a nuclear attack.

Would the result have been any different if Labor had been in power? Not necessarily. In 1946, Chifley had established Woomera Rocket Range, an Anglo-Australian joint project that many assumed would be used to test atomic weapons. At the same time, he initiated a three-step atomic programme that encouraged uranium exploration, established nuclear physics and engineering laboratories at universities around the country, and eventually led to the commissioning of the Lucas Heights reactor in New South Wales. Even the famed Snowy River Scheme was designed to power atomic energy research at the brand new Australian National University in Canberra. If anything, Chifley might have been even more enthusiastic about atomic power than Menzies was, but it is hard to believe that he, or any other prime minister, could have signed off on Attlee's proposal more quickly than Menzies did.

After Garnett left, Menzies made a brief note at the bottom of the cable:

Have replied – 'Reference your Top Secret. We agree in principle and to proposed detailed reconnaissance'
Reply has gone through UK High Commissioner.
Robert Menzies 19.9.50

The following night, the prime minister delivered the first of his three defence addresses from the ABC Studios in Melbourne. In his sonorous baritone, he proclaimed:

Plain thinking and plain talk and clear action are all needed on the subject of defence. There has been far too much wishful thinking, far too much 'let's pretend' ...

Putting all diplomatic pretence on one side, who is the prospective attacker? Who is today breaking the world's peace in some places and threatening it in others? Who commands the allegiance of a gang of wreckers right here in Australia? A child could answer these questions, though a diplomat might prefer not to.

Do you think that this Communist enemy would hesitate to overrun Western civilisation if the United States did not have the atomic bomb? Don't let's pretend about the bomb. It's real. It is today keeping the world out of a tragic world-wide war. Horrible as it is (and I saw Hiroshima a few weeks ago), it is today not an instrument of war, but of peace. How many years do you suppose will elapse before the Communist has it in large quantities? Five? Four? Three? Two? Do you believe that when he has it he will then hold out the olive branch and cast his bombs into the sea? Dictatorial aggressors are made of sterner stuff than that ...

Let us come out of our self-delusion. Time runs in our favour only if we use it well. The only hope we have, the only hope the United Nations has, of keeping the peace is to prove to the potential enemy that, putting the bomb entirely on one side, we are as ready and as strong as he is.[11]

Menzies went on to outline the strategic roles for Australia's three services in the war against Communism: the Navy would focus on anti-submarine warfare to protect merchant ships from Soviet submarines; the Australian Military Forces (the regular Army), which until now had only been allowed to serve in Australian territory, would be sent to Korea and wherever else it was needed, doing away with the necessity of recruiting a separate volunteer force during wartime; and the Air Force would be prioritised with new aircraft and more air bases to help establish air superiority throughout the region.

Compulsory National Service would also be introduced for all three services, with all fit and healthy 18-year-old men required to commit to a minimum of six months in uniform.

In retrospect, one of the most interesting elements of the first broadcast was Menzies's mention of the bomb, and his assertion that it was 'not an instrument of war, but of peace'. Was that passage written before Garnett's visit or afterwards? It is interesting to speculate. But one thing is certain: Britain had no intention of putting the bomb aside, and neither did Australia.

# 3.

# EPICURE

It was a cloudy, windy morning when Lieutenant Commander Tony Cooper and a team of Naval ratings reported to the Boom Defence Depot in Fremantle, Western Australia.

A 30-year-old hydrographer from Burwood, New South Wales, Lieutenant Commander Cooper had just returned from London after two years on loan to the Royal Navy, and was due to take up a post as Deputy Senior Officer Hydrographic Service of the Royal Australian Navy. He was supposed to be home on leave in Sydney, catching up with family and friends, but the Naval Board had cut short his leave and despatched him to Western Australia on a secret mission instead.

Cooper's orders were to temporarily assume command of boom defence vessel HMAS *Karangi* and proceed to Onslow on the North West Coast, where he was to embark four VIPs for passage to the Montebello Islands. The purpose of the cruise, as far as he knew, was to survey the islands 'to determine their suitability for testing ship-borne GW [guided weapons] and rocket projectiles which would have to be fired over shore-based recording instruments'.[1] This was a cover story, cooked up in London, and inspired by real but unrelated plans to extend Woomera Rocket Range all the way out to the North West Coast. The true purpose of the cruise, codenamed

Operation Epicure, was to reconnoitre the Montebellos for their suitability as an atomic test site.

At first glance, Cooper's new command did not look like much. Berthed among the passenger liners and cargo ships at Victoria Quay, the 768-ton *Karangi* was small and squat. Designed to lay anti-submarine netting across the mouth of a harbour, the boom defence vessel had two distinctive 'horns' extending from her bow, powerful winches fore and aft, and a round, ribbed stern. During the war, she had been equipped with two machine guns and a 12-pound anti-aircraft gun, but she had since been defanged. Owing to her ungainly appearance, her nickname in the service was the Pregnant Porpoise.

As per Naval tradition, Lieutenant Commander Cooper was piped on board, at which point he officially assumed command from the *Karangi*'s long-time skipper, Senior Commissioned Boatswain JE White, a 41-year-old former rating from Fremantle, who had 'come up through the hawse pipe' from the lower deck and earned his commission the hard way. The seasoned boatswain duly handed over the keys to the ship and moved into the wardroom, where he was joined by the ship's new navigation officer, Lieutenant John Ferguson, DSC, a 30-year-old staff officer on loan from HMAS *Leeuwin*, Fremantle's main Naval base.

At the same time, the hydrographic ratings from HMAS *Kuttabul* in Sydney were allocated berths in the crowded mess decks below deck, where they found the ship's company buzzing with excitement. The *Karangi* had a complement of 30-odd tough, sunburnt ratings, mostly from Western Australia. Like the ship's officers, they had all been screened for security and ordered to sign papers promising not to reveal to anyone, including their families, where they were going or what they were doing. Punishment for talking was ten years in prison under the Commonwealth *Crimes Act*. Naturally, all this made for great scuttlebutt. Any change to the dull routine of tending Reserve ships and teaching part-timers to tie knots was good for morale, but a secret mission to parts unknown? That was really something.

Over the next few days, the ship was fuelled, watered, victualled, stored and boilers were flashed up. To the skipper's frustration, a shipment of surveying equipment arrived too late to be embarked because the crates had been stowed at the bottom of a cargo ship's hold, and local waterfront workers either could not or would not get them out. Worse still, the echo-sounding boat was weeks behind schedule because the master of another cargo ship had refused to embark it. The lack of cooperation from wharfies and merchant seamen was profoundly irritating for the Navy men. Unions such as the Waterside Workers Federation and Seamen's Union of Australia were dominated by Communist Party members, and frequently obstructive in their dealings with the services.

Over at the Naval Staff Office in Cliff Street, Captain Harry Howden, CBE, Naval Officer in Charge (NOIC) Fremantle, was forced to make alternative plans for the missing equipment. A dapper New Zealander in his fifties, Howden had responsibility for most of Western Australia's coastline, including the Montebello Islands, despite which he too had been given the Woomera cover story. Epicure's true objective was only divulged on a 'need to know' basis, and as far as the Naval Board was concerned, the NOIC Fremantle did not need to know. Under Howden's direction, plans were made to send the surveying equipment to Onslow via RAAF Dakota, while the State Shipping Service was engaged to take up the echo-sounding boat if and when it ever arrived.

Early on the morning of Saturday 4 November 1950, the *Karangi* slipped from alongside and proceeded for the Montebellos via Geraldton, Carnarvon and Onslow. With a top speed of 9 knots, the long journey up the coast took four days. For Cooper and his team from Sydney, this was an adjustment.

Compared to most ships in the 'Big Navy' (those based on the east coast), the *Karangi* was as slow as a wet week, with none of the mod cons like air-conditioning or radar. Navigation was done the old-fashioned way, with a compass and chart. If you wanted to have a shower, you pumped up the water yourself with a hand pump on the upper deck.

Despite her many drawbacks, the *Karangi* was a tough little ship. On 19 February 1942, she was stationed in Darwin, operating the anti-submarine boom net across the harbour mouth, when the Japanese attacked. Over 240 bombers, dive-bombers and fighters descended on the city in two waves, hitting the Army barracks, the Air Force base, the civil airfield and the many ships in the crowded harbour. The *Karangi* responded immediately, going straight to action stations and slipping her anchor to the bottom of the harbour. As Japanese Zeroes streaked past, strafing the hospital ship *Manunda*, the *Karangi* returned fire with machine guns and ack-ack, pumping out shells as fast as she could. On her port quarter, American destroyer USS *Peary* came under sustained attack from Japanese dive-bombers. The Americans fought back with everything they had, but a direct hit on the magazine blew the *Peary* to pieces, rocking the nearby *Karangi*. The horrified Australians could only watch as the destroyer went down by the stern, the forward gun crew still firing as they went under.

When the Japanese finally withdrew, Darwin was in ruins, the air full of smoke and cordite, 11 ships sunk, dozens more listing, and at least 297 servicemen and civilians dead.

Somehow, the *Karangi* escaped virtually unscathed.

•

Following an uneventful voyage, the *Karangi* secured alongside Onslow Jetty on Wednesday 8 November.

With a population of approximately 150, Onslow was a port town that existed primarily to service nearby lead mines and sheep stations. It was hot and dusty, with a mile-long jetty, a main road wide enough to drive stock down, and one pub – the two-storey Beadon Hotel (plus a tea room called the Snifter for those with a more refined sensibility). Cyclones frequently battered the town and damaged the jetty, which was constantly in need of repair. A few miles down the road, on the banks of the Ashburton River, lay the ruins of Old Onslow, the original town site, long since abandoned owing to its lack of suitability as a port.

Onslow was also bombed during the war, albeit on a much smaller scale than Darwin. On the night of 15 September 1943, a single Japanese flying boat appeared in the skies overhead, dropping 16 bombs and incendiaries as the locals ran for cover. The small port was not without strategic military value: American submarines on patrol out of Fremantle regularly refuelled at the jetty, and the RAAF occasionally used the airstrip outside town as a base for operations. Luckily, the bomber was ineffective, ignoring the jetty and missing the airstrip. There were no casualties.

Lieutenant Commander Cooper was pleased to find the missing surveying equipment waiting for him, but the echo-sounding boat was nowhere to be seen. After ordering the crew to embark the gear, he rendezvoused with his VIP passengers.

There were four of them. The senior officer and expedition leader was Air Vice Marshal ED 'Dizzy' Davis. A big, blustery sort of fellow, Davis had recently retired from the RAF to take up a senior post at the Ministry of Supply. It was up to him to decide whether the Montebellos would make a suitable test site. Charles Adams represented the scientific side of the operation. A buck-toothed boffin from High Explosive Research (HER), he would eventually be named Deputy Technical Director for the trial. Lieutenant Charles Scott was one of the Royal

Navy's best hydrographers. It was his job to complete the preliminary hydrographic charts for the Admiralty. Finally, there was Lieutenant Colonel Max Phillipps, head of security for Woomera Rocket Range. A former military intelligence officer, Phillipps was on secondment to ASIO, which he would soon join on a permanent basis. He handled security for the operation, and his presence had the added benefit of strengthening the Woomera cover story.

The four men had flown up from Perth in the same Dakota that had delivered the missing hydrographic equipment. On arrival, they went straight to the pub, where they tried their best to look inconspicuous in patchless Army khakis. It did not work. A couple of locals, aware that the *Karangi* was due in port, sized them up immediately and deduced that they were heading out on an expedition of some sort. This was quite a blow for the visitors, but to their relief the barflies guessed that they were either prospecting for oil or reconnoitring a potential submarine base in Exmouth Gulf. 'These conjectures were, of course, not denied', Davis noted in his report.[2]

Meanwhile, Lieutenant Colonel Phillipps spent the afternoon visiting local press representatives to make sure word of the visit did not leak out. He met with the Onslow postmaster and his assistant, both of whom represented Western Australian newspapers; another resident representing the ABC; and a radio operator from the Department of Civil Aviation (DCA) who represented Aeradio. Phillipps informed the men that the visit was 'associated with defence' and asked them to keep it hush-hush.[3] All four men were loyal Coastwatchers, and vowed the news would go no further, but the DCA man had recently controlled an aerial reconnaissance of the Montebellos by the RAAF and could not help telling Phillipps that he had guessed their destination. Phillipps's response was a masterclass in disinformation. In hushed tones, he swore the man to secrecy and gave him the cover story, divulging the plan to extend Woomera Rocket Range. The DCA man swallowed it hook, line and sinker.

By the end of the day, the hydrographic gear had been stowed in the holds and the VIPs had been accommodated in the upper-deck sleeping quarters. The *Karangi* now had six extra officers (including Adams, an honorary officer) on top of her usual complement of one, but according to Davis 'the party was cheerful and relatively comfortable'.[4]

The *Karangi* was now ready to depart, but Lieutenant Commander Cooper was sceptical about the accuracy of the antique charts for the surrounding waters, which dated from the turn of the century, and elected to proceed in daylight. The *Karangi* slipped from Onslow Jetty at 0500 the following morning, cautiously steaming up the Mary Anne Passage, through treacherous waters dotted with reefs and shoals, stopping every quarter of an hour to take soundings. At 1200, she reached her destination.

•

The Montebello Islands comprise about 175 islands scattered across 50 square miles of ocean, varying from rocky islets a few yards across to larger islands several miles wide. They are flat, barren and windswept. From the air, they are laid out roughly in the shape of an arrow pointing north-west.

The two largest islands, Hermite and Trimouille, are situated on opposite sides of the central lagoon. Hermite lies to the west, about 6 miles long and 2 miles wide, with a coastline so irregular that it is rarely more than a mile across at any given point. To the east lies Trimouille, only 3 miles long and 1 mile wide, but much more uniform in shape than Hermite. The only other islands of any real size are Alpha, off Hermite's northern tip, and North West, the island that forms the northern limit of the group (or the arrowhead).

According to most encyclopaedias available in the 1950s, the history of the Montebellos began in the 17th century, when British and Dutch trading ships first visited the west coast of Australia. In reality, though, Aboriginal people had beaten the Europeans by about 50,000 years. A few decades after the *Karangi*'s visit, expeditions to the Montebellos and nearby Barrow Island led by archaeologist Peter Veth would find evidence of prehistoric Aboriginal habitation, including stone tool fragments, charred animal bones and shellfish remains, in multiple caves. Carbon dating puts the oldest of these deposits at between 46,200 and 51,100 years old.[5]

Back in those days, during the last Ice Age, sea levels were a lot lower and the Montebellos were still joined to the mainland, comprising rocky peaks on what was then the continent's north-west coast. Then, about 10,000 years ago, the ice caps began to melt, causing sea levels to rise, and cutting off the islands from the mainland. At first, they formed a single landmass with nearby Barrow Island, separated from the mainland by a narrow passage easily crossed by canoe, but eventually, as sea levels continued to rise, they were reduced to distant outliers far off the coast. At that point, Aboriginal visitation appears to have ceased.[6]

When Europeans finally did turn up, it was only by accident. In 1622, a British East Indiaman called the *Trial*, bound for Java with a cargo full of silver, struck upon a reef near the islands. The *Trial*'s master, John Brooke, had been ordered to sail to the East Indies on a new course, making use of the strong westerlies in the southern latitudes to cross the Indian Ocean in quick time, but a costly navigation error had taken him too far east before turning north, bringing him close to the treacherous shore of 'Terra Australis'.[7] Disaster struck on the night of 25–26 May, when the *Trial* crashed into submerged rocks at full speed. Captain and crew fought desperately to save the ship and her valuable cargo throughout the night, but to no avail. In the early hours of the following morning, Brooke took to the skiff with nine others, while trader Thomas Bright led 36 into the longboat. All in all, 93 souls were lost to the deep that night.

While Brooke sailed straight for Java, over 1000 miles away, Bright headed for a nearby island (probably North West) and spent seven days preparing for the long voyage ahead. The two boats arrived in Java separately about one month later, the survivors half dead from thirst and hunger, with both parties telling very different stories about what happened on the night of 25–26 May.

The *Trial* was Australia's first recorded shipwreck. To avoid the blame for the loss of his ship, Brooke falsified the reef's position in his report to the company, so thanks to his incompetence and dishonesty, its exact location remained a mystery for over 300 years. Wary mariners searched for the 'Tryal Rocks' in vain, looking hundreds of miles west of their true position. Finally, in 1969, divers found a wreck on a reef 9 miles north-west of the Montebellos. Due to the passage of time, it was not possible to identify the wreck conclusively, but it was almost certainly the *Trial*. That reef is now known as the Tryal Rocks.

As for the Montebellos, their name came from another European visitor. At the turn of the 19th century, French explorer Nicolas Baudin led an expedition to 'New Holland' in the *Géographe* and the *Naturaliste*, visiting the low-lying desert islands in 1801. Presumably to curry favour with Napoleon, he named the islands after the Battle of Montebello, a triumphant victory for the Emperor's forces in the Italian Alps the previous year. Montebello means 'beautiful mountain' in Italian, but there are no mountains of any kind in the Montebello Islands.

The Royal Navy sent numerous ships to explore the area in Baudin's wake, most notably HMS *Beagle*, on her first voyage since the one described by Charles Darwin in *Voyage of the*

*Beagle.* On 31 August 1840, Lieutenant JL Stokes deposited a survey team led by Mr Fitzmaurice on 'a cliffy islet' called 'Tremouille' with a small boat and orders to chart the main islands. 'The fact that these and their neighbours are not separated in the charts fully evinced the necessity of our visit', wrote Stokes.[8] After exploring nearby Barrow Island, Stokes returned a few days later to pick up Fitzmaurice and his team, 'having completed the examination of the Montebello Group, a large proportion of chart material, in a very short space of time, considering the number of small islands'.[9] To celebrate a job well done, Stokes formed a hunting party and went off to shoot wallabies, which he considered 'excellent sport', bagging about 20 in a couple of hours. However, the English sailors found that 'the flesh was by no means good to eat, tasting very strong; this was the only instance in which we found wallaby at all unpalatable'.[10]

Ultimately, it was the marine life for which the Montebellos became famous. In 1884, the Singaporese schooner *Sree Pas Sair*, sailing in company with another vessel, brought pearlers to the islands for the first time. A pair of colourful adventurers led the expedition: Captain Edward Chippindall, an ex-Royal Navy officer, and Mr Thomas Haynes, an agent for wealthy London jeweller EW Streeter. The crew comprised Malay sailors and native divers from Sulu in the Philippines. Like the Aboriginal divers working on pearling boats up and down the North West Coast, the native divers were indentured labourers.

The *Sree Pas Sair* stayed in the Montebellos for months, making a good haul, including a 40-grain pearl judged to be 'the finest pearl seen in England for years'.[11] But many of the divers fell sick with beriberi, and seven died before they made it home. Haynes himself was lucky to survive the homeward journey when a mutinous crew member smashed his skull with a 9-pound lead weight. He had a dent in his forehead for the rest of his life. On a subsequent voyage, Chippindall died in mysterious circumstances, with rumours that he had been murdered by the crew. Clearly, pearling was a dangerous business.

Haynes returned to the North West numerous times over the years. In 1902, he was granted an exclusive 14-year pearling licence for the Montebellos, where he established the first commercial pearl-shell farm in Western Australia. Completed in 1904, Haynes's 'tidal pool' comprised a walled-off lagoon on North Delta Island with a floodgate that could be opened and closed with the tide. It was not a success. Plagued by financial difficulties and bureaucratic red tape, Haynes struggled to produce pearl shells for years, and when his house was destroyed by a cyclone in 1911 he gave up and returned to England.

Haynes died in 1929 at the age of 76. According to Debbie Cameron, a volunteer researcher at Manchester Central Library in England, he insisted on being buried alongside Chippindall at the Pioneer Cemetery in Broome, Western Australia, despite being survived by a widow and seven children in England.[12] In accordance with his wishes, Haynes's body was shipped halfway around the world to be interred alongside a male travelling companion who had died almost half a century earlier.

Since then, the Montebellos had only been visited by the occasional pearler or fishing trawler – until now.

•

As the *Karangi* approached the islands, Lieutenant Commander Tony Cooper grew concerned. His orders were to take the ship into the lagoon via the southern entrance, where a channel of 5 to 6 fathoms ran between two small islands, and anchor off Trimouille Island. But the approaches were clearly dangerous, with rocks breaking the surface all around, and the water shoaling in places. Lowering a boat, Cooper personally took soundings with Lieutenant Scott. Sure enough, the two hydrographers found that the entrances were too shallow for the *Karangi* to navigate at low tide. For safety's sake, the skipper elected not to enter the lagoon. This decision was justified a few days later when the *Karangi*'s anchor cable parted (or snapped) in gale-force winds and she was forced to put to sea. Had she been trapped in the lagoon at the time, surrounded by reefs and shoals, the results could have been disastrous: injuries, deaths, the ship wrecked, a court martial.

Cooper's caution also had drawbacks though. One reason the Admiralty wanted the *Karangi* to anchor off Trimouille was to provide the reconnaissance party with a dummy target vessel for the purpose of making observations. Now that would not be possible. The decision to remain in the outer anchorages also meant long, uncomfortable boat rides through unprotected waters for the landing party, cutting hours off the workday.

The reconnaissance began immediately. For the next three weeks, Davis, Adams and Phillipps went ashore each day. They traipsed all over the islands, trudging up and down sand dunes, wading through fields of spinifex, taking hundreds of photographs, and collecting dozens of samples. It was hot, exhausting work. The sun beat down constantly and the bare rock baked beneath their feet. The glare was often blinding. Sometimes the breeze brought relief, but at other times it whipped up sandstorms that stung the eyes and skin. 'In general, living conditions ashore for a prolonged period would be somewhat severe and can only be called inhospitable', reported Davis.[13] At the end of each day they returned to the ship drenched in spray.

Early in the operation, the British officers realised it would be impossible to achieve all their objectives without the full cooperation of Lieutenant Commander Cooper, so Air Vice

Marshal Davis made the command decision to brief him on the true purpose of Operation Epicure. The *Karangi*'s skipper took this astonishing news in stride and adjusted the daily programme accordingly.

While the landing party explored the islands, Lieutenant Scott and the hydrographic team surveyed the lagoon, erecting at least a dozen sounding marks, triangulation marks and tide poles. Once the echo-sounding boat finally arrived (about two weeks late), the survey proceeded swiftly. The lagoon was quite shallow in places, and dotted with submerged coral heads, which represented hazards to navigation, even for shallow-draught boats. Some islands possessed sandy beaches suitable for landings, but many had rocky shores undercut by tidal action, meaning that jetties would be required if they were to be used by boats and landing craft. A few islets thought to be suitable observation sites were surrounded by cliffs on all sides, and could only be accessed by ladders at high tide.

Depending on which area was under reconnaissance that day, the *Karangi* anchored to the north or south of the islands. The ship's company took hourly meteorological observations and recorded a fortnight's worth of tidal data. The ratings spent their days in shorts and sandals, bare torsos baking in the sun, and their nights sleeping on mats up on deck or under the open hatch to escape the stifling conditions in the mess decks.

With the *Karangi* rapidly running out of supplies, an RAAF Dakota airdropped fresh fruit and vegetables. Twice, the *Karangi* left the islands and rendezvoused with merchant ships to top up with water and refrigerated stores, leading to a mix-up when one of the supply ships headed for Sunday Island, way off in Exmouth Gulf, instead of the designated meeting place at Sandy Island in the Mary Anne Passage. A furious exchange of signals finally set them right. Dizzy Davis was amused by this episode, which seemed to indicate that the merchant seamen had been thrown off the *Karangi*'s scent by rumours of a submarine base in Exmouth Gulf. But the mix-up may have had a more prosaic explanation: the *Karangi*'s leading signalman reported that radio reception in the area was extremely erratic, and prone to fading or cutting out while sending and receiving.

One message that did get through was an official broadcast about the development of Woomera Rocket Range. Although the Montebellos were never mentioned, the broadcast hewed closely to the official cover story, leading members of the ship's company to exchange knowing nods and winks. They were delighted to be in on the big secret – which, of course, they were not.

By the end of the month, Davis's report had begun to take shape. The islands consisted primarily of limestone, with an average elevation of 10 feet above sea level, and a peak of 120 feet in the form of a hill at the northern end of Trimouille. Other islands featured hills of between 40 and 80 feet, offering suitable observation sites for the many cameras and other devices required to record the blast. Hermite was clearly the most logical place for a base camp, being both the largest island and the furthest upwind of the target vessel, but it was swarming with white ants that would devour untreated wood. Roads and tracks would need to be built on various islands. There was no suitable site for an airstrip on Hermite or anywhere else. Seaplanes could alight on the lagoon up until the day of the test, but after that the water in the lagoon would be radioactive. There was no fresh water to speak of. Aside from spinifex, there was very little vegetation, just a few low shrubs and mangrove swamps. No trees, and no shade anywhere.

The landing party found a few signs of previous human habitation: a dry well, a couple of ruined buildings, an abandoned oyster farm. This was Haynes's old tidal pool.

There was no sign of any wallabies. They were long gone, having been wiped out by feral cats and rats introduced by European visitors. 'Except for lizards, birds and insects, no animal life was seen on the islands, but the sea abounds with shark, sting-rays, coral snakes and other unpleasant species,' noted Davis.[14] In addition to those 'unpleasant species', the archipelago was home to turtles, dugongs, schnapper, grouper, tuna, cod, Spanish mackerel, mullet, flathead, crayfish, mud crabs and oysters. It was, in fact, a fisherman's paradise.

On Monday 27 November, the *Karangi* finally weighed anchor and headed for Fremantle, leaving Lieutenant Scott and the hydrographic party with the echo-sounding boat and orders not to return to the mainland until the survey was complete. They eventually made it back to civilisation a few weeks later.

In January 1951, Air Vice Marshal Davis submitted his report. The reviews were mixed. Although impressed by Australia's servicemen, Davis was not so keen on the troublesome left-wing unionists who had disrupted the operation. Any future plans would need to take them into account. After outlining the islands' drawbacks in some detail (the heat, the wind, the sharks), he concluded:

> Though there will undoubtedly be many difficulties to overcome, I am of opinion that, from the administrative aspect, the site would prove suitable for the trial.[15]

Back at HER, William Penney agreed, going as far as to say that it was 'the only site suitable to meet the planned date'.[16] From that point on, all thoughts of holding the trial in Canada or anywhere else faded away. Attlee and Penney still hoped for a change of heart from the Americans but, failing that, Britain's first atomic test would be held in the Montebello Islands.

# 4.

# THE WESTERN ISLANDS

At 10.00 a.m. on Thursday 15 March 1951, Prime Minister Robert Menzies left The Lodge, the official prime ministerial residence, and drove to Yarralumla to ask Governor-General William McKell for a double dissolution.

Menzies was fed up with Labor's efforts to block his agenda in the Senate. The final straw was not the incendiary Communist Party Dissolution Bill, which Labor had reluctantly allowed to pass (it was eventually struck down in the High Court), but the innocuous-sounding Commonwealth Bank Bill, which sought to re-establish the Commonwealth Bank Board, previously abolished by Ben Chifley. When Labor intentionally delayed the bill by referring it to committee, Menzies had all the excuse he needed to call for a double dissolution.

The election was set for 28 April. During the brief campaign, Menzies cleverly appropriated Labor's own rhetoric by saying that the government deserved a 'fair go' to implement its policies.[1] He also played the hits, claiming that Labor was 'on the side of the Communists', while fellow Liberals used the slogan 'Menzies or Moscow'.[2] It worked: this time the Coalition won both houses.

That was good news for the British atomic programme. Right in the middle of the election campaign, Menzies had received another cable from Clement Attlee, divulging the results of the Epicure reconnaissance. Attlee's experts had advised him that it would be possible to conduct an atomic test in the Montebellos, but only in the month of October, owing to the prevailing winds. It was still Attlee's preference to use an American site, but with negotiations going nowhere he was obliged to make a back-up plan. He asked if Menzies was prepared to formally agree that:

(a) if necessary the trial should be held next year in the Monte Bello Islands and (b) that preparations to this end should begin forthwith between the authorities concerned in our two countries. We hope that you will be willing to help with the logistic support of the expedition which will be needed to conduct it; we should be glad to arrange for your experts to take part in observation of the effects of the test. We can settle later details of finance and machinery.[3]

He also offered Menzies a warning:

There is one further aspect which I should mention. The effect of exploding an atomic weapon in the Monte Bello Islands will be to contaminate with radio activity the north east group and this contamination may spread to others of the islands. The area is not likely to be entirely free from contamination for about three years and we would hope for continuing Australian help in investigating the decay of contamination. During this time the area will be unsafe for human occupation or even for visits by e.g. pearl fishermen who, we understand, at present go there from time to time and suitable measures will need to be taken to keep them away. We should not like the Australian Government to take a decision on the matter without having this aspect of it in their minds.[4]

Nobody knows where Attlee got the figure of three years. Even in 1951, there was plenty of evidence that radioactive contamination could last a lot longer than that. Maybe his scientific advisers had come up with an estimate for when the islands would supposedly be safe to re-enter, and Attlee had misquoted them, either intentionally or unintentionally.

Menzies was naturally inclined to accept Attlee's proposals, but had put off giving his approval until after the election. Now he was free and clear. He readily accepted each proposal, making no demands and setting no conditions of any kind. He even volunteered to pay for Australia's entire contribution to the project, even though Attlee had not asked him to. His compliance stunned even the Brits. As Margaret Gowing, official historian of the British atomic programme, later wrote, with some understatement: 'The Australians agreed to this without striking a hard bargain over technical collaboration, and were most co-operative throughout ...'[5]

The two governments now started working in unison. In London, the proposed trial was given the codename Operation Hurricane.[6] A panel of service chiefs called the Hurricane Executive (Hurrex for short) was established to plan the trial on the service level, with Vice Admiral Sir Edward Evans-Lombe, KCB, Deputy Chief of Naval Staff, as chairman. In Melbourne, the Hurricane Panel was set up to coordinate with Hurrex, with Evans-Lombe's opposite number, Captain Alan McNicoll, GM, Deputy Chief of Naval Staff, as chairman.

Hurrex's first missive to the Hurricane Panel explained that a Royal Navy task force would be sent out in two phases. In Phase One, a landing squadron comprising two landing ships tank (LSTs) would transport a squadron of Royal Engineers to the proposed test site along with the equipment and materials necessary to lay the groundwork and build a command centre on one of the islands. In Phase Two, a special squadron comprising a headquarters ship (escort carrier HMS *Campania*), a frigate and a third LST would bring out most of the scientists, scientific equipment and, most importantly, the bomb itself.[7]

What followed was a three-page list of requests that sounded a lot like orders: a more comprehensive hydrographical survey of the islands and the surrounding waters; detailed meteorological information for the months of August to October; moorings and marker buoys to be laid in the lagoon and the outer anchorages prior to the arrival of the Special Squadron; roads and landings to be constructed on all four major islands; air transport throughout the operation; security patrols in the lead-up to the test; surface communications; medical facilities; refuelling facilities; provisions ... Hurrex was certainly making the most of Menzies's generosity.

For the detailed survey, the Hurricane Panel tabbed HMAS *Warrego*, an elegant 1060-ton sloop with white sides and a buff funnel, denoting her status as a survey ship. The *Warrego* had been laid up at Garden Island in Sydney for the past two years. On Thursday 14 June, she was recommissioned under Commander George Tancred, DSC, a 44-year-old hydrographer from Nanango, Queensland, who had been decorated in 1943 for charting the coast of New Guinea 'under the very guns of the Japanese'.[8]

Following a brief but intensive working-up period, the *Warrego* proceeded to sea at the end of June. As far as the ship's company knew, they were heading out on a 17,000-mile cruise to survey the north coast of Australia, including channels that had not been charted since Matthew Flinders's voyage in HMS *Investigator*. All this was true, but it was not the full story, as Commander Tancred was about to find out.

Three days later, the *Warrego* secured alongside at Port Melbourne, and Tancred reported to Navy Office at Victoria

Barracks, then home of the Department of Defence and headquarters for all three services. While the Army was based in the historic 19th-century bluestone building on St Kilda Road, the Navy and Air Force were housed in a more recent red-brick extension to the rear. There, Tancred met with the top brass: Vice Admiral Sir John Collins, KBE, CB, First Naval Member and Chief of Naval Staff; and Captain Alan McNicoll, GM, Deputy Chief of Naval Staff and Chairman of the Hurricane Panel.

Already a legendary figure in the RAN, Admiral Collins was the first graduate of the Royal Australian Naval College to rise to Chief of Naval Staff (before him, only Royal Navy officers were considered up to the task). A 52-year-old gunnery expert from Deloraine, Tasmania, Collins had overall responsibility for Australia's contribution to Operation Hurricane, and generally displayed more sense than his civilian bosses, encouraging the Menzies Government to keep the Australian public informed with official statements and pushing for Australian scientific representation at the test. After retiring in 1955, he would become Australia's High Commissioner to New Zealand.

A 43-year-old destroyer man from Hawthorn, Victoria, Captain McNicoll was on the fast track to flag rank, and would also rise to Chief of Naval Staff (and, later still, Ambassador to Turkey). As Chairman of the Hurricane Panel, it was Captain McNicoll who presented Commander Tancred with detailed orders for the survey of the Montebello Islands. Since the Admiralty wanted the results by the end of the year, Tancred was ordered to finish the survey by the end of October, when cyclone season would commence. It was estimated that the job would take three months, so the *Warrego* was to be at the survey ground, ready to begin, by 1 August.

The *Warrego* left Port Melbourne on Wednesday 4 July and reached Fremantle one week later, having battled terrific winds, towering waterspouts and persistent mechanical problems in the Great Australian Bight. Some welcome shore leave was followed by the voyage up the west coast, during which the *Warrego* stopped to search for uncharted shoals reported by cargo ships off Lancelin and Dirk Hartog Island. Having found evidence of neither, Commander Tancred reported that the false readings were probably the result of untrained merchant seamen misreading high-tech echo-sounding machines that were 'too efficient' for them; the Admiralty and Navy Office were so fed up with such false reports that they had instructed all ships to check their readings with old-fashioned deep sea lead lines before reporting them.[9]

On Wednesday 18 July, the *Warrego* anchored off Onslow Jetty and collected a party of mysterious passengers by boat, before weighing anchor and proceeding for the survey ground. Among the ship's company, only Commander Tancred knew where they were going and why. Like the members of the *Karangi*'s company before them, they had all signed papers promising not to divulge details of their mission. As an added layer of secrecy, they were ordered to refer to the islands only as the 'Western Islands', even on plotting sheets.[10]

The *Warrego* arrived at Montebello on the morning of Friday 20 July, only to be met by gale-force easterlies that made boat work impossible. The survey ship could do nothing but anchor in the lee of the reef on the seaward side of the islands and ride out the storm. Commander Tancred spent most of the following day at the masthead, looking for a gap through the breakers, but saw none. He finally spotted one on Sunday morning, and, despite a heavy swell, hopped in a boat and personally charted and marked a shallow boat channel between two islands.

With no time to lose, Tancred ordered the echo-sounding boats to be lowered immediately. The hydrographic teams spread out around the islands taking soundings in the many nooks and crannies beyond the scope of the original Epicure survey. Owing to the jagged reefs, narrow channels and strong tidal streams, they found the archipelago to be a difficult survey ground.

At the same time, the mysterious passengers went ashore to conduct their own investigations. One of them was Noah Pearce, a top explosives expert from HER. It was Pearce's job to decide on the exact placement of the devices that would measure the blast. He visited each island with a line of sight to Ground Zero – the point where the target vessel would be moored – calculating heights and distances and taking photographs from all angles. Then there was Major Pat Smith, Commander Royal Engineers. Major Smith was in charge of the massive construction effort required to develop the desert islands into an atomic test site. He spent most of his time taking measurements on Hermite, Trimouille, Alpha and North West, where the biggest installations were planned. He also took loads of geological samples, eventually lugging ten sacks of rocks and sand back to the UK for examination.

Despite the difficult conditions, the *Warrego* made reasonable progress until the morning of Thursday 26 July, when a sudden change of wind forced the sloop to shift anchorage. As soon as the anchor was weighed, the windlass broke down, rendering the ship effectively anchorless. With no alternative, Commander Tancred opted to return to Fremantle to effect repairs, leaving a shore party of 14 to continue boat sounding in his absence.

Unfortunately, the *Warrego* did not return for nine days, leaving the shore party stranded. Noah Pearce, who was among those left behind, later described the ordeal in Brian Cathcart's *Test of Greatness: Britain's Struggle for the Atom Bomb*:

Our food got down to some biscuits and some not very nice water. Our radio didn't have the range to reach the mainland to send an SOS. The Australians were getting a bit edgy. I was sitting in my tent one day and suddenly there was a boom and two Australians said, 'It's the *Warrego*!' and scrambled up the hill waving. We were rescued.[11]

The sloop had been delayed by bad weather and the captain's meticulousness; Commander Tancred had stopped twice more to search for the reported shoals, on the way to Fremantle and on the way back again. To the dismay of the bedraggled shore party, he rated their progress in his absence only 'fair'.[12]

Having lost a considerable amount of time, Commander Tancred now drove his crew even harder, ordering the entire ship's company to undertake hydrographic duties in addition to their own duties as seamen or stokers. Boat sounding took place from dawn to dusk every day, coastlines were charted and recharted, and semi-permanent leading marks and navigational buoys were established in the northern and southern entrances. Alarmed by the many reefs and shoals in the surrounding area, the skipper also extended ship sounding miles beyond his orders to establish a safe approach channel.

Finally, on Friday 17 August, the weather moderated enough for the *Warrego* to enter the lagoon. Even the saltiest old sea dogs on board were relieved to drop anchor in sheltered waters after weeks of constant rolling in the outer anchorages.

As the survey neared completion, Commander Tancred drew up sailing directions that doubled as a guide to life in the islands. He included detailed descriptions of the local fauna, a glowing report of the fishing, and a pointed warning about the sharks: 'Bathing is not recommended anywhere'.[13]

On Wednesday 29 August, the *Warrego* headed off to survey the Rowley Shoals near Broome, fleshing out the Woomera cover story by charting another so-called 'instrumentation site' on the opposite side of the rocket range's centre line, thus drawing the attention of hypothetical Communist spies away from the Montebellos.

The Admiralty had predicted that the survey would take three months. The *Warrego* had done it in less than half that. Even the British admirals were impressed, noting that the *Warrego* had completed its task 'in a remarkably short space of time'.[14]

The detailed survey formed the basis of the charts used by the Royal Navy Task Force throughout the trial. Some features were given appropriate names: the *Karangi* had a small island named after her, and the outer anchorage where her anchor line had snapped during a storm was dubbed 'Parting Pool'. The trial planners took a rigorously scientific approach with most of the other features: channels were named after scientists; islands after flowers; points after British prime ministers; and bays after drinks. The main channel where the target ship would be moored was named Bunsen Channel. Bluebell, Primrose and Daisy were among the islands named after flowers, and Gladstone, Disraeli and Churchill were some of the prime ministers honoured with points. As for bodies of water, Hermite alone featured Vermouth Lagoon, Stout Bay, Whisky Bay, Hock Bay, Brandy Bay, Claret Bay and Sherry Lagoon (a wit in the hydrographic office noted parenthetically that it was 'dry').[15]

•

One week before the *Warrego* sailed from the Montebellos, HMAS *Karangi* arrived at Onslow with a 40-ton Army Landing Craft (ALC 40) in tow.

The boom defence vessel was now under the temporary command of Lieutenant Commander Tony Synnot, a 29-year-old staff officer from Corowa, New South Wales. A rising star of the RAN, Synnot was so intelligent and industrious that he sometimes made his bosses at Navy Office suspicious. 'In fact, he seems at times almost too good to be true', wrote Captain McNicoll, 'but he may of course have a more fallible side which has been concealed from me.'[16] (Not really. He would eventually retire as Admiral Sir Anthony Monckton Synnot, KBE, AO, Chief of Defence Force Staff.)

According to McNicoll's brief report, the *Karangi* 'arrived with her tow at Onslow after some vicissitudes', a classic piece of Naval understatement that suggests they were lucky to make it there at all.[17] The problem was the landing craft. The ALC 40 was on loan from the Army, which immediately made it suspect in the eyes of the Navy, and was an awkward, unreliable beast that shipped water at an alarming rate. The sailors hated it with a passion.

At Onslow, Lieutenant Commander Synnot waited impatiently for an advance party from No 5 Airfield Construction Squadron RAAF (5ACS) to arrive. Affectionately known as the Flying Shovels, 5ACS had just been re-formed at Bankstown, New South Wales, partly to build tracks and landings in the Montebellos prior to the arrival of the Royal Navy Task Force. The four-man advance party, led by Corporal Tom Sugrue, had been ordered to transport hundreds of tons of heavy equipment, including bulldozers, generators, tip trucks and refrigeration units, to the islands prior to the arrival of a larger detachment. The airmen accompanied the plant to Geraldton by rail before hauling it the rest of the way by road with the help of drivers from Perth. But the sealed road on the North West Coastal Highway ran out at Northampton, just north of Geraldton. For the next 500 miles, there was nothing but a dusty, corrugated dirt road that wound its way across sheep stations, mining tenements and dry riverbeds.

Filthy and exhausted after days on the road, Corporal Sugrue and his men eventually rolled into Onslow, where they were met by a freshly shaven officer in a crisp new uniform who had just flown in by Dakota. Flight Lieutenant John Devaney was a 25-year-old ex-Army meteorologist from Adelaide, South Australia, who had just been appointed to the Citizens Air Force (the Reserves) and called up for active duty. His orders were to establish a meteorological station on Trimouille and run it with the help of Sugrue and his men.

As soon as the advance party arrived, Lieutenant Commander Synnot ordered his ship's company to begin embarking the first load of heavy equipment. The ship's derrick strained under the weight of the 25-ton bulldozers. The power grader was so big that it had to be dismantled to fit into the landing craft. A prefabricated Nissen hut – a semi-cylindrical donga made out of corrugated iron – was also hauled on board to house the meteorological station and give the airmen somewhere to sleep.

Loading cargo at Onslow was difficult work. The mile-long jetty was buffeted by wind and subjected to tides up to 10 feet. At low tide, the *Karangi*'s deck was far below the height of the jetty, and the ALC 40's deck was lower again. On a later trip, Leading Seaman JH Coff, an experienced rating, would be swept off the jetty while steadying a sling and fall 15 feet to the ship's deck, fracturing an ankle and a wrist.

Fully laden, the *Karangi* made the first of several trips to the Montebellos with the ALC 40 in tow. It was a fraught voyage, with the landing craft constantly in danger of foundering, breaking its tow, or running onto the rocks, but thanks to a combination of luck and skill, disaster was averted.

The *Karangi* arrived in Parting Pool just in time to meet the *Warrego*, which was still wrapping up the survey. Commander Tancred, who was by now quite at home in the islands' dangerous waters, came aboard and piloted the boom defence vessel into the lagoon, presenting Lieutenant Commander Synnot with a preliminary chart and sailing directions before returning to the *Warrego* and sailing for the Rowley Shoals.

Meanwhile, the *Karangi* anchored off Gladstone Beach, alongside Gladstone Point at the northern end of Trimouille, and began landing heavy equipment. It was now that Flight Lieutenant Devaney's inexperience became painfully clear.

Undoubtedly a top-notch meteorologist, the Reservist had no command experience and no idea how to set up camp in a remote location. Luckily for him, Lieutenant Commander Synnot was the sort of officer who knew how to seize the initiative. After selecting the best campsite, Synnot directed the sailors and airmen to assemble the Nissen hut and other camp facilities, while a relieved Flight Lieutenant Devaney kept out of the way and tinkered with his weather balloons.[18]

The airmen spent the next ten weeks recording wind velocity, temperature and humidity in one of the most isolated weather stations in Australia, if not the world. It was a lonely, monotonous existence in extremely harsh conditions. They all got sunburnt. At night, when the wind howled off the Indian Ocean, there was nothing to do but hunker down in the Nissen hut and play cards. They could not even listen to the radio because of the poor reception.

The *Karangi* kept the airmen company for the first couple of weeks, but once the boom defence vessel had finished delivering heavy equipment to Trimouille and stockpiling mooring gear on the floor of the lagoon, the ship's company wished the airmen well and departed.

The Naval Board had not completely forgotten about the airmen, and had in fact recommissioned a little wooden ship named HMAS *Limicola* (a.k.a. *GPV 948*) to support them, but unfortunately she was running behind. Before leaving Fremantle, the *Limicola* had experienced a 'series of unforeseeable main engine and auxiliary defects' that delayed her departure for days.[19] She eventually put to sea on Wednesday 12 September, under the command of Lieutenant GD Moore, a 26-year-old intelligence officer from Brisbane, Queensland. Escorted by corvette HMAS *Mildura*, the little ship could manage little more than 8 knots in near perfect conditions on her passage north. She eventually arrived at Trimouille about a week late, having rendezvoused with the homeward-bound *Karangi* for a handover en route. Engine problems would be a feature of the *Limicola*'s time in the Montebellos, but despite her limitations, she provided a welcome lifeline for the airmen, with regular deliveries of morale-boosting mail and provisions from the mainland.

•

In late October, the meteorological party received a visit from an even more unlikely vessel.

The *Nicol Bay* was a 65-foot coastal lugger that had been employed as an auxiliary refuelling vessel in Broome during the Second World War. The skipper was a tough old Norwegian named Harold Mathieson, who had been sailing the North West Coast for 25 years and was said to know the surrounding waters better than anyone alive. His crew consisted of a mate who was an ex-Army officer from Melbourne and a long-serving Aboriginal deckhand.

On Saturday 20 October, the *Nicol Bay* collected a group of high-ranking officers from Onslow. The senior officer was Rear Admiral AD Torlesse, DSO, RN, Task Force Commander Designate for the proposed trial. A posh 49-year-old former aircraft carrier captain with bushy black eyebrows, Admiral Torlesse was in overall command of Operation Hurricane, outranking even HER's Technical Director (a point he insisted on repeatedly, and was sure to get in writing). Accompanying him on his inspection of the proposed test site were Captain Frank Lloyd, OBE, RN, of the UK Service Liaison Staff; Commander Derek Willan, DSC, RN, the admiral's top staff officer; Captain Alan McNicoll, RAN, Deputy Chief of Naval Staff and Chairman of the Hurricane Panel; and Group Captain Bill Hely, AFC, RAAF, Officer Commanding Western Area. Based at RAAF Pearce near Perth, Group Captain Hely was the senior Air Force officer in Western Australia. He was in charge of coordinating air support for the trial, and would soon be promoted to air commodore.

With the officers on board, the *Nicol Bay* set off in a strong westerly crosswind that caused the lugger to roll considerably. Along the way, the passengers killed some time by dropping a few lines in the ocean, catching Spanish mackerel, trevally and queenfish. Mathieson and his crew had an unusual method of cooking fish: after being cleaned, they were cut into steaks, dipped in salt water, and hung between the shrouds to cook in the sun. Once the steaks were done, they were slapped between two pieces of bread and served up as sandwiches. This was not quite how it was done in the Admiralty dining room.

On arrival at Trimouille, the high-ranking officers were greeted by a nervous Flight Lieutenant Devaney. The meteorologist and his airmen had been roughing it for about eight weeks by this stage, and were looking a little worse for wear, but had done what they could to make themselves and their makeshift barracks presentable.

Admiral Torlesse's visit had been planned to give him an idea of the conditions likely to prevail at the time of the test. Over the next couple of days, he and his colleagues inspected the islands and the surrounding waters, examining navigational leads and marker buoys laid by the *Warrego*, and selecting suitable sites for moorings, shore camps and other facilities. With no guarantee that the test would go ahead, and cyclone season fast approaching, they decided to withdraw the advance party and leave the heavy equipment in situ to await the arrival of the main construction party in the new year, should the operation be approved.

After just 48 hours in the Montebellos, the officers returned to the mainland at Point Samson, where they graciously thanked Mathieson and his crew for a memorable experience. From there, they climbed into the back of a ute for a bumpy

15-mile drive to the airstrip at Roebourne, followed by an aerial inspection of the islands en route to Onslow.

When Admiral Torlesse and Commander Willan arrived back in London, they found that events had moved quickly in their absence. Throughout 1951, the Brits had been bombarding the Americans with requests to use an established US site while proceeding with preparations for the use of the Montebellos. In September, the Americans finally made an offer, but it was one the Brits found difficult to accept: a joint test carried out in Nevada, with the US Government given complete details of the bomb to ensure the safety of the American public. Chief Superintendent of High Explosive Research William Penney flew to Washington for further discussions, and ultimately recommended accepting the American offer, even though it meant sacrificing the data that would be gleaned by detonating a ship-borne bomb. Many in London, however, felt that there would be major political advantages in keeping the trial within the British Empire, and proving, as Defence Minister Manny Shinwell said, 'that Britain was not merely a satellite of the United States'.[20]

The final decision was put off until after the October election, which was a disaster for Attlee: despite winning the popular vote, Labour lost the election to Churchill's Conservatives.

The British Bulldog was back in Number 10.

Winston Churchill, now 76, had been critical of Labour's atomic programme while in opposition, but was surprised and impressed when he learnt how much work had been done in secret under Attlee's watch. He agreed that the programme should proceed more or less unchanged. He also took one look at the terms offered by the Americans and rejected them flat. This was a British bomb, and the UK Government did not need any help from the Yanks to make it work.

Operation Hurricane was go.

# 5.

# CYCLONE SEASON

On Thursday 27 December 1951, UK High Commissioner to Australia Edward Williams officially notified Prime Minister Robert Menzies that Operation Hurricane was to proceed.

Thanks to Britain's dithering over the American option, there was now less than a year to prepare the test site – very little time considering the difficulties of the location. Despite the fact that it was still cyclone season in the North West, HMAS *Karangi* was ordered back to the Montebellos to begin laying moorings as soon as possible.

One week later, Lieutenant Commander LN Morison assumed command of the *Karangi*. The new skipper was a 54-year-old Liverpudlian expatriate who had specialised in working up minesweepers during the Second World War. For the crew, it was getting hard to keep track of all the commanding officers coming and going. Able Seaman Derek Longworth, a 26-year-old boom technician from Lancashire, England, remembered it as a period when the *Karangi* 'had about five different captains in a matter of months'.[1]

The next few days were spent storing ship and flashing up boilers at North Wharf, Fremantle Harbour. That was where the *Karangi* was at 1335 on Monday 7 January when an explosion rocked the ship. The blast came from the engine room, destroying the main feed tank, shattering the skylight, and sending glass flying in all directions. The skylight's steel framework was severely buckled and the awning over the quarterdeck was blown to pieces. Miraculously, no one was killed, but six ratings were injured, including one who was struck in the head by a metal fragment that cut a deep gash in his forehead.

Fires and mechanical faults were all too common in the Navy, and there was no indication that this explosion was suspicious, but its effect was one of which any Communist saboteur would have been proud: the *Karangi* was forced to remain in port effecting repairs for the next seven days, delaying the beginning of preparations for Operation Hurricane by over a week.

Finally, on Tuesday 15 January, the *Karangi* proceeded to sea with the dreaded ALC 40 in tow once again. After stopping at Onslow, the ship and her tow arrived in the Montebellos fully laden with mooring gear. Already awaiting them was a stockpile of gear established on the floor of the lagoon during the ship's last visit.

The first moorings on the *Karangi*'s programme were two six-boat trot moorings in Bunsen Channel and two fourth-class moorings for the ships of the Landing Squadron. Trot moorings are designed to secure numerous boats or landing craft in a line. They consist of long, heavy ground chains bedded down by single-fluke anchors, with multiple mooring buoys connected at regular distances along their length. Ship moorings are classified by the size of the ship they are rated to hold, with first-class moorings being the largest, for giant ships like 15,000-ton aircraft carriers. Fourth-class moorings are designed to secure 2500-ton ships, such as landing ships tank. There are various designs for fourth-class moorings, but the ones the *Karangi* was ordered to lay were made up of three arms of heavy mooring chain bedded down by single-fluke anchors at the outer ends and concrete clumps in the middle, with a single mooring buoy connected to a central span of slack chain designed to stop the anchors from dragging across the seabed.[2]

Right throughout cyclone season, the *Karangi*'s boom technicians ('boomers') utilised the ship's horns, winches and derrick to connect and lay the individual mooring components, each of which weighed several tons. Dressed in shorts and sandals, the boomers toiled away in thick humidity punctuated by violent bursts of rain that did little to cool them down. Once each mooring was laid, the ship's divers went down to examine the connections and make sure the anchors were properly bedded down, while up on deck their mates kept a lookout for sharks. Below deck, the stokers toiled in the engine room and boiler room, where temperatures sometimes topped 140 degrees Fahrenheit. Sweat poured off them in rivers. An electric fan was eventually installed in the boiler room; it made life a little more bearable, but not much.

Despite the temptation of the cool, clear water, members of the *Karangi*'s company could not go for a swim because of all the sharks. But there was one upside to life in the Montebellos: the fishing. Whenever the ship's anglers had half a chance, they would drop a line in the ocean, often catching enough fish to feed the whole ship's company. Men fishing off the side could simply turn and sling their catches straight into the galley for the cook to fry up for dinner.

Lieutenant Commander Morison had an ingenious method for night fishing that he had developed during the war. Before retiring for the night, he dropped a line in the water, ran it up over the bridge, through the hatch, and into his cabin, where he placed the reel in a wastepaper basket beside his bunk. Whenever he had a bite, the sound of wastepaper rustling in the basket woke him up and he dashed out on deck to land the fish.

•

On the morning of Sunday 24 February, the *Karangi* was in the Mary Anne Passage, en route to the Montebellos after a brief visit to Fremantle, when the barometer began to plummet and dark, glowering clouds rolled in, blanketing out the sun. Recognising the ominous signs, Lieutenant Commander Morison gave the order to batten down the hatches and scuttles.

It was a cyclone.

At 1225, the *Karangi* was hit by a line squall that passed directly overhead, buffeting the ship with north-east winds Force 7 (about 30 knots). The little ship managed to ride out the first storm, anchoring in Parting Pool three hours later, but was soon hit by a second, fiercer one. This time, the winds were Force 8 (40 knots). Conditions continued to worsen throughout the afternoon.

Lieutenant Commander Morison reported:

> 1640. Wind increasing in velocity and sea rising. Hove the stern anchor wire through a fisherman's block forward, and veered to 130 fathoms. The ship now lay head to wind and sea. Barometer 1001.5 and falling.[3]

The ship was battered by wind and sea throughout the night, and the morning brought no relief:

> 0815. Hove in 70 fathoms on the stern anchor wire. Let go port bower anchor, sheered to starboard and let go starboard bower. Both bowers were then veered to 40 fathoms and the main anchor wire veered to 130 fathoms. Port and starboard bowers were then veered to 55 fathoms and dragged until they shared the strain with the main wire.[4]

Wind and sea increased throughout the day, the lowest barometer reading being 995.5, recorded at 1500. Two hours later, winds increased to Force 10 to 11 (50 to 60 knots), with torrential rain reducing visibility to nil, and breaking seas completely obscuring nearby Peanut Island. The *Karangi* was now fighting for her life. All throughout the first watch, Morison was forced to engage main engines to keep her on station. The situation remained unchanged throughout the night, and as the wind never changed direction from the north-east, it became clear to all on board that the ship was right in the path of the storm.

Throughout the cyclone, one unlucky seaman was stationed on the horns with a signal lamp at all times, watching the anchor wires and hollering out to the officer of the watch whenever they became too taut. Heavy spray and wild seas continually crashed on deck. Sub Lieutenant PM Cumming, a 22-year-old officer from Nedlands, Western Australia, improvised a helmet from the brass binnacle cover to help battle the driving rain while peering to windward, and was soon imitated by the older officers, all pride gone by the wayside. Constant bearings were taken of the surrounding islands through the brief gaps in the rain, the fear of running onto the rocks all too real.

Finally, on the morning of Tuesday 26 February, the weather abated just enough to weigh anchor and head for the shelter of Bunsen Channel. Conditions were still rough, and the helmsman was forced to take evasive action to avoid crashing into the navigation buoy in the entrance to the channel, but at 1300 the *Karangi* moored in the deep, riding out the rest of the storm in relative safety after forty-eight hours of sheer terror.

The next day, the tough little ship went right back to work as if nothing had ever happened. A few days later, she left the lagoon and headed to Darwin to collect 90 tons of pierced-steel planking (PSP) for the construction of roads and landings. One night, on her passage north, it was so hot that a fire broke out below deck, sending the entire crew to fire stations. The blaze was soon extinguished, with little damage to the ship, but the result could have been much worse. 'It was apparently caused by the spontaneous combustion of cleaning materials (new) stowed in the Engineer's store on the port side of the tiller flat', reported Lieutenant Commander Morison.[5]

•

While the *Karangi*'s company laboured in the extreme heat and humidity of the North West, government officials and service chiefs plotted in cosy firelit chambers in London and air-conditioned offices in Melbourne and Canberra.

Up until now, Prime Minister Menzies had given remarkably little thought to the issue of radiation. It was only when prompted by Admiral Collins, Chief of Naval Staff, and Sir Frederick Shedden, Defence Secretary, that he finally broached the topic in official correspondence with the UK Government. In a letter dated 24 January 1952, Menzies drew attention to the 'possible after-effects of this project on the Australian Mainland and its inhabitants':

The only persons in a position to make an authoritative statement in this regard are the United Kingdom scientists who know the precise nature of the experiment and who are now in possession of the necessary meteorological data to estimate its after-effects. From the point of view of the Australian announcement, some categorical and authoritative statement will be necessary that the effects will be innocuous.[6]

In response, the UK High Commission promised that London would consult with Canberra on a suitably reassuring official announcement. The British diplomats added that they hoped to forward a memorandum full of 'technical and highly confidential' data on the subject of after-effects 'very shortly', but they never sent it, probably for security reasons.[7] Instead, they offered Menzies a personal assurance on behalf of William Penney and his scientific colleagues:

> Meanwhile the United Kingdom scientists concerned give a categorical assurance that the explosion will take place only when conditions are such that there will be no danger from radio-activity to the health of animals or people on the mainland of Australia. There is a slight risk of minor damage to property from reverberation (for example, perhaps a few broken windows) but this will be no greater than the risk caused by distant gunnery practice.[8]

Distant gunnery practice! That statement was as ludicrous as it was disingenuous. The British scientists were well aware of the risks inherent to an atomic test – that's why it was happening in the Montebello Islands and not the Scilly Isles off the coast of Great Britain. Possible accident scenarios included a larger-than-expected explosion impacting the surrounding ships or a last-minute change of wind carrying dangerous levels of fallout across the mainland. The British scientists were literally asking Menzies to take their word that nothing like that would happen. Naturally, Menzies accepted their assurance in the spirit in which it was offered. The atomic programme proceeded on what amounted to a gentlemen's agreement between the two nations.

On Monday 18 February 1952, just a few days after the death of the ailing King George VI and the accession of Queen Elizabeth II, the British and Australian governments simultaneously announced plans to conduct an atomic test in Australia. The carefully worded statement was brief and intentionally vague, with no specific reference to where or when the test would take place:

In the course of this year the United Kingdom Government intend to test an atomic weapon produced in the United Kingdom. In close co-operation with the Government of the Commonwealth of Australia, the test will take place at a site in Australia. It will be conducted in conditions which will ensure that there will be no danger whatever from radioactivity to the health of people or animals in the Commonwealth.[9]

The Australian press did not react to the news with alarm, but with patriotic pride. 'Britain, with her resources of scientific talent and technical skill, is again effectively demonstrating her ability to increase the power of the free world', proclaimed the Adelaide *Advertiser*.[10] 'It is fitting in all the circumstances that Australia, with the useful contribution she can offer, should be associated with the practical side of the British experiments', added *The West Australian*.[11] The Melbourne *Age* at least acknowledged the potential downside of atomic testing, before quickly glossing over it: 'Such is mankind's natural dread of the unknown in atomic weapons that the first reaction of most men and women is one of trepidation at the announcement that Britain's first atomic weapon is to be exploded in Australia. It is a fearful weapon; the most indiscriminately destructive yet devised by the ingenuity of man. Such fears should be allayed however, by consideration of the hard realities of science and international relations.'[12]

Much of the ensuing coverage was given over to excited speculation about the location of the test site (the smart money was on Woomera Rocket Range) and the nature of the test (many experts believed that multiple weapons would be tested because a British official had said that the UK would test 'atomic weapons' [plural] in Australia).[13] The assurance that the test posed no danger to Australians was generally accepted as a matter of course.

A rare voice of dissent came from Henry Wardlaw, Secretary of the Council for Aboriginal Rights. 'Atomic tests over the Woomera Rocket Range would be the most barbarous of all the barbarous acts yet perpetrated against the aborigines', he said.[14] The rocket range covered vast areas of desert populated by Aboriginal people living traditional nomadic lifestyles. 'The danger to human life from an explosion or contact with contaminated material is obvious', he noted.[15] Wardlaw was wrong about the test being held at Woomera, but he was right about the dangers of testing on the mainland, as later events would prove.

●

On Tuesday 11 March, HMAS *Mildura* anchored off Onslow Jetty.

A Bathurst Class corvette (or Australian Minesweeper), the *Mildura* was a small warship, similar in size to the *Karangi* but lighter, more manoeuvrable, and much better armed. Built quickly and cheaply during the war, the *Mildura* was already showing her age, despite which she had recently been recommissioned as a training vessel for Western Australian Reservists and National Servicemen. Her orders were to rendezvous with the airmen of No 5 Airfield Construction Squadron (5ACS), transport them to the Montebellos, and remain on hand to facilitate the construction of roads and landings.

The captain of the *Mildura* was the recently promoted Lieutenant Commander John Ferguson, DSC, previously the *Karangi*'s navigation officer. A Scottish-born hard-arse decorated for his actions while commanding torpedo boats off Normandy, Ferguson was well suited to the task of training raw recruits and part-timers. Following one of his ship's earliest training cruises, he remarked:

Conduct has not been all that is required of a training ship, and discipline therefore is inflexible. It is considered that a good number of ratings entered during the post-war period feel that a 'draft' to a ship operating from their home port lends itself to relaxation and may be treated as a 'holiday', and that the comparative youth of the Senior [RAN] ratings lacks the authority necessary to govern experienced Senior [RANR] ratings. These impressions are being corrected, and it is confidently expected that the required standard of conduct will be maintained.[16]

Translation: they copped a bollocking.

In addition to her normal complement of 85, the *Mildura* was carrying a draft of 48 National Servicemen, six Reserve ratings, three Reserve officers, three National Service instructors from HMAS *Leeuwin* and one staff officer from Navy Office. Consequently, the mess decks were crowded and malodorous, with seasickness rampant among the green trainees. The hold was also crammed from stem to stern with Air Force stores and equipment loaded at Fremantle. 'It could be observed that the RAAF appear to have a propensity for understatement of cubic capacity and are not overwell acquainted with the hold capacity and accommodation spaces of a Fleet Minesweeper', grumbled Ferguson.[17]

The following day, the *Mildura* secured alongside the jetty and embarked the 30-strong 5ACS Detachment. This time, the Flying Shovels were led by Squadron Leader Ken Garden, a 41-year-old engineer from Sydney who had led the old 5ACS into Japan in 1946 as part of the British Commonwealth Occupation Force (BCOF). The detachment included a high number of experienced non-commissioned officers, including the newly promoted Sergeant Tom Sugrue. Large quantities of petrol, oil and lubricants were also embarked, as well as a motorboat for the use of the airmen. 'The hull condition of this motorboat resembled that of a strainer, and it was accordingly hoisted for caulking and tingling as necessary', complained Ferguson. 'Additionally, the engine was defective to the extent that it was deemed necessary to lift it for a complete refit.'[18]

On arrival at the Montebellos, the *Mildura* found the place deserted. The *Karangi* had recently gone to Darwin to collect 90 tons of PSP and was yet to return. Thanks to her shallow draft, the *Mildura* negotiated the southern entrance with relative ease and anchored in Bunsen Channel. Lieutenant Commander Ferguson, Squadron Leader Garden and Lieutenant Commander Tommy Clarke, the visiting staff officer, then went ashore to look for suitable campsites on Trimouille, eventually opting to stick with the old one at Gladstone Beach.

Returning to the ship, Ferguson ordered a working party to bring forward the heavy plant and refrigerating machinery stored the previous year. To everyone's surprise, the equipment had survived the recent cyclone intact. More alarming was the state of the poor old ALC 40, which was found 300 yards inland at medium tide and side on to the beach. After a failed effort to refloat it that night, the sailors succeeded the following day, with the assistance of an RAAF bulldozer. A sustained effort by the *Mildura*'s stokers soon had the landing craft operational again.

Meanwhile, the seamen landed hundreds of tons of equipment, stores, fresh meat and tinned vegetables at Gladstone Beach in the motorboat and whaler. To make room for the camp, the airmen removed the side of a huge sandhill with a bulldozer. Next, they put up tents, connected electric lights to generators, and ran pipes to water tanks set up on higher ground. The original 5ACS had done this sort of thing to great acclaim in places like New Guinea and Borneo during the war, but Lieutenant Commander Ferguson did not rate the new lot at all. 'Naval working parties continued to assist the

RAAF shore party in the establishment of the camp and, as was expected, again showed superior initiative, versatility and industry', he commented, unnecessarily editorialising in an official report to the Naval Board.[19]

By Tuesday 18 March, the camp was up and running and the heavy machinery was 90 per cent operational. Right on cue, the *Karangi* returned with a hold full of PSP, but not as much as expected. Owing to the breakdown of the only available forklift in Darwin, Lieutenant Commander Morison had been forced to leave behind 30 tons to be collected another day, giving the airmen 60 tons to begin with. The *Karangi* immediately began offloading PSP into the ALC 40 to be landed at Gladstone Beach, but the sailors were dismayed to discover that the landing craft – which they optimistically expected to carry 55 tons – was 'in imminent danger of foundering with only 31 tons embarked'.[20] From then on, they never exceeded that amount, but the bloody thing still almost sank on at least two more occasions.

At Gladstone Beach, the airmen bulldozed and graded a landing and started laying PSP. Working in small teams, they connected each 10-foot by 15-inch plank to the one alongside by fitting the hooks on the long side of one plank into the slots on the opposite side of the other. Although the short ends were straight, the airmen interlocked the planks lengthwise by laying them in a staggered pattern, ensuring that each plank was connected to two planks on either side, thus allowing no movement in any direction. In no time at all, the airmen constructed a sturdy landing for boats and landing craft, and a nearby hardstand for stockpiling stores and equipment, thereby expediting the unloading process considerably. They would spend the next six months doing the same sort of jobs.

•

At dawn on Saturday 5 April, a merchant ship appeared in the offing at the Montebellos. SS *Dorrigo* was a 2500-ton steamer from Western Australia's State Shipping Service. In her hold was an additional 250 tons of PSP from Darwin, including the 30 tons short-shipped by the *Karangi*.

In an era before railway lines and sealed highways, the State Shipping Service provided a crucial lifeline to the remote communities of the North West. State Ships delivered fresh fruit, vegetables, mail and (most importantly) beer to Geraldton, Carnarvon, Darwin and ports in between, bringing back beef, wool, asbestos, lead ore and crates full of empties. Some State Ships also carried passengers, but the *Dorrigo* was strictly a cargo ship.

The State Ships often delivered supplies to Onslow during Operation Hurricane, but, surprisingly, they also made the occasional delivery directly to the Montebellos. Security on board was the official responsibility of the ship's master, but ASIO men also kept an eye on suspect individuals while in the vicinity of the test site. All photographs, sketches and notebooks were strictly forbidden.

On arrival at the Montebellos, the *Dorrigo* was led into Parting Pool by the *Mildura*, which directed the State Ship's movements with signal flags. The *Dorrigo*'s master, Captain WE Hardman, rather enjoyed this exercise in seamanship, but his mood soon fell when work began and the state of the ALC 40 became clear to him:

Our worst fears were realized when discharging started and the barge built to carry 50 tons could only take a maximum of 25 tons in smooth weather. The gear to handle the cargo ashore was just inadequate and in spite of great efforts by Officers and men of the Navy – on the first day we discharged 35 tons, the second 43½ tons, the third (bad weather), 16 tons.[21]

Lieutenant Commander Ferguson was also frustrated. The ALC 40's lack of seaworthiness, combined with the unreliability of its engines, led to the decision to embark the PSP into the *Mildura* for transfer to the landing craft in the sheltered water of Bunsen Channel. Even that effort failed when the RAAF crane on shore broke down, followed by the ALC 40 itself. As a last resort, the *Mildura*'s hard-working sailors unloaded the PSP into the motorboat and whaler while the airmen allegedly watched from the shore. Tension had been building between the two services ever since the 5ACS Detachment had embarked in the *Mildura*, and now it reached breaking point. Lieutenant Commander Ferguson unloaded on the Air Force in his report to the Naval Officer in Charge (NOIC) Fremantle:

> In this regard as in some other minor matters it was felt that the RAAF party was less co-operative than was possible. Observing that Naval Parties manned all boats, worked continuously in three watches, were entirely responsible for embarking cargo and bore the brunt of the labor [sic] of discharge, while RAAF parties in three watches with one watch standing down waited idly until machinery was repaired; and further noting that the Shore party depended for its existence and to a large degree for its technical maintenance and Stores upon the Naval service, it was considered that greater endeavour from that quarter could have been expected. Disgruntled RAAF whisperings concerning the paucity of the tobacco ration, the normal Naval ration, were not unheard by ratings, who also remembered that the RAAF beer ration, supplied entirely by the ship, was more than double their own. Naval comment did not waste words with innuendo but was unmistakeably plain. Inter-Service relations however did not suffer unduly, but it is ventured as an opinion

that an overall command, preferably Naval, would be an advantage in operations of this nature."[22]

Captain F Bryce Morris, the new NOIC Fremantle, was not too fazed by the diatribe, probably because he knew what Ferguson was like. 'The party concerned were mainly technicians and as such seemed to lack the initiative and ability to improvise of the seamen and are rather lost without their cranes, bulldozers, etc. with which they normally work', he explained, rather condescendingly, in his cover letter to the Naval Board. 'It is agreed, however, that an overall command is most desirable in such cases.'[23]

It is not clear whether the airmen felt the same way, because Squadron Leader Garden declined to record his thoughts on the matter, showing more restraint than his Naval counterpart.

Meanwhile, poor Captain Hardman was tearing his hair out. A delay like this was a nightmare for the master of a merchant ship, with a strict itinerary he was expected to stick to come hell or high water. As Hardman's desperation rose, it became clear to the Navy officers that the only solution was to bring the *Dorrigo* into the lagoon. On the morning of Tuesday 8 April, the *Mildura* led the State Ship through South Channel, right into the middle of the top-secret test site.

Now the unloading picked up pace. The RAN supplied enough men for the *Dorrigo* to work two gangs, and over 113 tons were discharged the first day. The next day, the *Karangi* finished a mooring job and embarked 100 tons of PSP to capacity, while the *Mildura* embarked the balance of 34 tons. Finally, the job was done. At high water on Thursday 10 April, the *Mildura* acted as a tugboat by turning the *Dorrigo* about and leading her out of the lagoon, to Captain Hardman's evident relief. The *Dorrigo* eventually arrived in Fremantle on Friday 18 April, three days behind schedule.

The role of the State Shipping Service was one of the most unusual elements of Operation Hurricane. The *Dorrigo* made three more trips to the Montebellos, sustaining hull damage from Naval lighters on two separate occasions, to Captain Hardman's dismay. Passenger/cargo ship MV *Kabbarli* also visited the islands in May, anchoring in Parting Pool with a full complement of 37 civilian passengers on board, including a senior member of the editorial staff of West Australian Newspapers Limited, publisher of Perth's two daily newspapers.

The additional duties inevitably impacted the State Ships' normal services to the North West, leading to a heated debate in State Parliament. In September, Labor's Loy Rodoreda launched a broadside at the Liberal Government, alleging that the prioritisation of the atomic test was delaying the delivery of vital provisions to northern ports. 'Because of the huge quantities of petrol being sent to the atomic project, supplies in the North West are in a parlous position', he stated.[24] Almost alone among Australian politicians, he also expressed concern about the environmental impact of the bomb, lamenting that 'the islands could have been one of the finest tourist resorts that ever existed'.[25]

Premier Ross McLarty dismissed these concerns as 'either without foundation or extremely exaggerated'.[26] He admitted that there had been some delays, but argued that these were due to other factors, such as the temporary absence of State Ship *SS Dulverton* on duties in the eastern states. 'The Navy has cooperated closely with the management of the State Shipping Service to ensure that the normal service should not be disrupted.'[27]

Captain Hardman might have begged to differ.

# 6.

# THE LANDING
# SQUADRON

It was early on the morning of Wednesday 16 April 1952 when the Royal Navy's 4th Landing Ship Squadron arrived at Fremantle, Western Australia.

HM Ships *Zeebrugge* and *Narvik* were a day late, having been delayed by a fierce storm in the Indian Ocean. The rough seas meant slow going for the fully laden landing ships tank (LSTs), with their flat bottoms and shallow draughts, which pitched and rolled up and down the waves in a sickening, corkscrewing motion. At the height of the storm, a bulldozer in the *Narvik*'s tank deck broke free, threatening life and limb until it was caught and lashed down.

The storm had since abated, and the weather was fine as the two ships rounded Rottnest Island in the dawn light and steamed into Gage Roads, Fremantle's outer harbour. The *Zeebrugge*, under the command of Captain George Colville, Senior Officer of the 4th Landing Ship Squadron, was the first to enter the inner harbour, securing alongside at H Shed, Victoria Quay, at 0935. One hour later, the *Narvik*, under Commander Derek Willan, berthed alongside.

The security arrangements at Victoria Quay that day were unlike anything seen in Fremantle since the Second World War.

Barbed-wire barricades surrounded the wharf. Commonwealth Peace Officers, Naval Dockyard Police and Naval ratings patrolled the area. Armed guards manned the only gates in and out. All along the fence line, warning signs read:

Defence (Prohibited wharves and public buildings) Regulations: Entry on this wharf is prohibited except under the authority of a permit issued in pursuance of Regulation 6 of the above-mentioned regulations. Penalty: A fine of £20 or imprisonment for three months.[1]

The notice was signed by Captain F Bryce Morris, Naval Officer in Charge (NOIC) Fremantle.

Only a handful of press men and waterfront workers were on hand to watch the Landing Squadron arrive. Among them was Norm 'Myrtle' Milne, a 25-year-old reporter from *The West Australian*, Perth's long-running morning paper. A keen yachtsman and former RANR rating, Milne was *The West*'s man on the waterfront. Alongside him were mates and rivals from the evening *Daily News* and *The Sunday Times*.

The press men watched intently as the LSTs came into port. The UK Ministry of Defence had said nothing about the Landing Squadron's movements, but the two ships had snuck out of Portsmouth just one day after the announcement that Britain's first atomic test would be conducted in Australia sometime that year. The press in both countries had immediately concluded that the ships were heading Down Under to prepare for the test, and no one had bothered to deny it.

When the ships docked, scores of Royal Marines and Royal Engineers lined their upper decks, looking sharp in their crisp uniforms. Other than a few crates stacked up on deck, there was nothing remarkable about the *Zeebrugge*'s appearance. By contrast, the *Narvik*'s upper deck was covered with landing craft: five larger landing craft, known as landing craft mechanised (LCMs), which were designed to carry tanks and personnel carriers; and two smaller ones, landing craft assault (LCAs), which were designed to carry troops. As a Navy man, Milne immediately understood the significance of their presence.

Ever since the test had been announced, most experts had assumed that the bomb would be detonated at Woomera, in the heart of the South Australian desert. But the landing craft on the *Narvik*'s upper deck told a different story. Amphibious assault vehicles would not be of much use in the desert, but they would certainly come in handy on a remote beach somewhere. But where? Australia had over 30,000 miles of coastline and thousands of offshore islands, from Heard Island in the southern reaches of the Indian Ocean to Norfolk Island, way off in the South Pacific.

Milne and his colleagues speculated on these and other matters as they milled about on the dock, watching proceedings through the barbed-wire fence. Despite the fearsome defences and air of grave mystery, the scene was punctuated by a moment of slapstick worthy of an Ealing comedy. As *Sunday Times* gossip columnist Richard Murray reported:

> It is to be hoped the scientists at the rocket range are better shots than some of the sailors and seagoing soldiers aboard the hush-hush ships *Zeebrugge* and *Narvik*. Attempts at throwing lines ashore and between the 2 ships gave some of the onlookers a laugh when the ships berthed. If anyone wants a good mooring line there is one on the harbor [sic] bottom at H shed. They forgot to fasten one end before they threw it out.[2]

The following day, the officers of the Landing Squadron were officially welcomed to Fremantle at a Town Hall function hosted by Mayor Bill Samson. Also in attendance was Fremantle's

Federal Member of Parliament, Labor's Kim Beazley (senior), who proclaimed the Landing Squadron's visit 'unique in the history of Fremantle'.[3] Beazley also took a swipe at the Menzies Government over rumoured plans to sell South Australian uranium deposits to the USA. 'These resources should be kept within the British Commonwealth', he insisted, to murmurings of assent.[4]

As senior officer, Captain Colville spoke on behalf of the Landing Squadron. The 48-year-old former cruiser captain was the grandson of a lord, the son of an admiral, and the brother of the Queen's press secretary. It would be fair to say that handling the niceties of a civic reception was well within his wheelhouse. Rising to speak, he graciously thanked his hosts for their hospitality and apologised for the Landing Squadron's late arrival. Brushing off questions about their ultimate destination, he stuck to the official line and told reporters, 'I will be honest and tell you that I've not yet got my final orders and am in the happy position of not knowing where we are going from here.'[5] With a twinkle in his eye, Colville revealed that he had been keeping track of all the rumoured destinations to appear in the press, and currently had 19 places checked off on his map! His remarks were met with gratifying laughter.

Commander Willan, captain of the *Narvik*, kept his face impassive throughout. A 34-year-old Dunkirk veteran with a keen interest in philately, Willan would go on to write a book called *Greek Rural Postmen and their Cancellation Numbers*, which would win the *Bookseller* award for Oddest Title of 1996.[6] Commander Willan had already been to the Montebellos with Admiral Torlesse, and definitely knew where they were going, even if Captain Colville did not – which he clearly did. But Willan was in for a surprise of his own when the local Qantas representative stood up and presented him with a plaque. It was his ship's own plaque – a solid brass lion from the city of Narvik, Norway – which had mysteriously disappeared during the recent visit to Cocos that had resulted in the deaths of several men. The culprits were the larrikins from No 2 Airfield Construction Squadron RAAF, who had made off with the lion during a raucous farewell bash, only to return it via Qantas courier in a box labelled, 'Wardroom, *Narvik*'.[7] The lion had come the long way around, with stops in Djakarta, Singapore and Sydney on the way to Perth.

The official reception was just the beginning of the Landing Squadron's festivities in Western Australia. According to Lieutenant Peter Bird of the *Narvik*, the locals put on 'a quite staggering programme of entertainment':

> That weekend many of us accepted an invitation from the West Australian Turf Club to a race meeting at the lovely Headquarters track – an occasion blessed with glorious weather and, for two of us, the smile of Lady Luck: we 'went through the card' for eight winners.
>
> That evening the Victoria League entertained us to a barbecue party. To take up all the other invitations showered upon us we had to split up into small groups; official occasions led to private parties – dances and outings to the West Australian beauty spots like Araluen and Canning Dam. Our timetable was not elastic, and six short days was not enough to accept all the hospitality offered.[8]

While the officers wined and dined with society types, the men of the lower deck attended dances organised by the Naval Association and Returned Servicemen's League, or made their own fun in the many bars and brothels in Perth and Fremantle. Most of the servicemen comported themselves admirably, but inevitably a few troublemakers took things too far. On the day the Landing Squadron arrived in Fremantle, three sailors from the *Zeebrugge* were arrested for brawling in Hay Street, Perth. The men were charged the following day, but the charges were almost immediately withdrawn, with the prosecuting sergeant informing the magistrate that he had been ordered to drop the case for 'security reasons'.[9] Instead, the men would be dealt with by the Navy.

Later that night, two British servicemen stole a taxi from outside a house in Fremantle. Several taxi drivers inside the house heard the engine start and dashed out in time to see the servicemen tear off. The furious drivers then jumped in their vehicles and gave chase through the streets of Fremantle. The troublemakers were eventually caught and hauled into Fremantle Police Station, only to be released to the Royal Navy Shore Patrol soon after.

In a separate incident, three British soldiers, two Australian sailors and one 18-year-old civilian were seriously injured when a packed automobile crashed into a parked truck in Queen Victoria Street, Fremantle. The servicemen were all admitted to Hollywood Hospital with a collection of lacerated scalps, fractured skulls and broken arms, and the 18-year-old was admitted to Fremantle Hospital with a fractured jaw, fractured skull and dislocated hip. The authorities initially refused to confirm or deny that British servicemen were involved, citing 'security reasons' just for a change, before reluctantly releasing the names of the injured men under pressure from the press. Once again, no charges were laid.

This was all highly irregular. While it was not unusual for visiting servicemen to get into trouble on shore leave, the normal procedure was for offenders to face a civil court before being dealt with by the services. Now it seemed as though shadowy figures were lurking in the background, pulling strings and prioritising British security over the safety of Australians.

When grilled about the special arrangements, the relevant authorities pleaded ignorance. The *Narvik*'s first lieutenant,

Lieutenant Commander Mark Kerr, DSC, said he had 'no knowledge of men from his ship being released from police custody' and 'knew of no arrangement for this procedure' (a statement that notably excludes the *Zeebrugge*).[10] Regarding the brawling charge, an RAN spokesman said that 'as far as he knew there had been no arrangement or instruction to the RAN locally to have the disorderly charge withdrawn from civil court'.[11] The Western Australia Police Commissioner refused to comment on the situation, and the Police Minister claimed to know nothing about it. The Federal Defence Minister, Philip McBride, washed his hands of the matter entirely, saying, 'These ships are under Royal Navy command and they act under their own regulations.'[12]

Dismayed by the arrogant flouting of Western Australian laws, and the submissive response of the local authorities, the *Daily News* published a scathing editorial:

SO MUCH FOR 'SECURITY'
Security here has run amuck [sic], produced an intolerable and dangerous situation, and is now in process of making a shambling retreat.

By some mystery of meddling and muddling, servicemen on shore leave from the atomic-gear ships now nearing the end of their stay at Fremantle were conceded immunity from the law of the land.

Instead of being hauled into court as anyone else would be – serviceman or civilian – to answer charges of disorderliness by fighting and so on, those who came under police notice were handed over to their own authorities 'for security reasons'.

'Security' – rubbish and humbug ...[13]

Much to his chagrin, Captain Morris, NOIC Fremantle, was forced to deal with the growing controversy. A 49-year-old destroyer man from Wycheproof, Victoria, Captain Morris was in charge of service security for Operation Hurricane. It was his job to safeguard all military equipment and establishments associated with the test and prevent any subversion of (or by) service personnel. As NOIC Fremantle, he had the full resources of the Naval Staff Office and the Naval Dockyard Police (the Navy's equivalent of the Military Police) at his disposal, but ultimately the responsibility was his.

Responding to the *Daily News*'s editorial, Captain Morris insisted that the whole thing was one big misunderstanding. 'I am unable to ascertain where the mistake arose, but it was never the intention that men on shore leave from the visiting ships would be immune from the normal processes of the law', he explained. 'As soon as my attention was drawn to this matter, the authorities were informed that the men were to be dealt with in the normal manner. The only provision was that care should be taken that questions to which the answers might, perhaps, disclose confidential information as to the ship's movements, etc., should be avoided.'[14]

Captain Morris's statement did the trick and tamped down the furore, but it also raised a significant question: If the NOIC Fremantle and his staff did not intervene on behalf of the British servicemen, who did?

It could only have been ASIO.

The newly formed Australian Security Intelligence Organisation was in charge of civil security for Operation Hurricane. It was their job to keep all known and suspected subversives under close observation, especially the Communist rabble-rousers in the Waterside Workers Federation and Seamen's Union of Australia, and prevent any loose talk among the civilian population.

ASIO's involvement in Operation Hurricane went right to the top. Colonel Charles Spry, Director General of ASIO and former Director of Military Intelligence, was one of five members of the Hurricane Panel in Melbourne coordinating the operation with their counterparts in London. Among the small number of people in Spry's office with codeword clearance was Miss MJ Tucker, his personal secretary. His wartime driver, Lieutenant Colonel Max Phillipps of Operation Epicure, was in charge of coordinating security arrangements with the Navy. Though based in Melbourne, Phillipps visited Western Australia frequently, and was almost definitely in Perth when the Landing Squadron arrived.

Local security was handled by Colonel Tom Cotton, MC, DSO, head of ASIO's Perth office. A bone fide war hero, Cotton had been seriously wounded and had a metal plate in his head, which gave him headaches and apparently caused him to act erratically. Cotton had officers lurking in pubs and nightspots all around Perth and Fremantle eavesdropping on unsuspecting patrons. ASIO officers did not have the power to arrest anyone, so if and when they picked up on any subversive activities they called in Commonwealth Peace Officers to slap on the cuffs. If anyone told the Western Australia Police to drop the Hay Street case, it was probably someone from Cotton's office.

Finally, two other senior ASIO officers joined the Task Force to coordinate security between the Montebellos and the mainland: Leo Carter and Jack Clowes. Carter, a former RAAF officer, was attached to the *Zeebrugge*, and remained in the islands right throughout the operation. Jack Clowes was based in Onslow, where he operated 'under cover' for six weeks before setting up an office at the local police station.[15] From then on, all civilians were required to report to Clowes upon arrival in town, which they apparently did willingly. A devoted Catholic from Queensland, Clowes would spend eight months away from his family on Operation Hurricane.

Meanwhile, the press men were keeping a close eye on developments down at Victoria Quay.

Every day, reporters and photographers watched from behind the barricades as hundreds of crates were trucked in and loaded onto the LSTs. This seemed to be further evidence that the test would not be conducted at Woomera. If the Royal Engineers were heading to South Australia, then the LSTs would probably be unloading supplies for transport by rail, not taking on more by the truckload.

The next big clue was the arrival of two RAN vessels: Motor Water Lighter (MWL) 251 and Motor Refrigerator Lighter (MRL) 252. The 200-ton lighters were designed to resupply ships at sea with food and water. MWL 251 had just been brought out of mothballs at Garden Island, Western Australia, while MRL 252 had been towed around from Melbourne by the Naval tug HMAS *Reserve*. Both ships were now berthed outside the wire barricades protecting the LSTs, but subject to security restrictions regarding their future movements.

The inference was clear: the lighters would be used to resupply the LSTs at sea. That meant the Landing Squadron was probably heading to an offshore island, or group of islands, for an extended period.

The puzzle was coming together.

It was Norm Milne who got the scoop. As a former Naval rating, Milne knew how to talk to men of the lower deck. Just before the squadron was due to leave port, he struck up a conversation with a British sailor. Almost as an aside, he asked where they were heading.

'Some bloody place called the Monte Bellos', was the reply.[16]

Eureka! The Montebello Islands! The uninhabited archipelago off the North West Coast would make an ideal test site. All of a sudden, the recent movements of HMA Ships *Karangi* and *Mildura* began to make sense. Both ships had been seen towing landing craft and other small vessels up and down the coast with no explanation from the Navy. The *Mildura* had just returned from a so-called 'training cruise' to the North West, and the *Karangi* was up there right now.

Hoping for confirmation, Milne went to the Navy for comment, but a spokesman refused to confirm or deny the story, saying only: 'We have no information.'[17] Corroboration soon arrived from Canberra, however, when *The West Australian*'s correspondent reported that the Commonwealth Government was planning to declare prohibited areas around the Montebellos, Barrow Island and the Rowley Shoals 'for the testing of war material [sic]'.[18] The prohibition was due to be gazetted in just over a week. The penalty was a £200 fine and/or six months in gaol.

That was enough for *The West Australian*'s editors. Milne's carefully worded article, which described the Montebellos as the 'likely' test site, appeared on the front page on Tuesday 22 April:

ISLANDS OFF W.A. FOR ATOMIC TESTS
The Monte Bello Islands, about 85 miles north-east of Onslow, are believed to be the site chosen by the British and Australian Governments for the first British atomic tests which are to be held later this year.

The atomic expedition, consisting of two Royal Navy tank-landing craft and two Royal Australian Navy lighters, is due to leave Fremantle at 10 a.m. today for the testing site.

Aboard the tank-landing ships the Narvik and Zeebrugge are 100 technicians of the Royal Marines and the Royal Engineers who will prepare the area for the explosions ...[19]

Milne's story, which would go on to win the Lovekin Prize for Best Western Australian News Story of 1952, was just the beginning of his company's groundbreaking coverage of Operation Hurricane.

•

On the same day as Milne's editors were debating whether to run his article in Perth, 11 senior RAAF officers met at Air Force HQ in Melbourne to discuss 'RAAF aspects of Operation Hurricane'.[20]

The meeting was held in Room 212 in N Block, the new red-brick extension behind the original Victoria Barracks, and commenced at 1430 precisely.

Air Vice Marshal Val Hancock, DFC, Deputy Chief of Air Staff, chaired the meeting, which was also attended by representatives from Eastern Area HQ in Sydney, North Eastern Area HQ in Townsville, and Western Area HQ in Perth. Air Vice Marshal Hancock was a 44-year-old Western Australian who had commanded No 71 Wing RAAF, a Beaufort bomber wing operating out of New Guinea, during the Second World War. (He was also the cousin of iron ore mining magnate Lang Hancock.) He began by explaining that the purpose of the conference was to discuss the problems that might arise from the provision of aircraft for Operation Hurricane.

Several months earlier, the UK Hurricane Executive (Hurrex) had sent Australia's Hurricane Panel a long list of requests for the RAAF, including security patrols, a courier service, communications facilities and medical evacuations (if and when required). Most of those tasks were fairly routine, but a couple were anything but. To prove that the UK Government was taking its safety commitment to Australia seriously, and to gather valuable scientific data on the performance of the weapon, Hurrex had asked the RAAF to carry out 'coastal monitoring duties on the day of the explosion and the one following to determine whether any fission products had been deposited on the mainland' and 'air sampling sorties up to 25,000 feet and at approximately

500 miles range from the Monte Bello Islands on the same days'.[21]

Air sampling meant flying through the radioactive cloud to collect samples for scientific analysis. The proposed programme was based on one carried out by the RAF over the North Atlantic, in which bomber crews collected long-range radioactive samples from atomic tests carried out in the US and the USSR for analysis by the Atomic Energy Research Establishment (AERE) at Harwell, Oxfordshire.

Clearly, air sampling and coastal monitoring both involved a significant risk of radioactive contamination of aircraft and exposure of aircrew, a fact of which Hurrex was well aware. At the beginning of the North Atlantic air-sampling programme, the AERE had come up with a series of radiation guidelines for RAF aircrews:

1. The radiation dose received by aircrews while actually flying through an atomic explosion cloud could be expected to be well below the lethal level at times later than 15 minutes after the burst.

2. The contamination of the aircraft was likely to cause radiation exposure quite as serious as that arising from direct exposure from the cloud.

3. The breathing of contaminated air during passage through the cloud at speeds of the order of 300 mph was found to be rather less serious than the exposure to the external gamma radiation in the cloud and no long-term injury was likely to arise from this cause for times later than 15 minutes after the burst.

4. The simple rule that aircraft must avoid flying through the visible cloud following an atomic bomb explosion was sufficient to guard against injury and at the later times when the visible cloud had dispersed there will be no danger to aircrews.[22]

The AERE guidelines were pretty inadequate by today's standards, and even compared to the strict procedures used by the US Air Force in the 1950s, but they were better than nothing. Hurrex had those guidelines on file, but for unknown reasons – probably to do with security – neglected to pass them on to the Hurricane Panel. Instead, they sent the Australians a vanishingly brief document entitled 'Hazard to Flying Personnel' as an appendix to an appendix to an outline of the air-sampling programme.

This is what it said:

The radioactive hazard to aircrews in flying through this cloud is negligible and there is no fear of the aircraft becoming contaminated.[23]

That was it. No warnings, no safety procedures, no nothing.

With that advice in mind, Air Vice Marshal Hancock and his colleagues examined Hurrex's many requests in detail. It was a big ask for a service already stretched thin by deployments in Malaya and Korea. It meant minimising normal operations, juggling available aircraft, cannibalising other aircraft for spare parts, and cancelling several long-planned exercises and air shows. Despite the fact that the whole point of the conference was to discuss problems arising from participation in an atomic test, there was no medical officer in attendance, and the issue of radiological safety was never even discussed.

The RAAF accepted all commitments without reservation.

# 7.

# THE GODDAM ISLES

HM Ships *Zeebrugge* and *Narvik* slipped from Fremantle Harbour at 1030 on Tuesday 22 April, stopping in Gage Roads to take the two RAN lighters in tow before heading north. Even now, the Navy refused to confirm or deny that the ships were heading to the Montebello Islands. 'All I know is that the ships are under operational control of the British Admiralty', said Captain F Bryce Morris, Naval Officer in Charge (NOIC) Fremantle.[1]

The passage north was uneventful, and frustratingly slow for the British sailors, with the lighters acting as drags on the landing ships tank (LSTs). As the small convoy rounded the North West Cape, near Carnarvon, the lighters were released to head into Onslow for supplies, and the LSTs steamed towards the test site. Just as when the two ships arrived at the Cocos Islands, hundreds of men lined the upper decks, straining for a glimpse of their final destination. But when the Montebello Islands finally hove into sight, British hearts sank. There were no palm trees, coconuts or comely native girls here – only barren rocks.

According to Lieutenant Peter Bird of the *Narvik*, the islands were immediately christened the 'Goddam Isles':

This was the nickname given to the islands at an early stage [of planning] to shroud their true identity and, on seeing the

Monte Bellos for the first time, the name appeared so apt that it stuck. Their proper name was rarely used, except in official correspondence, for the remainder of the operation.[2]

It was 1220 on Saturday 26 April when the two ships anchored in Parting Pool. As a first order of business, Captain George Colville, Commanding Officer of HMS *Zeebrugge* and Senior Officer 4th Landing Ship Squadron, ordered all clocks set forward one hour to 'daylight saving' time (GMT + 0900, known in the Navy as I or Item time).[3] To make the most of the daylight hours, the Landing Squadron would be getting up one hour earlier than everyone else in Western Australia.

Weighed down by heavy equipment, and buffeted by a strong nor'-easterly, the LSTs were forced to remain in the outer anchorage until high water the following day, when an improvement in the weather provided a brief opportunity to enter the lagoon. The *Zeebrugge* went first, scraping over the shallow bottom of South Channel with inches to spare, as every man on board peered nervously over the side, watching for rocks and coral heads. The *Narvik* soon followed, but even then both ships had to 'crab' their way up Bunsen Channel against wind and tide, eventually securing to their moorings off Trimouille's Main Beach with relief.

Captain Colville found HMAS *Karangi* moored off Gladstone Beach, with 5ACS Detachment camped nearby. Ever since the departure of HMAS *Mildura*, the two Australian outfits had been working double time laying moorings and tracks in anticipation of the Landing Squadron's arrival. They now came under Captain Colville's operational control.

On the *Narvik*, Commander Derek Willan gave the order to begin unloading landing craft. The 8-ton LCAs were hoisted out over the side, then the heavy derrick was rigged, and one by one the 28-ton LCMs were brought aft on the upper deck's railway system and hoisted out. Right forward, the LST's bow doors opened up and steel ramps were lowered into the water. Lieutenant Bird marvelled as Royal Marines drove the LCMs straight up the ramp and into the loading bay:

> The craft had to be driven squarely between the bow doors – despite crosswinds and currents, and at just the right speed, fast enough to reach the loading point but not so fast as to damage the craft in steel-to-steel contact. Little guidance could be given to the coxswains; from the high fo'c'stle the loading point was obscured, while from the loading point, down in the tank deck, visual communication was entirely cut off over the last fifty yards or so of the run in by the high ramp bow of the craft. The skill with which this manoeuvre was carried out, time and time again, by the Royal Marine corporals in charge of the craft warrants the highest praise.[4]

Once in position, the LCMs were secured with wires and loaded up with Land Rovers, trailers, trucks, bulldozers and crane excavators for transport to the islands. At the same time, nets full of tents, stores and camp equipment were slung out of the aft hatch and into boats alongside. In other words, both LSTs were being unloaded from both ends simultaneously. Soon after arrival, the weather took a turn for the worse, but despite a torrential downpour that lasted for days on end, the unloading process continued almost without pause, often through the night.

The Royal Marines deposited the heavy equipment on landings laid by 5ACS Detachment at beaches on Trimouille and Hermite. In just six weeks, the Flying Shovels had bulldozed and graded 6½ miles of tracks and landings across all four major islands, laying 300 tons of pierced-steel planking (PSP) in the process. They now came under the command of Lieutenant Colonel Pat Smith, Commander Royal Engineers, who was rapt with their efforts. 'They gave us a flying start', he later wrote in an enthusiastic testimonial.[5]

Lieutenant Colonel Smith's main force, 180 Engineer Regiment, comprised the 200 officers and other ranks of 71 Field Squadron RE and an attached troop of Royal Electrical and Mechanical Engineers. The regiment had been raised specifically for Operation Hurricane and spent six months training at Longmoor, Hampshire, prior to departure. Most of the sappers were quartered on board the LSTs and run out to the islands by landing craft each day, while a detachment working on Hermite, on the opposite side of the lagoon, was simply deposited on the island with food and water and resupplied twice a week.

The engineers wasted no time in getting to work. First, they set fires to clear the sites of spinifex, then they used explosives to cut quarries out of the rock and blast passes through the hills. Before long, the whole archipelago was transformed into a giant construction site. Concreters, steel benders, welders, carpenters and plant operators swarmed all over the islands, destroying the peace and quiet with a cacophony of hammers, drills and heavy machinery. Over the next few months, the sappers laid an additional 9 miles of roads and built 80 concrete instrumentation platforms, 15 Anderson shelters (bomb shelters constructed from corrugated iron and reinforced with sandbags), nine jetties, five concrete bunkers, four scaffolding towers and a permanent command centre on Hermite.

Sapper Peter Fletcher was a 20-year-old boxer from Lancashire, England, who would later recall some questionable workplace safety practices. 'We were building the ramps for the small boats to come as close in as possible, bringing stores and stuff in. No snorkels and things like that. It was just a matter of diving down, coupling up your tube with your scaffolding, and coming back up, holding your breath. Today they'd do it totally different, I suppose. They'd have snorkels on, and diving equipment. It was all so primitive in them days ... there was always somebody who had to be on top with bits of stone, bits of rock, in case any of the big fish came in. We saw these big manta rays, and the occasional shark, and it was just a matter of throwing the stones or rock in to scare them away while you were under water fixing up the coupling and things like that.'[6]

To combat these predators, the engineers installed shark nets across the mouths of two shallow tidal bays, thereby creating safe swimming baths. The nets were constructed from 2-inch steel scaffolding and heavy wire mesh and installed at low tide. Fish and other creatures unlucky enough to be trapped in the baths were caught or dynamited. NAAFI (Navy, Army and Air Force Institutes) canteens serving ice-cold beer and soft drinks were established nearby, so ratings and other ranks could unwind over a beer at the end of a long day. The sappers also built a number of sports grounds, including a football pitch and a hockey field, with goalposts made out of tubular steel scaffolding.

All this was made possible by the Royal Marines, who ran the daily 'bus service' from dawn to dusk, ferrying sappers and equipment back and forth in landing craft and supplying landing parties with water and victuals. The Royal Navy was also busy, plotting and marking boat channels across the lagoon and laying 150 miles of cable across the seabed, carefully avoiding jagged rocks and coral heads, to link dozens of remote instrumentation sites to the command centre on Hermite.

On weekends, members of the Landing Squadron played sports, attended movie screenings, and went on picnics and sailing trips to the outer islands. Fishing, as always, was highly popular, and the biggest catches were recorded in a game book. Captain Colville topped the list of anglers with a 73-pound grouper caught while trailing from a landing craft. Sailors from the *Narvik* also landed a 500-pound bluefin shark, while the *Zeebrugge*'s best effort was a 256-pound tiger shark.[7]

•

The Landing Squadron's main link to the mainland was provided by the RAN fleet train, initially comprising small ships HMAS *Warreen*, MWL 251 and MRL 252. The three ships, which usually sailed in company, constantly shuttled between Onslow and the Montebellos, resupplying the Task Force with water, food and mail.

The *Warreen* (formerly known as HMAS *Stella*) was a small survey vessel that had passed back and forth between the Navy and the Council of Scientific and Industrial Research (CSIR – forerunner to the CSIRO) numerous times over the years. In April, she had been recommissioned yet again and sent up to the Montebellos to act as the Task Force's despatch vessel. Lieutenant Ray Pioch, a 27-year-old ex-rating turned intelligence officer from Brisbane, Queensland, was captain of the *Warreen* and senior officer of the fleet train. Unfortunately, Lieutenant Pioch suffered from recurring eye problems throughout the operation, forcing him to return to Fremantle for treatment on multiple occasions.

The *Warreen* turned out to be an extremely unlucky ship (possibly because her renaming ceremony had not been carried out properly, superstitious mariners have suggested). In addition to her captain's eye problems, she was immobilised by a fouled propeller on her first trip to the Montebellos and taken in tow by MWL 251. The weather then deteriorated and the seas became too rough to proceed without parting the tow. As a result, the entire fleet train was marooned off North Sandy Island for days until the *Karangi* mercifully appeared and Lieutenant Commander Morison ordered his divers to clear the propeller.

A few weeks later, the *Warreen*'s engine broke down from near constant use. The small survey vessel was towed back to Fremantle for refit and HMAS *Limicola* was brought up to act as despatch vessel in her place. The *Limicola* was the wooden general-purpose vessel that had previously supported the meteorological party, with mixed results. Unfortunately, she was still not up to the task. With a maximum cruising speed of 6 knots, no passenger accommodation, no refrigeration, very little stowage for fresh vegetables, and an unreliable engine, she was basically useless as a despatch vessel. Consequently, the more reliable MWL 251 was used for most of the routine journeys to Onslow in the *Warreen*'s absence.

•

One day not long after the Landing Squadron arrived at the Montebellos, members of the Task Force discovered a small boat with a ragged crew of civilians tucked away in a secluded bay. The intrepid mariners were not fishermen or pearlers – they were press men from Perth.

On the same night that Norm Milne filed his award-winning story, Jim Macartney called a late-night meeting in his office at Newspaper House on St Georges Terrace, Perth. As Managing Editor of West Australian Newspapers Limited, Macartney was in overall charge of both *The West Australian* and the *Daily News*. Except for a wartime stint in the RAAF, he had been with the company since 1928. The atom bomb was the biggest story to happen on his patch in years, but the experienced news man knew that covering it would not be easy. The Montebellos were almost 800 miles from Perth – greater than the distance from London to Berlin – and over 50 miles offshore. The islands and their surrounding waters were due to be declared a prohibited area in a week's time. A press expedition would be dangerous, difficult and expensive, with no guarantee of success. Was it worth it?

Macartney weighed up all the factors and decided that it was. 'We have to go to those islands and find out just what is going on', he announced. 'No one is going to tell us, so we must do it within the week's grace we have to get there.'[8]

Four men were selected for the expedition: Norm Milne from *The West Australian*; Jack Coulter, veteran police roundsman for the *Daily News*; Harold Rudinger, an ace photographer who would provide images for both newspapers; and Jack Nicoll, circulation manager for *The West Australian* and close mate of Macartney. As a former lieutenant commander and corvette captain in the Royal Australian Naval Volunteer Reserve (RANVR), Nicoll was the obvious choice as expedition leader. He also just happened to know a bloke who owned a pearling lugger based at Onslow.

'Our briefing was short – to make the best time we could to Onslow, sail in the lugger and report back what was happening at the island group', Coulter recalled in his memoir, *By Deadline to Headline*.[9]

All efforts to purchase seats on a commercial flight or charter an aircraft to Onslow failed, so the press men went by road. After a false start in a Holden sedan with dodgy suspension, the small expeditionary force left town in Macartney's brand new Ford V8 at 2.30 a.m. on Tuesday 22 April.[10] For the next three days, they travelled on dirt roads, ate hard tack out of tins, and slept by the side of the road. River crossings were especially punishing, with all four men wincing as the V8's undercarriage took a pounding on jagged, boulder-sized rocks in the dry riverbeds. They finally made it into Onslow with the gear rods smashed to pieces and the car stuck in top gear.

The press men were amazed to find that the sleepy town had been transformed into a busy Army base. A few days earlier, a convoy of trucks had rolled into Onslow and set up a temporary camp on the edge of town. The Western Command Transit Camp Detachment, under the command of Captain Tom Carlin, comprised 35 drivers, cooks, engineers and batmen stewards from Perth. Most of the troops were now hard at work establishing a permanent camp, situated opposite the hospital, to serve as a staging post for personnel and supplies en route to the islands. Other teams were busy stocking a 4000-gallon fuel dump near the cemetery and upgrading the airstrip on the claypan a few miles out of town.

The first thing the press men did was head to the post office to report back to Newspaper House. Onslow was not yet equipped with telephones, so all messages to the big smoke were sent by telegram, manually transmitted by a telegraphist trained in Morse code. It was a cumbersome way to get copy back to Perth, making it harder to file stories by deadline.

While Jack Nicoll went off to find his mate with the lugger, the rest of the team took the V8 to the local garage for some much-needed repair work. They learnt, to their surprise, that the people of Onslow had been watching RAN and RAAF personnel shuttling backwards and forwards to the Montebellos for 18 months. The failure of the usually reliable bush telegraph was the result of Lieutenant Colonel Phillipps's visit during Operation Epicure. The ASIO man had asked the local press representatives to keep quiet about the unusual service activity, and to a man they had kept their word.

Soon Nicoll returned, looking grim. 'It looks as though it is all off', he announced.[11] The lugger was out of commission due to an overdue delivery of essential rigging. This stroke of misfortune was not exactly a coincidence: later on, the press men learnt that ASIO had got wind of their plans and arranged for the rigging to be 'delayed' until the prohibited area had been gazetted.

The owner of the garage was Billy Clark, an experienced sailor who had served with the Army's Small Ships Section in the Pacific campaign. It was Clark who saved the day. 'I have a bit of a boat which might get you to the islands', he said. 'I'm happy to give it a go, if you are.'[12]

Clark took the press men down to Beadon Creek and showed them a dilapidated old boat moored offshore. The *Thelma* was a 22-foot yacht with a jib and mainsail, a two-stroke engine, and a forward half-cabin with sleeping berths for two. She was too small for a crew of five to comfortably take on an offshore voyage, and she had clearly seen better days, but she was better than nothing. After a quick conference, the press men decided to give it a crack.

The *Thelma* slipped from Beadon Creek at 11.00 a.m. on Saturday 26 April, towing a dinghy astern, with Jack Nicoll as skipper and Billy Clark as his first mate.[13] A handful of locals turned out to see them off, while others placed wagers on the expedition's prospects of success. Word of the adventure even travelled as far as Navy Office in Melbourne, where Admiral Collins reportedly said: 'If they are mad enough to try it, good luck to them.'[14]

The *Thelma* island-hopped by day, often against wind and tide, sometimes making as little as 3 knots. At night, the press men anchored in bays protected from the wind and slept ashore, eating crayfish and oysters caught by hand, or bully beef stew cooked on a primus stove. As Coulter later wrote:

> Our party was wet with spray for almost the entire trip and even the gear we stowed in the leaky cabin was soaked. We had no change of clothing. Disdaining wet clothes as useless, Jack Nicoll spent most of the daytime hours wearing only his hat. This was 'to keep his smokes and matches dry'.[15]

Nicoll had experienced worse in his time. In 1943, he was serving in HMS *Bredon*, an auxiliary minesweeper on escort duty in the Atlantic, when she was torpedoed by a German U-boat off the Canary Islands. The ship sank in less than a minute, taking 43 men – almost the entire crew – with her.

Fortunately, Nicoll was able to save himself and one shipmate by jury-rigging a raft from driftwood and life jackets. The two survivors were eventually plucked from the sea and taken to Algiers. Nicoll was later awarded an MBE (military division) for bravery.

The *Thelma* reached the Montebellos on Sunday afternoon, anchoring in a secluded bay. The press men rowed ashore in the dinghy and climbed a nearby hill, where an incredible sight unfolded before them. Amidst the scattering of barren islands, what looked like a full-scale invasion was under way: the two LSTs were riding at anchor in the channel, troops in jungle fatigues were ferrying stores ashore in landing craft, and shirtless men were hard at work bulldozing roads through the scrub. Elsewhere in the lagoon, small boats were taking soundings, and a funny-looking ship with two big horns was laying moorings – the *Karangi*.

The press men cheered. This was a major coup, especially for Milne – the Landing Squadron was exactly where he had said it would be. There were slaps on the back all around.

With night coming on, the press men returned to the secluded cove where the *Thelma* was anchored and spent the night camped on the beach, sharing a bottle of Captain Kettle rum. In the morning, they set out to explore in the *Thelma*. As Coulter recalled, they were soon discovered:

> Met by a landing barge manned by Royal Marines with automatic weapons at the ready, we were cheered to see they were getting as thoroughly wet as we were. With them were a couple of terribly serious Australians in service dress and slouch hats, but without any distinguishing colour patches. They demanded to know our business.
>
> We asked them to declare theirs and they reluctantly announced themselves as Commonwealth Security officers and ordered us to leave the area. They did not press the

point when told that we were aware that prohibitive legislation had not yet been passed and they called off their troops, allowing us freedom to sail around taking note of the preparations at the Monte Bello Islands, but barred us from going ashore.[16]

The two ASIO men (probably Lieutenant Colonel Phillipps and Leo Carter) could only watch, glaring, as the crew of the *Thelma* triumphantly sailed off.

The press men returned to Onslow the following day, having sailed right through the night. Coulter's story was published on Tuesday 29 April, beating the official security ban by two days. It began:

PRESSMEN FIND MONTEBELLOS LIKE WARTIME BEACHHEAD
ONSLOW, Tues: Among the Montebello Islands off Onslow are scenes reminiscent of a wartime beachhead. It is a combined operations job. The Royal Navy has landed in the lee of an island and is busily furthering the work started by RAAF men 12 months ago.
The islands, scene of activities so far cloaked in secrecy, have been visited by a party of four Pressmen who set out from Onslow by boat last Saturday ...[17]

On Wednesday 14 May 1952, the British and Australian governments finally confirmed Coulter's and Milne's reporting. The two nations were supposed to release identical statements simultaneously, but the Brits jumped the gun, leaving the Australians looking silly.

The statement read:

The test of the United Kingdom atomic weapon in Australia will be carried out at Monte Bello Islands off the north-west coast of Australia as a joint operation involving the three fighting services and the Ministry of Supply. The operation will be under the command of Rear-Admiral AD Torlesse, and the test will be under the scientific direction of Dr WG Penney, of the Ministry of Supply. Besides Her Majesty's ships *Zeebrugge* and *Narvik* which have already sailed carrying a detachment of the Royal Engineers, and stores, the Special Squadron will consist of Her Majesty's ships *Campania* Flag Ship, *Tracker* and *Plym*. These latter ships are being specially fitted to transport the scientific staff and test equipment and are expected to sail in about two months' time. Units of the Royal Australian Navy and Royal Australian Air Force will work with the Special Squadron in Australian waters.[18]

Despite intense public interest, the governments announced that no press correspondents or politicians would visit the test site to witness the trial. The Montebellos would be a closed shop.

To ensure that secrecy was maintained, the Australian Government passed the *Defence (Special Undertakings) Act* of 1952, expanding the prohibited area around the Montebellos to a 40-nautical-mile radius around Flag Island. The punishment for entering the prohibited area without authorisation was up to seven years in gaol. The Department of Civil Aviation (DCA) also announced security restrictions on all civil flights across a swathe of territory stretching from Woomera in South Australia to the Montebellos and the Rowley Shoals off the North West Coast (the restricted zone had been designed with the cover story in mind). Pilots were instructed to confiscate all cameras from passengers prior to departure, and hostesses were required to ensure that all passengers complied with security procedures during flights. Aircraft not equipped with radio were forbidden from flying in the restricted zone, and non-scheduled flights were required to obtain permission from the DCA and call in their positions every 20 minutes. The penalty for noncompliance was two years in gaol.

With all these new developments, there was increased speculation about the nature of the test. Many experts still assumed that Woomera would be involved somehow: one theory was that a Canberra bomber flying out of Woomera would drop a bomb on the Montebellos; another was that guided rockets armed with atomic warheads would be aimed at the islands from the rocket range. These were the sensible guesses. Some of the more outlandish theories included pilotless planes operated by remote control dropping sticks of small atomic bombs, atomic anti-aircraft guns capable of demolishing squadrons of raiding aircraft, and 'an atomic ray dealing death by radio-activity'.[19]

Funnily enough, one *Daily News* reader just about nailed it. 'Observer' from West Midland wrote:

> It seems a clear indication that the atomic tests are going to have plenty to do with the water. Otherwise, why would the expedition ships bring out so many landing barges? Maybe we can expect underwater atomic tests similar to those conducted by the Americans at Eniwetok atoll.[20]

In London, Labour MP Tom Driberg (who was later revealed to be a Communist spy) used question time to ask Prime Minister Winston Churchill what, if anything, was being done to protect Aboriginal people in the vicinity of the blast. In reply, Churchill reiterated his statement that the test would be conducted in conditions 'which assure that there is no danger whatever to the health or safety of people in Australia'.[21] Conservative MP Martin Lindsay received cheers when he dismissed the matter as something that 'could well be left to the common sense of the Australian Government'.[22]

The entire issue was reduced to comic fodder when Welsh Labour MP Emrys Hughes asked the prime minister if he was aware that certain Aboriginal people, having been converted to Christianity, were now thinking of sending missionaries to the UK 'because they think the atom bomb could only have been invented by savages'.[23] But Hughes was outclassed by Churchill, a masterful orator with a rapier wit. 'I hope Mr Attlee will not be unduly hurt', he smirked.[24] Cheers and laughter ensued.

British planners had clearly not given much serious thought to the health and safety of Aboriginal peoples. For reference, they relied primarily on a slim document entitled 'Some Notes on North-West Australia', prepared by HER scientist ER Woodcock, whose main source was apparently *Encyclopaedia Britannica*. According to Woodcock, 'the area to the south, south-east and east and within 150 miles of the Monte Bello Islands' had a population of 715 people, 'excluding full-blooded Aboriginals, for whom no statistics are available'.[25] But that was not true. While Aboriginal people were still excluded from the Commonwealth Census, Western Australia's Department of Native Affairs kept extensive demographic data which revealed that approximately 4538 Aboriginal men, women and children were living in surrounding regions at the time.[26]

Emrys Hughes tried another line of attack a few weeks later when he asked Churchill if the safety of bird and animal life in the Montebellos had been considered. The ensuing exchange was printed in *The Times* of London:

MR. CHURCHILL (Woodford, C.). – The report of a recent special survey showing that there is very little animal or bird life on the Monte Bello Islands was one of the factors in the choice of the site for the test of the United Kingdom atomic weapon.

I should add, however, that an expedition which went to the islands 50 years ago reported that giant rats, wild cats, and wallabies were seen, and these may have caused the hon. member some anxiety. (Loud laughter.) However, the officer who explored the islands recently says that he found only some lizards, two sea eagles, and what looked like a canary sitting on a perch. (Renewed laughter.)

MR. EMRYS HUGHES. – Will we get some report which will satisfy civilized human beings that no unnecessary destruction of wild life is taking place?

MR. CHURCHILL. – Yes. Everything should be done to avoid the destruction of wild life and also of human beings. (Cheers.)[27]

One of Australia's leading ornithologists was unimpressed with Churchill's flippant attitude towards the local wildlife. AH Chisholm, a Fellow of the Royal Zoological Society, pointed out that there were at least twenty kinds of birds in the Montebellos, some of which were not found anywhere else, including the pipit and the spinifex bird. Nearby Barrow Island was also home to wallabies, bandicoots, a rare species of kangaroo and the black-and-white fairy wren, which was only found on one other island. 'It will be very regrettable if these notable birds and animals are blasted out of existence', he warned.[28]

When pressed on the matter, Churchill remained true to form, quipping, 'Every effort will be made to inconvenience them as little as possible.'[29]

•

Back in the Montebellos, plans were underway to provide the Task Force with a much-needed supply of fresh water. The Landing Squadron was small enough to get by on occasional deliveries from visiting ships, but the Task Force would quadruple in size when the Special Squadron arrived, and the demand for water would skyrocket. Although most of the ships were equipped with desalinators capable of producing potable water from seawater, the resulting product tasted stale and chlorinated. For obvious reasons, everyone preferred drinking fresh water.

Early in the planning stages, the Hurricane Panel had identified the Fortescue River as the source of fresh water nearest to the islands. The Fortescue sprang up near Roy Hill in the middle of the Pilbara and wound its way through the Hamersley Range before reaching the coast at Mardie Station, an enormous spinifex-covered sheep station about 60 miles north of Onslow. The estuary was tidal and brackish, and for much of the year the river was dry, but at various points along its course deep waterholes retained water all year round. The Hurricane Panel's idea was to build a pipeline from one such pool to a disused landing near the river mouth, where MWL 251 could top up with water on a regular basis.

The owner of Mardie Station was a lean nor'-wester named Bob Sharpe, who, in an admirably patriotic gesture, agreed to let the Task Force use his water free of charge. Following a series of exploratory investigations, Squadron Leader Ken Garden, Officer Commanding 5ACS Detachment, then surveyed a 7-mile-long pipeline route from Mungajee Pool to Fortescue Landing.

On the morning of Wednesday 21 May, the *Karangi*'s sister ship, HMAS *Koala*, secured alongside Onslow Jetty and began unloading pipes with the ship's derrick. The boom defence vessel had come all the way from her homeport of Sydney via Port Augusta, South Australia, and had 71 tons of piping and mooring gear stowed in her holds and up on deck. The captain was Lieutenant CF Young, a 59-year-old Reservist and former merchant seaman from Kent, England, who, incredibly, had learnt to sail in three-masted sailing ships. It was the ageing skipper's last cruise before retirement, and it had proven unusually tiresome: rough seas in the Great Australian Bight had flung him from his bunk in the middle of the night, fracturing one of his ribs, and obstreperous waterside workers in Fremantle had refused to assist the *Koala*, echoing the earlier treatment dished out to the *Karangi* during Operation Epicure.

The ship's company spent the next three days unloading pipes, carefully lowering each length into racks on the jetty by hand. The pipes were second-hand 4-inch quick-coupling pipes, and they were not in great shape. About half of them had been provided by the Department of Works in Sydney, and the rest had come from Woomera Rocket Range. The sailors finished unloading on Saturday afternoon, and several men were nearly trampled as they ran the last pipe the length of the upper deck, their haste motivated by the prospect of shore leave. 'No damage or loss occurred, though it was noted that many of the pipes came aboard in a bad condition', observed Lieutenant Young.[30]

From Onslow Jetty, the pipes were transported to Mardie Station by road, a 100-mile journey across terrain so rough that Squadron Leader Garden recommended going by sea. The Australian Military Forces, however, scoffed at such concerns. After conducting his own reconnaissance, Captain Tom Carlin, Officer Commanding Western Command Transit Camp Detachment, proclaimed the road 'a veritable bowling green'.[31] Over the next few weeks, two Army Mack trucks made half a dozen trips from Onslow to Mardie, hauling a total of 7½ miles of piping, one engine and three trailer pumps in 16-ton loads. Despite Carlin's optimistic appraisal, the truck drivers soon discovered that the road was only passable when dry, and it was not always dry. The first team to make the trip was cut off by a flash flood and stranded for days, forcing

Bob Sharpe to ride to the rescue and deliver emergency supplies on horseback. Hauling was delayed by a week or more.

Having spent the past 10 weeks in the Montebellos almost without a break, 5ACS Detachment now relocated to the mainland to begin work on the pipeline. Owing to a shortage of operational landing craft and cranes in the islands, they were forced to leave behind all their heavy equipment, along with a section of men to maintain it, so they were significantly understrength when they arrived at Mardie Station. At about the same time, the highly experienced Squadron Leader Garden was ordered to return to Richmond, leaving Pilot Officer LE Johnson in command.

After setting up camp on the red gum-lined banks of the Fortescue River, the airmen began the arduous task of constructing a pipeline across the rugged Pilbara landscape. For the next six weeks, they battled heat, flies and flash floods to connect the quick-coupling pipes. Without their beloved bulldozers, they were forced to go over and around boulders and sand hills instead of through them, lengthening the pipeline and causing them to run out of pipes. An emergency order was placed with a firm in Melbourne, which sprang into action. First, the pipes were rolled, then they were driven to Port Augusta and loaded onto the express train for Kalgoorlie in south-east Western Australia. From there, they were hauled to the opposite end of the state by road – a distance of about 1000 miles. The pipes arrived at Mardie less than two weeks after they were ordered – an unheard-of delivery time for an order from the North West.

While the pipeline was under construction, a section of four sappers from Western Command Transit Camp Detachment, led by Corporal RL Crosby, rebuilt the dilapidated landing so it was safe for MWL 251 to use. Once the pipeline was finished, the airmen went back to the Montebellos, while the sappers stayed on at Mardie to service the pipeline for months – a lonely, thankless task in tough conditions many miles from the relative comfort of life in Onslow.

The Fortescue pipeline was the subject of a triumphant press release from the Department of Defence, which lauded the project as 'a striking example of the excellent team-work' between multiple government departments and all three services, crowing that 'a practically unlimited supply of fresh water, at present capable of providing 3,400 gallons an hour, was obtained'.[32]

Except, the bloody thing did not work.

Corporal Rex Raph was a 24-year-old non-commissioned officer who was in charge of the RAAF communications section at Onslow Airfield. Many years later, he wrote about what he called 'the ill fated water pipeline' from Mardie Station to Fortescue Landing: 'Months of work had gone into constructing the line from old second-hand pipes ... The pipe was rotten and blew out under pressure each time it was tested. Next, the water level at the lagoon dropped and the pumps were ineffective. Pits were dug to get the pumps closer to the water and this caused further problems. The whole thing seemed to have become an engineering nightmare and I don't believe that more than one water lighter was ever filled from this system.'[33]

Raph's unflattering account is supported by the fact that official accounts of the operation make no mention of a fresh water supply. In the report by Admiral Torlesse, Task Force Commander, the section dealing with the pipeline has been redacted, and his description of the role of MWL 251 states that the water lighter 'stored the reserve of water made by ships' distillers and also transported provisions between Onslow and the islands'.[34] No mention of fresh water.

Similarly, Lieutenant Colonel Alec Walkling, Assistant Director of HER's Radiological Hazard Division, stated that all ships in the Task Force were forced to distil seawater due to the absence of an 'external supply of drinking water'.[35]

The lack of fresh drinking water was not just disappointing – it would also have serious health ramifications during Phase Three of the operation – the aftermath – when ships would be forced to distil contaminated seawater to produce drinking water.

In the end, 5ACS dismantled the pipeline just four months after it was built.

•

In mid-June, the *Karangi* and the *Koala* returned to Fremantle for a most unusual task: the exchange of the ships' companies.

The *Karangi* had been working nonstop in the Montebellos for six months, and was long overdue for a refit, so the Naval Board had decreed that the *Koala*'s Sydney-based crew would sail her back to Sydney, while her Fremantle-based crew would remain in the Montebellos, sailing the *Koala*. To maintain consistency, captains and officers would remain with their ships. Immediately following the exchange, both ships would return to the Montebellos for a handover period, during which the Task Force's two biggest and most complicated moorings would be laid: the huge first-class mooring for the headquarters ship and the specially designed mooring for the target vessel.

The two ships conducted the exchange at No 1 North Wharf on Friday 20 June. All at once, 60-odd ratings disembarked and swapped places with their opposite numbers, while tons of dunnage were slung over the side of each ship, trundled along the bustling wharf, and hauled on board the other ship. The *Koala* was under orders to proceed to sea first thing Monday, so she was also being loaded with a fourth-class mooring and fuelled at the same time. Adding to the mayhem, the fuel line sprang a leak, spraying oil fuel everywhere and creating a fire hazard on top of everything else. 'The scene was one of indescribable chaos', lamented Lieutenant Young.[36]

The following day was spent turning over stores and victuals and getting settled in. Eventually, the *Koala* slipped from North Wharf and secured alongside HMAS *Mildura* at H Shed, Victoria Quay. At 1030 Sunday morning, the boilers were being flashed up when a 'backflash' blew Leading Stoker JW Barlow, a 24-year-old rating from Beverley, Western Australia, clear across the boiler room and set the oil in the bilges alight. Dazed and singed, Barlow scrambled to his feet and sounded the alarm. The ship's company immediately dashed to fire stations, while members of the *Mildura*'s company raced down the wharf to lend a hand. Soon, the fire brigade arrived.

The fire raged for over two hours. Fire fighters constantly sprayed water on the ship's oil tanks to stop them exploding and poured foam down the boiler-room hatchway for three-quarters of an hour. Once the blaze was finally brought under control, a fire fighter in a gas mask went down to investigate.

The ship was dead in the water: the main electrical leads were burnt out, and the repairs would delay her departure for at least a week. Leading Stoker Barlow, who was 'shaken about a bit' by the experience, spent a few weeks in Hollywood Repatriation Hospital but lived to tell the tale.[37] There were no other casualties.

This was the second incident to delay the departure of a boom defence vessel from Fremantle since the beginning of Operation Hurricane. It was beginning to look suspicious. An investigation was announced, and on Thursday 26 June a board of inquiry sat in the *Mildura*. The findings were surprisingly mundane: the investigators said that the *Koala*'s boilers and bilges were in a poor state and had been so for some time. The engineer officer at HMAS *Penguin*, the Navy base where the *Koala* was homeported, had been asked to clean them before the ship left Sydney, but had run out of time and ordered the *Koala*'s chief engine room artificer (senior engineering rating) to do it 'at the earliest opportunity'.[38] Clearly, that opportunity had not arisen.

Now, belatedly, the ship's stokers set to work cleaning out the bilges. To speed up the process, a working party of twelve stoker mechanics from HMAS *Leeuwin* and HMAS *Parkes* (the Reserve Fleet Detachment at Garden Island, Western Australia) was sent to help. The men were divided into three watches, working eight-hour shifts around the clock for the next four days. 'The work consisted of ridding the bilges of a considerable quantity of jellified fuel oil', reported Lieutenant Young. 'The sludge was too thick to be pumped and had to be scraped off the bilge plating with whaling spades etc., and hoisted out to the upper deck in buckets.'[39] At the same time, members of the ship's company mopped up the foam sprayed by the fire brigade, while a civilian firm repaired the electrical wiring. Gradually, over the course of a week, power was restored, the bilges were declared clean, boilers were flashed up, and the ship was stored and prepared for sea.

Discipline in the WA Navy was considered to be lax compared to that of the Big Navy over east, but Lieutenant Young was pleasantly surprised by the men's conduct:

> Contrary to opinions heard, the new Ship's Company, although not yet well known to me or my officers, have pulled their weight very well. Special mention is made of the Engine Room Branch Ratings who, though unfamiliar to this particular ship, took immediate and effective action against the fire, with complete calm. The thankless task of cleaning out the bilges was tackled by the stokers in good spirit.[40]

The *Koala* finally slipped from H Shed on Thursday 3 July, 10 days behind schedule, having been preceded to sea by the *Karangi*.

For Lieutenant Commander Morison and his officers, the *Karangi*'s cruise up the west coast was an opportunity to run the new ship's company through their paces; for the men, it was a chance to get to know the ship that would be their home for the next nine months. Although the boom defence vessels were built along identical lines, each had been organised according to the preferences of her captain and crew, with myriad refits over the years rendering them different in many ways large and small. In short, each ship had her own character and her own sailing qualities.

On arrival at the Montebellos, the *Karangi* secured alongside HMS *Zeebrugge* and began loading the first-class mooring for the headquarters ship, escort carrier HMS *Campania*. The *Karangi*'s orders were to lay the mooring in 10 fathoms (60 feet) of water in Parting Pool and then stand by to assist while the *Koala* laid the special mooring in Bunsen Channel. To ensure that both jobs were done to the Admiralty's specifications, the recently promoted Captain George Tancred, now Senior Officer of the RAN Hydrographic Service, joined the Landing Squadron with a survey party from HMAS *Kuttabul* in Sydney.

The first-class mooring was truly gigantic: it comprised four arms of heavy ground chain as thick as tree trunks, each seven shackles (630 feet) in length, ending with 10-ton single-fluke anchors. The contraption was so big that it took the better part of two days for the *Karangi* just to load and connect the first arm. For the next three days, the weather was too rough to leave the lagoon, and when the *Karangi* finally made it to Parting Pool on Monday 7 July, she was forced to seek shelter in the lee of her namesake island, Karangi Island. The next day, she commenced laying the first arm in conditions that remained less than ideal. To stretch the heavy ground chain taut along the seabed, the *Karangi* moved astern, hauling on her stern anchor, but despite the use of main engines, the combined force of wind and tide caused the stern anchor to drag home. Under the watchful eye of Captain Tancred, Lieutenant Commander Morison weighed anchor and brought the ship about, successfully stretching the ground chain by steaming ahead in the direction of the lay – the exact opposite of what it says to do in the Admiralty's *Manual of Seamanship*.

Over the next eleven days, the ship's company loaded, connected and laid the three remaining arms in similarly difficult conditions. On Saturday 19 July, two and a half weeks after they had begun, they connected the last couple of shackles on the fourth and final arm, while battling tides so strong that an LCM was used to hold up the ship's stern. 'This was ably done by the Royal Marine crew, and the final anchor was slipped, without regrets, at 1445', reported an exhausted Lieutenant Commander Morison.[41]

The *Karangi*'s work on the first-class mooring was praised by Captain F Bryce Morris (now known as NOIC West Australian Area), who noted that a '1st Class Mooring would, normally, only be laid in sheltered waters with the full assistance of a dockyard, including the provision of special mooring lighters, tugs, etc.'[42] To complete the job on her own, in exposed conditions, in only 12 working days, was quite a feat. The Naval Board agreed, conveying its pleasure to Lieutenant Commander Morison and the ship's company in a letter of commendation. It was a fitting culmination to six months of tireless, unglamorous work. At the end of the month, the *Karangi* returned to Fremantle, before eventually sailing to Sydney for her much-needed refit.

When her sister ship, the *Koala*, finally arrived in the Montebellos, Lieutenant Young and his officers immediately commenced preparations for their most important job: the laying of the special mooring. On Saturday 12 July, the ship's company began loading 10-ton anchors, concrete clumps and cable from the *Zeebrugge*, before proceeding to the position selected for the target vessel – a precise point in Bunsen Channel, 400 yards off Trimouille's Cocoa Beach.

The special mooring comprised six arms and six bridles, and was designed to hold the target vessel as still as possible. The first two arms were laid without incident, but then the *Koala* was ordered to embark the *Narvik*'s medical officer and a patient with an acute case of appendicitis, and proceed for Onslow 'forthwith'.[43] As soon as the patient was landed, the *Koala* turned around and steamed straight back to the Montebellos, but bad weather, stiff anchor rings and ill-fitting stocks meant that a number of frustrating days passed before the third and fourth arms were laid. With one boiler defective, the *Koala* was then forced to operate on a single boiler as the fifth and sixth arms were loaded, connected and laid. Final adjustments were made on Saturday 26 July – two weeks after the *Koala* had begun – with an LCM holding the ship broadside to the fast-flowing tide as she straightened the last arm.

The *Koala*'s sailors, now highly experienced after months of work in the *Karangi*, had acquitted themselves well during the laying of the special mooring and the emergency dash to Onslow. They soon made light work of the rest of the mooring programme, laying a boat trot in Stephenson Channel, a lighter mooring in Beadon Bay, and flying boat moorings in Parting Pool and the lagoon in short order. As a reward for all their hard work, Lieutenant Young granted shore leave at Onslow, a well-intentioned decision with what the skipper called 'disastrous results': the ratings returned to ship so legless that, for safety's sake, they were hauled on board in a cargo net by ship's derrick.[44]

With the special mooring in position, all was now ready for the arrival of the Special Squadron, the scientists and the bomb itself.

# 8.

# VOYAGE OF THE SPECIAL SQUADRON

On a grey and gloomy day at Portsmouth on the south coast of England, the main scientific party tramped up the gangway of the escort carrier HMS *Campania* in hats and coats with suitcases in tow.

About half the 85 scientists came from High Explosive Research (HER), while the rest were seconded from other departments in the Ministry of Supply or Home Office. There had been some debate as to whether they should travel to Australia by air or sea. Chief Superintendent of HER William Penney, who was flying out later on, thought they should travel by air: not only would a long sea voyage take up valuable preparation time, it would also add considerably to the length of the trip, hampering recruitment efforts. Air Vice Marshal ED Davis, the blustery leader of the Epicure reconnaissance, scoffed at such concerns. 'Any right-minded man would regard these trials as a grand experience combined with the fun of a picnic', he proclaimed; the long sea voyage would be like 'a prolonged rest cure', and anyone who didn't like it could resign or be sacked.[1]

They went by sea.

The leader of the scientific party was Dr Leonard Tyte, Technical Director of Operation Hurricane. Dr Tyte was

113

a bald, 44-year-old ballistics expert with a hard head and a prickly personality. As Technical Director, he was in charge of planning the scientific side of the trial, from the staff and apparatus required at the site to the organisation of teams and the allocation of duties. He was unhappy with the Montebellos as a test site, particularly the transport difficulties and the fact that the headquarters ship could not enter the inner anchorage. He would find a lot more to complain about later on.

The scientists spent their first day on board getting settled into their cabins and learning their way around the ship. Converted from a requisitioned cargo ship, the *Campania* was a 12,450-ton escort carrier with a complement of 640, commanded by Captain AB Cole, DSC. During the Second World War, the *Campania* had served on Arctic convoy duty to Russia; more recently, she had sailed around the British Isles as a gaily painted showboat for the 1951 Festival of Britain. She had since been repainted Navy grey and fitted out with everything she needed to serve as headquarters ship for Operation Hurricane, including extra cabins, offices, workshops, laboratories and desalinators. Stowed on her crowded flight deck were three Dragonfly helicopters, two ancient Sea Otter bi-planes, six Land Rovers, eighteen boats of various sizes, numerous stacks of crates, and a large metal shed for storing and filling helium weather balloons. Down below, hundreds of tons of scientific equipment were stowed in the holds and anywhere else there was room.

A thick blanket of fog kept the *Campania* in Portsmouth until the following afternoon, when she slipped from port under the flag of Rear Admiral Arthur Torlesse, Commander of the 4th Task Force. It was Tuesday 10 June.

Despite decades of experience, Admiral Torlesse was feeling the burden of command. For one thing, he was worried about the size of his task force. 'If this had been an American project, a great armada would have been employed', he later complained. 'I was given five ships and some 1,500 men and told that I must make do with them.'[2] (That was not quite true – Torlesse had neglected to count the Australian ships and personnel under his command.) He also had scores of pesky civilians to worry about. Although the trial was being conducted as a Royal Navy operation, it was in reality a combined operation with the Ministry of Supply, whose scientists had their own separate chain of command and their own distinct culture. In the Navy, perhaps the most conservative of all the services, discipline and tradition were paramount. By contrast, the scientists were iconoclastic by nature and training, encouraged to doubt received wisdom and question authority.

There was trouble right from the start. When the *Campania* left Portsmouth, all hands fell in on deck, per tradition, only to watch as the scientists embarrassed the ship by leaning over the side and 'waving to mum', as one disgusted officer put it.[3] The sailors had their revenge the following morning, when the entire ship was 'scrubbed over' at 0900. 'Simultaneously it seemed, all parts of the ship were in the process of being cleaned', wrote JJ McEnhill, a Scottish physicist who kept an official diary of the operation for HER. 'Cabins had to be vacated, the wardrooms had to be vacated, and it was not easy to know just what to do or where to go.'[4] Baffled scientists wandered onto gun platforms or congregated on the quarterdeck and were promptly chased off. It was only after the ship was declared clean at 1030 that they could get to work.

This daily ritual continued without alteration until the Navy finally relented and agreed to clean the various wardrooms at different times, leaving the scientists somewhere to work in the meantime. 'This should have been possible from the beginning, but for some reason it was ignored', grumbled McEnhill. 'Thus staff were made to feel that during certain hours they were an encumbrance in the ship and certainly not "of the ship". This was not very good for morale or efficiency.'[5]

Perhaps not, but in fairness the Navy did make a genuine effort to be accommodating – at least at first. One day after leaving port, Admiral Torlesse addressed the entire ship's company. Taking the *Campania*'s motto ('All of one company') as his theme, he exhorted servicemen and civilians alike to pull together as one for Queen and country. Over the next few days, officers and senior ratings conducted tours of the ship, including the engine room and the bridge, where many scientists took a turn at the wheel. The scientists were also made honorary officers, which gave them access to the wardroom (the officers' mess), where they significantly outnumbered the sailors. Some sailors would come to regret that decision.

A couple of days out of Portsmouth, the *Campania* rendezvoused with HMS *Plym* in the Bay of Biscay. The *Plym* was a 1400-ton frigate with a complement of 80-odd sailors and a handful of scientists under the command of Lieutenant Commander Peter Draisey. Though only ten years old, the *Plym* had been deemed surplus to postwar requirements, so she had been volunteered for one last mission: she was the target vessel.

Down below the water line, in the forward hold, was the bomb itself. The gadget, as the scientists called it, was a large sphere comprising multiple layers of high explosive encased in aluminium and attached to an elaborate support structure installed at Chatham Dockyards. Thankfully, it was not yet armed – the radioactive core would be flown out later on.

The weapon almost wasn't ready in time. HER's progress had been beset by a series of delays going back to 1950, when Penney had been forced, reluctantly, to alter the bomb's design.

One of the weapon's key components was a cylindrical cartridge that allowed the radioactive core to be inserted while airborne, mitigating the risk of a catastrophic accident on take-off. Upon examination, Wing Commander John Rowlands, GC, a scientific officer attached to HER to represent the interests of the RAF, detected a risk of the plutonium going supercritical during the arming process. If a chain reaction occurred at that stage, the delivery crew would be zapped with deadly neutron radiation and the bomb would probably detonate prematurely – exactly the sort of disaster the cartridge system was supposed to prevent. A disappointed Penney went back over his blueprints and made several adjustments.

The new design removed the risk of criticality, but also reduced the bomb's power considerably. Then his team came up with a third design, incorporating a gap between the core and the tamper, which promised an even greater theoretical yield than the original design. Ironically, the idea for the new configuration came from a paper written by Klaus Fuchs, the Communist spy who had given Britain's atomic secrets to Stalin.

All the tinkering with the bomb's design set back HER's scientists and technicians by 12 months. By the time the Landing Squadron sailed from Portsmouth in late February 1952, only one of the weapon's seven main components was ready: the detonators. The other components were having all sorts of issues: the firing system kept going off prematurely and had to be completely redesigned; many of the explosive lenses shrank during cooling and had to be rejected; a whole set of high-quality supercharges were accidentally cut to the wrong measurements and had to be thrown out. Then there was the tamper, which consisted of two thin domes of uranium fitted around the core. The domes were supposed to be machined to a perfect consistency, but in half a dozen attempts the metallurgists were unable to eliminate all the imperfections. It was too late to start again, so Penney decided he would have to use the best of the bunch, flaws and all. On top of all this, the Windscale Pile, Britain's first nuclear reactor, was yet to deliver any plutonium for the core or polonium for the initiator.

In the end, the weapon was assembled in a furious last-minute rush in the Explosives Preparation Laboratory at Foulness, a military firing range in Essex. Part of it was literally held together with sticky-tape. On Saturday 5 June, it was loaded onto the back of a lorry and driven to the seaside town of Shoeburyness, where it was transferred to a barge and transported across the Thames Estuary to the *Plym*'s berth at Sheerness, Kent. Carefully – very carefully – the bomb was hoisted up over the ship's rail, lowered into the holds, and brought forward to the specially designed weapon room. Five days later, the *Plym* left England for the very last time.

Given the unrest in the Middle East, where Egyptian nationalists were agitating against British and French control of the Suez Canal, it was thought best to avoid the region, so the *Campania* and the *Plym* took the long way around, via the Cape of Good Hope. Paradoxically, the Admiralty had also decreed that the voyage was to be conducted as a flag-waving tour, so stops were scheduled at Gibraltar, Sierra Leone, Cape Town and Mauritius en route.

Landing ship tank HMS *Tracker*, under the command of Lieutenant Commander RL Caple, DSC, proceeded independently for Australia via the Suez Canal. As health ship, the *Tracker* would be the most important ship in Phase Three of Operation Hurricane – the aftermath – when she would control the re-entry of the contaminated area.

For the benefit of the sluggish *Plym*, the Special Squadron steamed down the west coast of Africa at the stately rate of 10 knots. Contrary to Dizzy Davis's enthusiastic pitch, the eight-week voyage was anything but a pleasure cruise. There was plenty of work to do, beginning with the reorganisation of stores in the headquarters ship. Owing to a shortage of experienced stores officers, the packing and loading process at Chatham Dockyard had been a shambles. Hundreds of tons of scientific equipment from Woolwich, Aldermaston, Harwell,

Shoeburyness and Fort Halstead had arrived on the docks in badly packed boxes and crates, often unlabelled. With no time to lose, the whole lot was flung aboard the *Campania* in no particular order. HER staff now began sorting out the mess, going through every box and crate, cataloguing contents, labelling containers, and restowing cargo according to priority and site. It was a painstaking job that took the whole trip. Meanwhile, other teams were busy building and testing equipment, while Dr Tyte and his team leaders made detailed plans and preparations for the site.

One matter at the forefront of everyone's minds was radiological safety. From late June to late July, all personnel with special duties in Phase Three were trained in procedures for re-entering the contaminated area and recovering scientific data. Specialists from HER, the Civil Defence Corps and the services presented introductory lectures on topics like 'principles and description of an atomic explosion', 'radiological hazards from an atomic weapon' and 'the detection and measurement of nuclear radiations', illustrated with eye-opening films from American tests at Bikini and Eniwetok.[6] The personnel were then divided into groups for more detailed instruction. Officers and scientists serving as radiological surveyors and health escorts received instruction on radiac instruments, maximum permissible doses and medical aspects of exposure, while Naval ratings detailed for re-entry teams and decontamination parties were instructed in protective measures and decontamination procedures, and coxswains were trained in communication and navigation.

For the bemused servicemen, the training programme amounted to a crash course in nuclear physics. They learnt that there were four main types of ionising radiation produced by an atomic explosion: alpha, beta, gamma and neutron radiation. Alpha particles, which had a positive charge, were too weak to penetrate skin but dangerous if ingested. Beta particles were high-speed electrons, negatively charged, and strong enough to travel a fraction of an inch into human tissue before being absorbed. They could be blocked by light metal, like aluminium. Gamma rays were like X-rays: electromagnetic waves capable of penetrating and irradiating the whole human body. They could only be stopped by heavy material like lead. Neutrons had a dangerous effect on humans – when passing through the body they would 'knock on' protons from hydrogenous materials, indirectly ionising everything in their path – but only presented a threat during the initial release of radiation from the exploding bomb.[7] Very few neutrons were emitted by the fission products in fallout.

The servicemen were also familiarised with radiac devices like Geiger counters, film badges and quartz-fibre electroscopes. The Geiger counter was a portable device, about the size and shape of a car battery, with a hand-held sensor attached by a cable. It would be used by radiological surveyors and health escorts to detect radiation and measure levels of exposure, and could distinguish between beta radiation and gamma or X-rays. Film badges and electroscopes were personal dosimeters that measured radiation doses received by personnel. A film badge was literally a piece of film in a metal cassette, usually worn pinned to the waist. Radiation exposed the film, which would later be developed – the darker the film, the greater the exposure. Film badges were to be worn by all personnel in the operational area, regardless of duties. The electroscope (commonly referred to as a dosimeter) was a small, pen-like device, usually worn on the chest, with a visible scale that displayed gamma dose. Dosimeters were to be worn by all personnel entering the contaminated area. If the dose went above a certain level, the man would be ordered to leave the area and return to the *Tracker* for decontamination.

The training programme culminated with a series of exercises in which servicemen used Geiger counters to find radioactive sources hidden about the ship, learned how to draw up isodose contour maps, and practised reading dosimeters. The exercises went off without a hitch, giving everyone a welcome boost of confidence.

Despite the success of the training programme, relations between the sailors and scientists on the *Campania* continued to deteriorate. Sadly, the Navy's well-intended decision to admit the entire scientific party to the wardroom had been a disaster. To the chagrin of the ship's officers, the scientists tended to behave and dress less formally than was expected, committing *faux pas* like chatting with wardroom stewards in a familiar fashion, and coming to dinner without jackets! Worse still, some junior scientists had been seen fraternising with ratings below deck, a major breach of protocol. Many officers came to believe that the scientific party's more lowly technicians really belonged in the petty officers' mess, but since they had already been admitted to the wardroom there was nothing to be done about it (other than grumble).

For their part, the scientists thought the officers were overly obsessed with ceremonial and the finer points of etiquette. Things came to a head when the *Campania*'s first lieutenant posted a decree saying that ties must be worn to the Sunday evening picture show. Most of the scientists showed up wearing ties but no shirts.

Such petty squabbles assumed greater significance as the weeks dragged on, and the two sides grew further apart instead of coming together as Admiral Torlesse had hoped. Towards the end of the voyage, communications broke down quite literally when the Navy neglected to pass on a series of important communiqués, infuriating the senior scientists.

Much of this drama could have been avoided with better leadership, but unfortunately the two men in charge of the warring factions were among the worst offenders. Admiral Torlesse and Dr Tyte bickered constantly. The sailor thought the scientist was thin-skinned, ungrateful and overly critical, while the scientist thought the sailor was pompous, snobbish and inflexible. They were probably both right. The two men were just too different. Admiral Torlesse was the son of a Royal Navy captain, and had joined up as a 13-year-old cadet midshipman in 1915. He knew no other way of life, and valued Naval tradition above all else. Dr Tyte, on the other hand, was an East Ender with a PhD from London University. He had come up the hard way, and often went out of his way to be difficult, intentionally needling Captain Cole and his officers by calling the *Campania* a 'boat' instead of a ship, and using lubberly terms like 'the right-hand side' and 'sharp end' of the ship.[8] Worse still: he was a teetotaller. Perhaps it was inevitable that the two men would clash. After an early, abortive attempt at sociability initiated by Torlesse, they avoided each other as much as possible for the rest of the voyage.

One man who did his best to improve relations was Captain Pat Cooper, an ex-Navy man attached to HER as Naval Liaison Officer. Prior to departing England, Cooper had written a memorandum called 'Some Aspects of Naval Life' to help the scientists adjust to life on a Royal Navy ship.[9] It is not clear whether any of them read it. According to McEnhill, Cooper 'worked indefatigably' as a link between the two sides.[10] Unfortunately, he was also overloaded with administrative tasks, including the reorganisation of stores and the drawing up of boat timetables, leaving precious little time for diplomacy. When he was able to attend meetings, Cooper was frustrated to find that scientific matters were rarely discussed at Naval meetings and vice versa, despite the fact that the success of the operation clearly depended on close cooperation between the two sides. Surprisingly, the ex-Navy man's sympathies were largely with the scientists. Cooper found Admiral Torlesse and his staff to be unusually formal, even by Royal Navy standards, and criticised them for the 'complete lack of understanding and unsympathetic interest for the conduct of the trial which arose again and again and which maintained a constant source of antagonism between the naval and scientific staff'.[11]

There were other problems too. The *Campania*'s recent conversion had been a rush job, and the newly installed ventilation system sucked exhaust fumes from the engine room straight into some of the scientists' sleeping cabins, rendering them uninhabitable. The problem could not be fixed at sea, so the spluttering boffins were forced to find other berths. Some ended up camping out on deck, while others squatted in empty cabins set aside for colleagues due to join ship in the Montebellos. Dr Tyte was furious, accurately but undiplomatically blaming the Navy for the stuff-up. In the tropics, the *Campania* became a sweatbox, so the scientists were given wind-scoops to help bring fresh air into their cabins, but the scoops were the wrong size, and did not fit the scuttles. During the day, most of the civilians wore Army khakis, which had been issued as tropical rig, but they shrank in the wash, making the men feel uncomfortable and silly looking. And, of course, many suffered from seasickness, especially on the *Plym*, which was more susceptible to the motion of the sea than the *Campania*. For the worst afflicted, the long voyage began to seem like a never-ending nightmare.

But it was not all bad! There was tennis and volleyball on the flight deck and badminton and table tennis on the hangar deck. The photographic club also proved popular, even though the darkroom descended into chaos in rough seas, and the traditional Crossing the Line ceremony was a great success: when the headquarters ship crossed the equator a tarpaulin tank was set up on the flight deck, and all first-time visitors to the Southern Hemisphere were dunked, regardless of rank. 'The greatest advantage of this function was that it brought the ship's company in close contact with the civilian company, and in the robust frolic which ensued a sense of good fellowship was engendered', wrote McEnhill.[12]

The weather grew cooler as the two ships made their way south, and the ratings changed from tropical rig to blues. At Cape Town, the *Campania* and the *Plym* were greeted by a spectacular sunrise over Table Mountain. For the next few days, the ships' companies enjoyed some much-needed shore leave in apartheid-era South Africa, highlighted by cocktails and dances at the Royal Navy Club.

The weather had been remarkably kind up until now, but as soon as the Special Squadron left Cape Town and headed out into the open sea an icy wind whipped up off the Southern Ocean, forcing everyone to don extra layers. A long swell from the starboard quarter set in, causing the ships to roll and pitch, sending many green-faced boffins to their cabins. A few days later, the wind increased to Force 6 (25 knots), and the ships began to pitch severely. The poor old *Plym* had an especially rough time of it, shipping enormous amounts of seawater over her bow as she crashed through the waves. The heavy weather continued for the better part of a week, a period of boredom and frustration for the scientists, who could neither work nor sleep.

The final stop before Fremantle was Mauritius, where the ships' companies enjoyed three days of shore leave. 'The island was interesting and beautiful, and the mixed population of British, French, Indian, Chinese, etc., quite colourful', wrote McEnhill.[13] Sadly, the visit was punctuated by a fatal accident when one of the *Campania*'s cooks fell from a boat and drowned, apparently too drunk to swim.

The Special Squadron left Mauritius in weather too good to last. A few mornings later, the scientists staggered from their cabins to find rough seas buffeting the ship and a cold wind howling across the flight deck. Fiddles (low rails) were fitted to the wardroom dining tables to stop people's dinners from sliding into their laps, and occasional gushes of water poured into the upper wardroom via the ventilation ducts. The ship was rolling dramatically, and as a result the scientific contingent suffered its first casualty of the voyage – junior scientist Percy Pridgeon, who was flung headlong into a truck, breaking both his hands. The unlucky boffin spent the next few weeks with both arms in casts.

Life on board the *Plym* was not much fun either. As McEnhill observed:

> After dark it was quite impressive to stand on the quarter deck of *Campania* and look aft towards *Plym*. All that could be seen were her lights, and the sense of motion was highly accentuated because in the blackness the sea could not be seen and the motion could only be judged relative to *Campania*. The rise and fall of the lights seemed out of all proportion and their apparent extinction as the frigate slid into the trough of the swell was uncanny.[14]

As the Special Squadron neared Fremantle, another series of lectures was held to educate the ships' companies about the many dangers awaiting them in Australia. First, Dr Tyte addressed the scientists on the subject of security. To their dawning shock and dismay, they found themselves being castigated for a series of security breaches that had allegedly occurred throughout the voyage. Many had written letters back home, or sent picture postcards from various ports of call, revealing the location of the Special Squadron (and therefore the weapon), despite an earlier warning not to do so. It seemed patently absurd to most of the scientists to be told off for giving away the squadron's location when the entire voyage was being conducted as a public relations tour, with the press reporting its progress at every stop. Nevertheless, the point was driven home: no loose talk. As Western Australia's press men were known to be especially industrious, the boffins were given an official line for answering all queries: 'I can neither confirm, nor deny or comment upon your information, aspertion [sic], or allegation, as the case may be.'[15]

Following Dr Tyte's address, the *Campania*'s doctors gave a series of compulsory lectures on first aid. Surgeon Commander GD Wedd, OBE, gave an introductory lecture on shock and various fractures, followed by Surgeon Lieutenant RH Etherington, whose more detailed talk 'was extremely well delivered even if perhaps it did stress the macabre and gory possibilities so much, that overactive imagination caused one or two people to leave somewhat abruptly', according to McEnhill.[16] Another lecture by Surgeon Commander Wedd covered asphyxiation, sunstroke and the treatment of bites and stings from the many dangerous sea creatures said to be lurking around the Montebellos.

By far the most memorable talk was the venereal diseases lecture delivered by Surgeon Lieutenant Etherington when the ships were a day out of port. 'His advice was a judicious blend both medical and fatherly with a dry turn of wit which made the talk a gem in its own right, highly enjoyed by all who heard it, and providing an oft talked of subject by staff, after the interlude to which it had been aimed, had passed and been forgotten', wrote an amused McEnhill.[17] As if to drive home the medico's point about the pitfalls of sex, *A Streetcar Named Desire* was screened in the wardroom that night. The scandalous Tennessee Williams flick, starring Vivien Leigh and Marlon Brando, created uproar with its controversial depiction of rape, leading to noisy arguments in the wardroom that lasted for hours.

Finally, after eight weeks at sea, the Special Squadron arrived at Fremantle on Thursday 31 July, berthing at H Shed, Victoria Quay. Security was the strictest ever seen in Fremantle, topping even the elaborate precautions rolled out for the Landing Squadron. Armed Naval ratings, Naval Dockyard Police, Victoria Quay Police, Military Intelligence troops, Royal Marines and Commonwealth Peace Officers patrolled the wharf, which was surrounded by wire barricades. Lights had been installed under the wharf, and an armed guard posted to prevent any possible sabotage from below. No doubt ASIO men were lurking in the shadows as well.

The precautions did little to dissuade the local press. Photographers with long lenses manned the barricades, and a light aircraft flew overhead taking photographs. In the following days, the boffins were amused to read that the bomb was probably concealed in the hut on the aft end of the flight deck. In reality, the tin shed was a helium-filling station for weather balloons.

Very little attention was paid to the vessel that actually carried the device, the *Plym*, which was quietly berthed on the outboard side of the *Campania*. The health ship *Tracker*, which had arrived in Fremantle a few days earlier, was secured to a buoy in the river. The newest member of the Special Squadron, HMAS *Hawkesbury*, had just arrived from Sydney. The frigate, under the command of Lieutenant Commander RJ Scrivenor, had been brought out of mothballs specifically for Operation Hurricane.

The Special Squadron's stay in Fremantle was packed with official meetings and functions. Admiral Torlesse and Dr Tyte both met separately with Captain George Colville, Senior Officer 4th Landing Ship Squadron, and Lieutenant Colonel Smith, Commander Royal Engineers, who had flown down from Onslow to report on progress at the site. They also met with some of Western Australia's most important personages, including Governor Sir Charles Gairdner and Premier Ross McLarty. At an official reception in Fremantle, Admiral Torlesse delighted the locals with the tale of his 'incognito' visit to Western Australia the previous year.[18] He also agreed to a demonstration flight of one of the *Campania*'s Dragonfly helicopters. It was the first helicopter ever seen in Western Australia, and it proved a smash hit with the local kids.

Admiral Torlesse also held a conference with representatives of the Australian services on board the *Campania*, including two senior Air Force officers: the recently promoted Air Commodore Bill Hely, now Air Officer Commanding Western Area, and Group Captain MO Watson, Director of Air Staff Plans and Policy. The airmen were ready to make detailed plans for the RAAF's role in Operation Hurricane, but were shocked to find that the meeting's agenda was almost blank. Due to a communication breakdown between Melbourne and London (almost certainly a result of the decision to separate the air-sampling programme from the main operation), several key pieces of information had not yet reached either side. Admiral Torlesse had no idea that the RAAF had agreed to carry out the many tasks allotted to it, beginning with security patrols, which were due to start immediately. He also stated 'very emphatically' that all radio traffic relating to the operation had to be in cypher, despite the fact that the RAAF had repeatedly been told that plain language would suffice.[19] 'These additional communications requirements at this late stage, necessitated a rapid and very considerable change in communication arrangements and in the provision of facilities such as cypher which necessarily had to be provided from Melbourne', grumbled Air Commodore Hely.[20]

The Air Force officers also brought up the issue of radiation. Following the RAAF's breezy acceptance of coastal-monitoring and air-sampling duties, Air Vice Marshal Ted Daley, Director General of Medical Services, had expressed alarm about the possibility of exposure to radiation. Daley's concerns were put forward by Hely and Watson, who were given a 'specific assurance that there was no danger to aircrew' by an unnamed 'senior Ministry of Supply officer with RAF connections'.[21] The Australian officers accepted this statement, with the result that the RAAF took no precautions of any kind against the exposure of aircrews during Operation Hurricane: no protective clothing, no film badges or dosimeters, no warnings about ingesting radioactive particles in the cloud. Nothing. Ground crews, who would inevitably be working on contaminated aircraft, were not even considered.

At a hastily organised follow-up conference, Admiral Torlesse and Air Commodore Hely hashed out detailed plans for RAAF involvement in Operation Hurricane. From the beginning of September, Dakotas from No 86 (Transport) Wing would fly security patrols out of Onslow until relieved by aircraft carrier HMAS *Sydney* with 805 Squadron RAN and 817 Squadron RAN embarked; two of the Dakotas would also be fitted out with sensitive radiac instruments for coastal-monitoring duties. Air-sampling duties would be handled by Lincoln bombers from No 82 (Bomber) Wing, operating out of Broome. Additional Dakotas from MacRobertson Miller Airlines and No 11 (General Reconnaissance) Squadron RAAF would provide a biweekly courier service from Perth. The RAAF would also establish or upgrade laboratory, cypher and communications facilities at Onslow and Broome. On the other side of the country, Lincoln bombers from No 10 (General Reconnaissance) Squadron, supplemented by aircraft from 82 Wing, would fly air-sampling sorties out of Townsville. (Across the ditch, the Royal New Zealand Air Force would also fly air-sampling sorties between New Zealand and Fiji.)

This was a massive commitment by the RAAF, but one that was made willingly, as a contribution to the defence of the British Empire.

Later that night, Captain Morris, NOIC West Australian Area, and his wife hosted a supper party for the British officers and scientists at their home in Claremont, attended by high-ranking officers from all three Australian services and their glamorous wives and fiancées.

While the officers were chortling over champagne and canapés, the ratings were getting up to their usual mischief. One drunken helicopter fitter from the *Campania* caused a stir by trying to force his way into the Embassy Ballroom in Perth and challenging a police constable to a fight. He spent the night behind bars.[22] In Fremantle, two sailors and a canteen assistant from the *Campania* were hauled in following a row in Mouatt Street, which ended with an unsuccessful escape attempt. The authorities had apparently learnt their lesson from the Landing Squadron's April visit, because this time all four men appeared in court. The helicopter fitter got off with a warning, but the Mouatt Street mob received a total of £19 in fines. Senior Commissioned Observer HJ Lambert, DSM, appeared for the men in court, defending their character and pleading mitigating circumstances.

'They underestimated the strength of West Australian beer', he said.[23]

After a few short days in port, the Special Squadron quietly slipped out of Fremantle Harbour and sailed for the Montebellos in glorious weather. While the *Hawkesbury* called in at Exmouth to pick up fuel lighter SSL 563 for use at Onslow, the other ships steamed ahead. At 1200 on Friday 8 August, the precise hour planned over a year earlier, the *Campania* dropped anchor in Parting Pool. As per Naval tradition, the Landing Squadron greeted the Special Squadron with a Bible verse, flashed by signal lamp: 'St Luke, 13, 24' ('Strive to enter in at the straight gate ...')[24] And that is what the *Plym* did, entering the lagoon and picking up the special mooring off Cocoa Beach.

It would be her final resting place.

# 9.

# THE BUILD-UP

When the Special Squadron arrived in the Montebello Islands, Phase Two of Operation Hurricane commenced. All units and detachments operating in the islands – including the Australians – now came under the operational control of Admiral Torlesse, Task Force Commander. As a first order of business, Torlesse ordered that the clocks be put forward from Item time (GMT + 0900) to Item King or IK time (GMT + 0930), so that the working day would begin at dawn. The Montebellos were now one and a half hours ahead of the rest of Western Australia.

Then: lunch.

After that, the ships began unloading. From the flight deck of the *Campania*, sailors and scientists watched as a convoy of landing craft mechanised (LCMs) emerged from the South Channel and made a beeline for the escort carrier. It was such a big job that almost everyone pitched in: all hands, plus many of the scientists, hauled crates from the hold to the lift, where they were taken up to the hangar deck. From there, they were loaded into LCMs in order of priority for transport to the main sites: Hermite, Trimouille, Alpha, North West and the target vessel.

Meanwhile, Dr Leonard Tyte and his senior staff went ashore to inspect the facilities prepared by the Royal Engineers. They were blown away by what they found. The Montebellos, mere desert islands two years ago, were now equipped with jetties, boat ramps, camera towers, 15 miles of tracks traversing all four major islands, and laboratory facilities equal to those at home, complete with electricity and fluorescent lights. 'Truly the REs are magnificent', marvelled Dr Tyte.[1]

The modest Lieutenant Colonel Pat Smith, Commander Royal Engineers, gave much of the credit to the RAAF. After six long months in the North West, the 30-strong 5ACS Detachment finally headed home soon after the Special Squadron's arrival with rave reviews from Lieutenant Colonel Smith:

> Detachment 5ACS, RAAF have been an essential component of the Force Engineers. Throughout, they have been outstanding, the speed and quality of their work both in earth moving and in general field engineering, and their contribution to the engineering effort has been out of proportion in its importance to their numerical strength. I have found it most valuable to have available this Detachment with its high degree and quality of Officer and NCO leadership.[2]

Expected to take a week, the Special Squadron's unloading process went remarkably smoothly, and was all but finished inside two days, a testament to all the hard work by Naval Liaison Officer Captain Pat Cooper and others on board the *Campania*. But on Day 4, the weather took a turn for the worse: Force 5 (20 knot) winds whipped in off the sea, and a heavy swell buffeted the escort carrier at its mooring in Parting Pool. Lined up at the disembarkation space that morning, the scientists stared in horror as they were told to climb down the ladder on the ship's side and jump into a lurching LCM. The bravest of the lot gave it a go, and four of them made it, but then the mooring rope parted, and the ship's executive officer,

Commander Douglas Bromley, DSC, ordered the landing craft to lay off. The commander, who was in charge of safety, was justifiably sceptical of the boffins' seamanship abilities, and immediately called a halt to proceedings. No more disembarkation attempts were made that day, or the next two.

As HER physicist JJ McEnhill wrote:

This was simply a foretaste of a feature of the weather and sea at Montebello which was often to cause frustration throughout the project. After days of quiet calm seas the wind would suddenly increase, the swell rise and movement of boats in Parting Pool and sometimes the lagoon would have to be cancelled. Such weather conditions could arise in a few hours and often they would abate just as quickly.[3]

Even when conditions improved, there were still problems. Captain Cooper's intricate boat timetables had been based on information from the Epicure reconnaissance, which proved to be outdated and overly optimistic. In reality, most journeys took considerably longer than anticipated. For example, the early morning boat ride from the *Campania* to Hermite Island took 90 minutes, while the run from *Campania* to Trimouille Island took about an hour – and that was on a good day. Consequently, the schedule was soon thrown into chaos. There were not enough boats to make up all the lost time, and many boffins found themselves stuck on islands for hours on end, waiting to be picked up. To make matters worse, the constant chop in Parting Pool made it impossible for the *Campania*'s pinnaces to secure to the nearby trot mooring overnight. The boats were ultimately forced to tie up at the Stephenson Channel trot, 5 nautical miles away from the *Campania*, cutting even more hours off the scientists' workday.

To cut down on travel time, Admiral Torlesse decided to establish shore camps at H1, the command centre on Hermite, and T2, the main scientific site on Trimouille. The camps were equipped with tented accommodation, powered lights, and separate messes for officers, senior ratings and other ranks, and junior ratings and other ranks. They were up and running within the week. Finally, the boffins could get away from the *Campania* and the ship's officers could have their own wardroom back.

Coincidentally, on Monday 18 August, the same day the camps were opened, the first planeload of reinforcements arrived from the UK. Early in the morning, a party of 25 senior scientists, led by Charles Adams, Deputy Technical Director of Operation Hurricane, landed at Onslow in an RAF Hastings loaded with 1½ tons of scientific equipment. They sailed to the Montebellos in HMAS *Hawkesbury* and arrived at dusk the same day.

Now the real work began in earnest. The Task Force's scientific contingent had been divided into divisions based on their areas of specialty; the divisions were in turn divided into smaller teams with responsibility for individual tasks. These teams now spread out around the islands, setting up hundreds of devices with military efficiency. Every day, boats and landing craft crisscrossed the lagoon, carrying boffins from ship to shore and from island to island, returning to the same sites day after day to test and maintain their equipment.

The main site was the command centre at H1. Situated 6 nautical miles from the target vessel, at the southern end of Hermite, the hilltop building was the only site in the islands that would be occupied during the test itself. The command centre housed darkrooms, offices, laboratories full of apparatuses, and the all-important control room where the master control desk was located. This was the domain of Ieuan Maddock, Assistant Director of the Telemetry and Communications Division, a diminutive 35-year-old Welshman with a wispy moustache and a mischievous elfin face. Sitting at the control desk, Maddock and his assistants would coordinate the elaborate 24-hour countdown and initiate the firing sequence. Maddock himself would push the button.

At the front of the building, facing the target vessel, were apertures for the pride and joy of HER: ultra-high-speed Kerr-cell cine-cameras. Developed specifically to study the early stages of an explosion, Kerr-cell cameras were reportedly the fastest cameras on Earth, capable of taking short bursts of photographs at the astonishing rate of 100,000 frames per second. The revolutionary cameras did not throw images directly onto film but onto stainless-steel mirrors that revolved 150,000 times a minute, reflecting the images through small lenses onto film. The cameras were so new that they had not even been tested in the field yet.

Next to the command centre was a camera tower for conventional high-speed cine-cameras with speeds of up to 8000 frames per second. These cameras would provide photographs of the development of the fireball, the water column, the mushroom cloud and other blast effects. To the rear was a lean-to which served as the charging station for the many batteries required to power apparatuses scattered around the islands. The tented camp where most of the staff lived was at the bottom of the hill, a two-minute walk away.

Almost exactly 6 nautical miles north of H1, in the middle of Bunsen Channel, lay the target vessel. HMS *Plym* was held virtually motionless by the special mooring's six bridles and connected to H1 by cables linking the weapon's detonators to the firing mechanism. To the annoyance of the ship's company, the frigate was now crawling with boffins eager to send her to oblivion. Down in the hold, teams from the Weapon Operation Division, Atomic Energy Division and Multiplication Rate Division all jostled for space. John Challens, a 37-year-old rocket expert from Northamptonshire, England, was the Assistant Director of the Weapon Operation Division. He monitored the device and tested the operation of the firing circuit, while his deputy, Londoner Eddie Howse, maintained liaison with the command centre. On the other side of the hold, the Atomic Energy Division installed ionisation chambers to measure the multiplication rate of the fission process, and the Multiplication Rate Division installed crystal and photomultiplier units to measure the same process by other means. Up on deck, the Telemetry and Communications Division constructed an antenna array on the metal gantry above the forward gun deck to send signals to H1. Meanwhile, the ship's company installed 1800 sandbags, eight tons of lead bricks, five tons of steel plate and several hundredweight of lead sheeting to protect the recording gear in the aft superstructure, which would transmit weapon data right up until the very last moment, millionths of a second after detonation, when the ship and everything in it would be destroyed.

Over the next few weeks, the *Plym*'s company was reduced in stages, stores were back loaded and victuals were run down – sometimes too efficiently. 'Prior to 31st August all fresh water tanks and a ballast tank were filled with freshwater [sic]', Lieutenant Commander Peter Draisey recalled. 'For various reasons only 77½ tons was available for use after the boilers were shut down on 31st August. Although strict rationing was enforced there was anxiety about ekeing [sic] out this amount, especially when the last 3 tons from the ballast tanks were quite undrinkable. However, the boiler fed water used next was considered a great improvement!'[4]

Opposite the *Plym* at Cocoa Beach was T2, the main hub of scientific activity on Trimouille. T2 was home to 60 permanent camp residents, whose numbers swelled each morning as scores of scientists and sappers came ashore from the LSTs in the lagoon. From T2, each team drove or walked across the island to its designated sites, lugging all sorts of bizarre equipment. The Mechanical Effects Division set up a bewildering array of devices, from simple jerry cans and toothpaste tubes to complex multi-piston blast gauges and seismographic gauges that would measure the power of the blast. The Thermal Effects Division placed calorimeters, thermometers and heat-sensitive paint at various points to measure the heat of the blast, and hung out samples of 144 different types of clothing, including 100 service uniforms, to investigate the effect of the blast on different materials. The Radioactivity Measurement Division – which comprised all of two people – laid out cylinders of paraffin wax filled with sheets of various materials to measure the neutron dose at different distances from the bomb, while the significantly larger Radiological Hazard Division set up ionisation chambers, rigged up with amplifiers, pen recorders and shockproof containers, to measure radiation levels all around the islands. Elsewhere, modified vacuum cleaners were deployed to suck up air samples. Spitfire and Lancaster components were positioned to see how they would withstand the blast. A scale model of a destroyer's funnel was built to test its durability, and a model deckhouse was built to practise decontamination procedures. Eight tons of foodstuffs, including meat, vegetables, sugar, butter and flour, were sacrificed to measure the effect of radiation on them and the degree of protection afforded by different packaging materials.

There were also biological experiments. Dr WJH Butterfield of the UK Medical Research Council was roped into the expedition at the last minute to study the biological effects of fallout on plants and animals. Butterfield's team dispersed boxes of seedlings around Trimouille to be harvested and tested after the blast, and put 50 pieces of surgical gauze on plastic sheets to collect fallout samples. To replicate the effect of fallout on new crops, the samples would be taken back to Harwell, dissolved in various solutions and used to grow barley hydroponically. After the explosion, Butterfield would also catch rats and fish to measure the amount of fission products like iodine-131 and strontium-90 in their systems. He would also feed radioactive samples to guinea pigs and rabbits in the lab back at Harwell to see what would happen to them.

Frank Hill of HER made a separate study of the archipelago's native fauna and flora. Hill was not a professional biologist but an electrical engineer whose main job was to look after the control system that sent the firing signal to the weapon. Hill was also a keen amateur naturalist and he volunteered to conduct a biological study because no one else was doing it. In collaboration with Surgeon Commander GD Wedd, who specialised in marine specimens, Hill collected samples of 400 different species of plants and animals, including over 270 different kinds of insect. He was disappointed not to find any wallabies or bandicoots, which had long since been wiped out by introduced pests, but his lizard collection was a great success. It included the Gould's monitor, which grew up to 4 feet long and swam in the ocean, and Gilbert's dragon, which could stand up and run on its hind legs. When Hill presented his findings to the Linnean Society of London, they included 20 species of insects, six plants and a legless lizard that were totally new to science.[5] Unfortunately, most of them would have been killed by the bomb he helped detonate. If the keen naturalist had any conflicted feelings about that, he did not mention it in his talk.

On the opposite side of the lagoon from Trimouille, just north of Hermite, lay Alpha Island. The main site there was A4, a small hill where the sappers built a concrete observation building with a spectacular and uninterrupted view of the lagoon and the far-off target vessel. At the top of the tower, the Optics and Photography Division set up a range of remote-control cine-cameras set to run at different speeds; down below, the Thermal Effects Division placed devices to measure thermal radiation.

On North West Island, at the northern end of the group, lay N4 – home to a 30-foot camera tower and a battery of remote-control rocket-launchers. Immediately after the blast, the overworked Captain Cooper would fire a staggered salvo of rockets through the mushroom cloud, collecting radioactive samples in special filters installed in the rocket heads. The samples would then be used to ascertain the efficiency of the weapon by comparing the ratio of unfissioned plutonium to fission products in the samples, thus revealing how much plutonium had been used and how much had been wasted.

With an operation the size of Hurricane, it was inevitable that some things would go wrong. Despite the decision to quarter men ashore at H1 and T2, boat transport remained problematic. The boat crews were among the hardest-working men in the Task Force, but they did not have enough boats, and the ones they did have were taking a beating. The landing craft were in particularly bad shape, their engines frequently breaking down from overuse, and their flat bottoms routinely holed by rocks and coral heads. It was not uncommon for scientists to spend a whole trip with water swishing around their ankles, and sometimes they were even forced to bail out. 'It seems incredible that the whole of this expensive operation should hang on the thin red line of 3 or 4 LCMs', wrote Dr Tyte, 'but that is, I fear, the grim truth.'[6]

Vehicles were also in short supply. On Trimouille, there was a pool of nine Land Rovers, two 3-ton lorries, two bulldozers and two mobile cranes. The lorries were almost always engaged in the daily bus service that ran up and down the island, leaving very few vehicles for the scientists to share. Each morning, the harried Army transport officer at T3 at Gladstone Beach would find himself surrounded by boffins pleading their case. Officially, the vehicles were supposed to be allocated in order of priority by the Technical Services Division on the *Campania*, but in reality it was usually first in, best dressed.

Communications were another issue. The VHF radio sets provided by the Admiralty were useless beyond a certain range, and the whole communication network would have broken down entirely if it had not been for Ieuan Maddock's forward thinking. Following an unsuccessful trial in the Thames Estuary earlier in the year, Maddock had purchased a set of cheap but effective taxi radios for use in the Montebellos. Admiral Torlesse was not too happy to find the head of the Telemetry and Communications Division using cheap taxi sets instead of Royal Navy ones, taking it as an insult to the service, but after testing them himself he was reluctantly forced to admit they were superior radios.

Many of these logistical and supply problems could have been solved, or at least ameliorated, if Admiral Torlesse had simply asked the Australians for help. Prime Minister Robert Menzies had already offered to give the Brits anything they needed, so a few boats or Land Rovers were certainly not out of the question. But for some reason, presumably a misplaced sense of pride, Torlesse refused to do this.

There were also what McEnhill called 'domestic problems'.[7] Over the course of Phase Two, the testy relationship between the Royal Navy and HER, epitomised by the open animosity between Admiral Torlesse and Dr Tyte, continued to worsen. The scientists could not help but contrast the positive attitude of the Royal Engineers – who were almost always happy to help – with that of the sailors, who seemed to think their job was done as soon as the boffins were safely ashore. There were more and more complaints about the food at the shore camps, mostly from senior scientists. Although there was a small fridge at H1, there was no cold storage at T2, which meant no cool drinks. The scientists were also annoyed to find that conditions at the shore camps seemed to magically improve any time a Naval officer arrived for an inspection.

A plague of flies on Trimouille made life even more uncomfortable. According to McEnhill: 'Their population had increased alarmingly, and in some of the concrete emplacements such as T5 they were a great nuisance to men attempting to adjust apparatus, with both hands occupied, while swarms of flies crawled over them.'[8] At H1, the problem was termites, which were so voracious that they threatened to devour the command centre before D-Day.

The accommodation spaces on board HM Ships *Zeebrugge* and *Tracker* were another source of friction. The Radiochemical Division, led by HER's Frank Morgan, was based on the *Zeebrugge*, where the Navy had constructed an ingenious foldout laboratory on the tank deck. Unfortunately, the sailors had not given as much thought to quarters for Morgan's team, so the four men were put up in a converted packing crate so small that they could hardly stand up in it. Things were not much better over in the *Tracker*, where the Radiological Hazard Division was allegedly packed in like sardines, while two whole compartments with 20 bunks each were used to store beer. The situation ultimately led to a major blow-up between Dr Tyte and Admiral Torlesse. In a series of heated meetings, the Technical Director called the conditions on board the *Zeebrugge* 'appalling' and compared the scientists' accommodation to a 'dog kennel'.[9] The Task Force Commander was predictably unsympathetic, silencing his opposite number with the astonishing statement that 'after all this was an operation of war' and the scientists would have to put up with what they got.[10] The next day, a fuming Dr Tyte demanded a written statement to that effect, since no one had told him that Operation Hurricane was an operation of war, but Admiral Torlesse fobbed him off.

And of course, many of the scientists remained hopeless landlubbers. For those not blessed with physical coordination, the task of climbing in and out of landing craft in the rough waters of Parting Pool was always fraught, the sarcastic witticisms of the sailors only adding to their humiliation. For reasons that were not always clear, the scientists were often required to use the vertiginous ladder on the *Campania*'s weather side instead of the more civilised companionway on the lee side. Sometimes it was because the *Campania*'s officers did not want them to spoil the companionway for the use of the admiral's personal barge or other Naval launches. 'The return of a liberty cutter from a fishing trip with a handful of Wardroom Officers on board usually occasioned more attention and assistance from the watch on the embarkation space than the return of an LCM loaded with disreputable looking civilians back from a day's work on the islands', complained McEnhill.[11]

One scientist's misadventure nearly ended in disaster. The hapless Percy Pridgeon, who had broken both of his hands on the long voyage to Australia, had recently had his casts removed and returned to active duty. One evening, he was returning to the *Campania* when he mistimed his leap from the landing craft and plunged into the sea. The coxswain immediately swung the landing craft away to avoid crushing him against the ship's side; at the same moment, Commander Bromley, watching from above, ripped off his jacket, dived in and hauled the spluttering boffin up onto the companionway. Soaking wet, the commander fixed Pridgeon's colleagues with a look and drawled, 'I suppose you did want that man?'[12]

•

While many British servicemen worked in and around the most sensitive sites in the Montebellos, Australians were excluded from any duties that might reveal technical information about the bomb. Instead, they were kept on the periphery of the operation and allocated mundane tasks like transport, supplies and – ironically – security.

One of the busiest ships in the islands was HMAS *Hawkesbury*. In addition to ferry duties, the frigate was tasked with patrolling the prohibited area to search for unauthorised vessels, such as Soviet submarines hoping to spy on the test or Asian fishing boats accidentally wandering into the blast zone. Unfortunately, there was some doubt as to what she could do if and when she came across such an intruder. The Menzies Government, it seemed, had been a little overenthusiastic when it banned entry to an area within 40 nautical miles of the Montebellos. In reality, Australia's territorial waters only extended 3 nautical miles out from shore. So what was the *Hawkesbury* supposed to do if she confronted an unauthorised vessel in international waters? The RAN asked the solicitor-general, Professor KH Bailey, who advised that such a vessel would be outside Australia's jurisdiction, and any action against it could be construed as piracy under international law.[13] This put the *Hawkesbury*'s captain in an awkward position. Lieutenant Commander RJ Scrivenor was a 29-year-old former intelligence officer from Hawthorn, Victoria. He was under strict orders to stop all unauthorised vessels from entering the prohibited zone – without using force or causing an international incident. That was easy for the Naval Board to say, but not so easy to do. A warning from the British Admiralty, advising all ships and aircraft to stay away from the test site for their own safety, helped a little, but not much.

At the end of August, the RAN received unconfirmed reports of four submarine sightings in northern waters. The first came from New Guinea, where a commercial aircraft pilot reported sighting an object resembling a submarine periscope heading west 40 nautical miles north-west of Rabaul. The next day, three soldiers reported similar sightings in Darwin Harbour, one in broad daylight, the others in clear moonlight. All three men were experienced soldiers and considered reliable.[14]

The *Hawkesbury* was now on high alert. Kelvin Gough of Glebe, New South Wales, was a 22-year-old assistant steward at the time. Years later, he told Frank Walker, author of *Maralinga: The Chilling Exposé of Our Secret Nuclear Shame and Betrayal of Our Troops and Country*, about a fifth and final unconfirmed submarine sighting:

> We picked up an echo on the sonar. It was a long way off but the skipper thought it was a Soviet submarine following us so he ordered we drop a couple of depth charges to warn them off. It must have worked because the mysterious echo disappeared.[15]

The *Hawkesbury* had one other job during Phase Two. In the days leading up to the blast, the frigate laid 24 temporary buoys (known in the Navy as dan buoys) in a 100-nautical-mile radius of the islands on behalf of the Radiochemical Division. The buoys were fitted with special containers to collect radioactive water samples after the blast. Rather ominously, the ship's sick bay was fitted with a Geiger counter at the same time.

The ship's company was working hard, so it was no surprise that they also played hard while on shore leave in Onslow. On one occasion, rowdy libertymen smashed about 30 lights on Onslow Jetty, severed a hose, and threw several drums of paint and an expensive paint-mixing machine into the bay. Not long after that, a rating stole a rifle from a parked car while his shipmates stole a case of beer from another. The beer belonged to a local lead miner, who was particularly annoyed since he had just shouted the sailors a case of beer as a goodwill gesture. To smooth things over with the locals, Captain F Bryce Morris, NOIC West Australian Area, was forced to fly up to Onslow to lay down the law.

●

In August, HMAS *Warreen* returned to the North West to resume despatch duties. A few weeks later, the unlucky ship suffered two tragedies in a matter of days.

At 0940 on Wednesday 10 September, the *Warreen* was fogbound in 9 fathoms of water off North Sandy Island when Engine Room Artificer (Second Class) Harry Flack was found unconscious in his bunk. The popular 35-year-old from Tasmania was the fleet train's chief engineer. For 20 minutes Flack's crewmates desperately tried to revive him, but there was no response.

The entire ship's company was shocked. Flack had been up on deck, looking 'hale and hearty', just a few hours earlier, when the *Warreen* had slipped out of Beadon Bay.[16] The circumstances were suspicious enough for Admiral Torlesse to send the following message to Lieutenant Commander RH Grant, Resident Naval Officer Onslow:

WARREEN REPORTS ERA FLACK FOUND DEAD IN CABIN CAUSE UNKNOWN POSSIBLE POISONING[17]

It was a scenario worthy of an Agatha Christie novel: a small ship with a complement of ten fogbound at sea, one man dead, and a murderer on board. Constable Bill Connelly from the Onslow Police Station opened an investigation, and four ratings from the *Warreen* were hauled in for questioning. The *Narvik*'s medical officer, Surgeon Lieutenant PG 'Doc' Pugh, conducted an autopsy, but the results were inconclusive and tissue samples were sent to Perth for analysis.

After that, the investigation petered out. There were no follow-ups in the press, and Flack's death certificate, issued three months later, was suspiciously vague, listing 'kidney and liver failure' as cause of death.[18] That is a little like saying someone found lying in a pool of blood died from 'loss of blood'. Indeed, 'kidney and liver failure' sounds like code for poisoning.

Harry Flack was buried in Onslow Cemetery with full Naval honours on Thursday 11 September 1952. He was survived by his second wife and two sons from his first marriage.

Three days later, disaster struck again. Lieutenant Commander Richard Thurman was a 46-year-old Reservist from Subiaco, Western Australia, who had filled in as captain of the *Warreen* and the *Limicola* during Lieutenant Pioch's medical leave. Following a recurrence of Pioch's eye condition, Thurman had just been ordered to return to the North West to take over as senior officer of the fleet train once again. He was due to fly out the following week.

On Sunday 14 September, Thurman was entertaining a lady friend aboard his launch, moored off Barrack Street Jetty in the Swan River, when he discovered that the dinghy was adrift. Improvising a flotation device from an oar and an empty oil tin, Thurman stripped off and dived in to retrieve the dinghy. It was almost midnight. There was no moon and the river was choppy. He was never seen alive again. Two days later, the police recovered his body in 6 feet of water just 50 yards from the jetty.

With Thurman dead and Pioch hospitalised, the WA Navy was rapidly running out of reliable officers. It was Senior Commissioned Boatswain JE White who saved the day. The *Karangi*'s former skipper was called up off the Reserve list after 18 months on Civvy Street and sent up to take command of the *Warreen*. The poor old *Limicola*, which continued to experience engine difficulties, was secured to a mooring in the lagoon and left there. She was eventually towed home just days before the blast. She had never been much use to anyone anyway.

•

Down at Onslow, the Army camp was growing in leaps and bounds. Originally designed to accommodate 20 to 40 transit personnel, the Western Command Transit Camp was now home to 83 permanent residents from the Army, Navy, Air Force, WA Department of Works and ASIO, with more overnight visitors en route to the test site arriving each day. Situated opposite the hospital, about half a mile from the pub, the camp offered tented accommodation for visitors, a wet canteen known as the Texas Canteen, picture shows three nights a week, and facilities for table tennis, darts and quoits.

The new Officer Commanding Western Command Transit Camp Detachment was Captain Vern Donegan, a 40-year-old former WANFL football player from Toodyay, Western Australia. Donegan had assumed command from Captain Tom Carlin in July, and had spent most of the time since then pleading with HQ for help with the growing camp, mostly unsuccessfully. Urgent requests for more staff, new pipes to upgrade the struggling plumbing system, extra tables for the crowded messes, and a Fowler's stove for the kitchen were met with curt replies like: 'does not warrant the high degree of priority called for by you', 'a more judicious approach by you would be appreciated', and 'in the light of the experience of the late OC ... it is not understood why such difficulty should exist'.[19] The camp had of course doubled in size since Carlin's departure, but that was neither here nor there.

Adding to Donegan's frustration was the fact that his predecessor had cut corners on a number of occasions, with consequences only coming to light after his departure. The first trap to snare Donegan was an unexplained shortfall of £26 in the officers' mess accounts, which Carlin had signed off on moments before hopping on the plane to Perth. The debt followed Donegan around for months. He ended up paying half of it out of his own pocket before the Army reluctantly wrote off the rest. He was also ordered to account for a speaker that had been damaged by an unqualified projectionist appointed by Carlin, and a brand-new water pump that Carlin had given to the Department of Civil Aviation (DCA) to replace one damaged by his men. Each incident was relatively minor in and of itself, but they were all blown out of proportion by the bean counters in Perth. Given the sheer number of irregularities, it must have been galling for Captain Donegan to hear his bosses make unfavourable comparisons with Carlin.

On the bright side, the troops had done an excellent job with public relations. Three nights a week, the people of Onslow were invited to the camp's picture shows, earning the Army the affection of the local kids. The soldiers also helped put out bushfires, played cricket matches against the town on a red pitch with a rusty locomotive engine at square leg, and even threw a dance at the Road Board Hall, where everyone enjoyed cutting a rug to the music of local pianist Wyn Davey and band. The dance was organised by Private Norm 'Snowy' Aitken, a batman steward who had just returned from Korea, and Corporal Teddy Aide, a strapping young electrical and mechanical engineer whom the ladies of Onslow considered Hollywood heart-throb material.

Aitken may have had an ulterior motive for throwing the dance: there was a romance brewing between him and local girl Patty Clark. They were eventually married on Friday 31 October, with civilians on one side of the church and servicemen on the other. The reception, which was held at the Snifter tea room, was a roaring success.

Two of the most important residents of the transit camp were the security men: Jack Clowes, ASIO's man in Onslow; and Major Stuart Kingwell, Australian Army Intelligence Corps. A 35-year-old former artillery officer from Geelong, Victoria, Major Kingwell was in charge of service security in the North West. He had a total staff of three NCOs and six guards to patrol Onslow and Broome, where another base was established.

One unsuspecting sailor who got a first-hand look at the security men in action was Brian Emmott. An 18-year-old National Serviceman from East Fremantle, Emmott was serving in HMAS *Mildura* when she visited the Montebellos in September to deliver Captain Morris, NOIC West Australian Area, to a conference with Admiral Torlesse. On the way home, the corvette called in at Onslow for shore leave.

'We were told before we left the ship, "Don't forget – don't tell anybody where you've been!"' Emmott later recalled.

Naturally, the young sailors went straight to the pub, only to find that the cooling works had broken down. Rather than drink warm beer, they went down the road to the Texas Canteen.

'You blokes look thirsty', said the bloke behind the bar.

'Yeah, we are mate.'

'So anyway, where you been?'

'Oh, just sailing around the Indian Ocean.'

Emmott and his mates weren't silly – they knew that some of the men in the canteen could have been planted there to spy on them – but one of their shipmates was not so sharp.

'It turned out that this junior officer's got a few beers under his belt, and somebody's asked him where he'd been', Emmott recalled. 'And he said, "Oh, out at the Montebellos atom test, you know?" Now, I personally, and several other guys were there, when two big fellas marched in, in plain clothes, just shirts and pants, and they arrested him, took him off. We never saw him again.'[20]

•

During August, the RAAF descended on Onslow as part of the Phase Two build-up. First, a detachment from RAAF Pearce arrived to upgrade communications at the airstrip and develop the dusty old claypan into a fully equipped airfield. Base Commander Onslow was Squadron Leader Leo Britt, a 31-year-old former Halifax pilot and intelligence officer from Brighton, Victoria, currently employed as a flying instructor. It was his job to control and coordinate all air operations in the area, including security patrols, couriers and RAF transports.

Then, towards the end of the month, the first echelon of 86 Wing Detachment arrived from Richmond, New South Wales. The first echelon comprised two Dakotas with three-man aircrews, plus a ten-man ground crew. The second echelon, which arrived in late September, comprised an additional three Dakotas. The Detachment Commander was Flight Lieutenant Clarence Donnelly, a 34-year-old former Lancaster pilot and POW from Gympie, Queensland, who had recently been awarded the Queen's Commendation for Meritorious Service in the Air in Korea. Second in command was Flight Lieutenant Ron Grace, a 33-year-old former Halifax and Mustang pilot from Wyalkatchem, Western Australia, who had come off the Reserve list to serve in Korea.

The RAAF's decision to send up a Base Commander who outranked the 86 Wing Detachment Commander was a last-minute one, and it immediately led to friction between the two men. Squadron Leader Britt's orders tasked him with coordinating security patrols conducted by 86 Wing Detachment, which he understood to mean that he had direct responsibility for the control of individual aircraft and crews. But Flight Lieutenant Donnelly disagreed strongly, insisting that the Detachment Commander must control the aircraft under his command. The inferior officer stood his ground and, perhaps surprisingly, won the argument: Britt agreed to allocate tasks to Donnelly, who would in turn allocate the tasks to the captain of the individual aircraft (in many cases himself). Thus the all-important chain of command was maintained.

Next the airmen devised a series of patrol routes with codenames like Axe, Scythe, Saw and Hoe.[21] The Dakotas' orders were to intercept and divert all unauthorised aircraft in the prohibited zone and locate, report and shadow all unauthorised surface vessels or submarines in the crystal-clear water below. For security reasons, they were prohibited from flying within 5 miles of the Montebellos, or taking photographs within 10 miles of the islands, unless it was necessary to intercept or identify an intruder. (The big hole in the middle of the search area was covered by HMS *Campania*'s Dragonfly helicopters, which carried out short-range air patrols around the islands.) In the event of a confrontation with an unauthorised aircraft, the Dakotas were to 'divert it by close manoeuvre'.[22] In reality, they could do little else: the Dakota was an unarmed transport aircraft. In the final days before the test, the more venomous Fireflies and Sea Furies of the RAN Fleet Air Arm would take over air patrol duties.

Flight Lieutenant Donnelly flew the first patrol on Monday 1 September, and for the next four weeks he and Grace flew sorties on alternate days (except Sundays). Each patrol lasted about five hours and took a different route around the prohibited zone, extending into the larger danger zone as far as possible. To keep any hypothetical Communist spies or Soviet submarine captains guessing, a different patrol was selected at random each day, with security and policemen like Major Kingwell, Jack Clowes and Constable Connelly often tagging along to keep an eye on things down below, on the mainland and out over the coast.

•

On Thursday 11 September, an RAF Hastings arrived at Onslow with a 30-strong party of scientists and technicians on board. Among those who disembarked were two boffins from the Atomic Energy Research Establishment (AERE) at Harwell: Doug Peirson and Frank Hale. The two men comprised the Radiological Survey Division team tasked with running the coastal-monitoring programme out of Onslow. Their brief was to conduct an aerial survey of the North West Coast to determine the position, extent and activity of any fallout that reached the mainland after the blast.[23] Peirson, a 31-year-old graduate of London University who specialised in geological radioactivity, was the team leader. His plan was to have two RAAF Dakotas fly along the coast from Onslow to Broome at 500 feet on D+1 (the day after the test), taking readings with ultra-sensitive radiac devices designed for geological prospecting. A third Dakota would remain on standby in Onslow, loaded with a four-wheel drive and Geiger counters, in case fallout was detected anywhere on the coast. If so, the vehicle would be flown to the nearest airstrip and driven to the contaminated area so a close inspection could be conducted.

One week after the boffins arrived, the second echelon of three Dakotas from 86 Wing touched down on the airstrip. Peirson arranged for two of these aircraft to be fitted out with his radiac devices. The Geiger Muller arrays each comprised seven 3-foot Geiger tubes and a pen recorder attached to plywood boards and screwed to the floor of the cargo compartment. To avoid interference from the radiation produced by the luminous displays on the pilot's instrument panel, each device was installed at the tail end of the fuselage. Following a pair of practice runs to calibrate the devices and establish normal background radiation levels, the coastal-monitoring programme was declared ready to go.

•

On Saturday 20 September, two huge four-engine Lincoln bombers landed on the airstrip at Broome, the Kimberley region pearling town about 500 miles up the coast from Onslow. Over the next few days, five more Lincolns touched down at Broome, while another remained on standby at RAAF Amberley in Queensland. Along with ground crew and support staff, the eight bombers comprised the 82 Wing Detachment, tasked with flying meteorological and air-sampling sorties for Operation Hurricane.

The 140-strong detachment was led by Group Captain Geoff Hartnell, a 36-year-old former Catalina and Sunderland flying boat pilot from East Malvern, Victoria, who had commanded RAF Station Driffield in Yorkshire during the war. Regarded as one of the best brains in the RAAF, Hartnell was pulling double duty in Broome as both Base Commander and Detachment Commander. He arrived to find that the advance party, which had flown out via Dakota a week earlier, had established the technical and operational camp at the airfield just as planned. The set-up included a control room, crew tent and a Nissen hut laboratory for the use of the boffins. The detachment was billeted at the Western Command Base Camp, a tented Army camp established on the grounds of the Broome Meat Works and commanded by Major IG Crockett, with accommodation for 200 airmen, soldiers and scientists. The camp was situated near the shark-proof baths, with facilities for cricket, tennis, shooting and fishing nearby.

Known as a 'sink of iniquity', Broome was a sprawling mess of palm trees, tin roofs and latticed verandahs overlooking the pearling luggers and mangrove swamps of Roebuck Bay.[24] Owing to the pearling industry's exemption from the White Australia policy, the port town had a uniquely multicultural population, comprising about 700 Europeans, 300 'Asiatics' and 600 Aboriginals.[25] That was a problem as far as Group Captain Hartnell was concerned:

If amenities are not good, there will be a tendency for personnel to drift into 'Chinatown'. This area is full of aboriginals, Chinese, Malays, Koepangers and numerous half castes and Eurasions [sic]. The complications of this particular community are apparent, and it will be desirable to keep personnel away from the Area at night as much as possible. Fortunately, the campsite is over a mile from 'Chinatown'.[26]

Luckily for Hartnell, no unfortunate incidents were reported, and the airmen were kept busy at a number of dances and other functions laid on by the locals. The detachment held an open day to return the favour, and just about every kid in town showed up to crawl all over the Lincolns. On another occasion, the detachment's amenities officer, Flight Lieutenant Keith Wilson, second pilot on Lincoln A73-61, organised a picnic for the local orphanage, which was home to about 40 children. (Many of the children were not actually orphans at all. They were from the Stolen Generation – mixed-race children taken from their parents, supposedly for their own good, by Western Australia's Department of Native Affairs.) The picnic was held on the beach and was a great success: the camp cooks whipped up some special treats, airmen donated their ice cream rations, and Flight Lieutenant Wilson's Lincoln flew by and buzzed the waving children.

At 1600 hours on Monday 22 September, a full briefing of aircrew and other key personnel was held in the crew tent. It was only then that the airmen officially learned what they were in for. Their main tasks were: wind-finding sorties for the meteorological team in the *Campania* prior to the blast; air-sampling sorties for the AERE on D-Day and/or D+1; delivery of samples to Darwin for transport to Harwell; and delivery of samples to Melbourne for transport to Melbourne University, where a Radiochemical Division team including two CSIRO scientists, GL Miles and JN Gregory, had been installed. At all times, one Lincoln crew would remain on standby as a search-and-rescue crew, in case of emergency.

The Lincoln was a long-range, high-altitude variation of the famous Lancaster bomber. It was a big aircraft with a crew of seven, whose jobs varied depending on the mission. For Operation Hurricane, each aircraft employed two pilots, two navigators, two signallers and a gunner. Unfortunately, the Lincoln was obsolete from the moment it came into service, having been superseded by jet-powered bombers like the Canberra. It was also unpressurised, meaning air could get in everywhere. In fact, it was known as a particularly draughty aircraft. 'The only time it was not draughty was when it was raining', said Flight Lieutenant Wilson. 'And then it was wet.'[27]

Wind-finding sorties commenced on the morning of Wednesday 24 September. At dawn each day, two Lincolns took off from Broome Airfield and headed out over the ocean, one dropping a sea marker 50 miles north of Broome, the other 50 miles south. Each aircraft then conducted a series of 'bombing runs' over its marker at various altitudes (15,000, 20,000 and 25,000 feet), all on the same heading (in the same direction). By calculating the amount of drift experienced by the aircraft, the aircrews were able to produce highly accurate estimates of the wind's velocity at each altitude. Each sortie lasted about two and a half hours, after which the crews returned to base for breakfast and showers.

The airmen spent the rest of the morning attending lectures, including a series of talks on nuclear physics and its applications by Hubert Gale of AERE Harwell. A 24-year-old Oxford graduate, Gale was the leader of the two-man Radiological Survey Division team overseeing the air-sampling operation. (His colleague, RN Crooks, was in Townsville, Queensland, looking after both the east coast and New Zealand efforts.) Gale did not consider his morning talks to be operational briefings, but, rather, general interest lectures designed 'to fill in the time' and 'keep everyone happy'.[28] Later on, when he appeared before the Royal Commission into British Nuclear Tests in Australia, he was extremely vague about the content of the lectures: 'These talks were given without notes but

I would assume that I would have touched generally on the hazards of radiation. However, I would not have stated, as far as I can recall, that there was likely to be any danger involved in the forthcoming operation.'[29]

Based on his limited experience with the North Atlantic air-sampling programme, in which aircrews generally returned with weak samples and little to no aircraft contamination, Gale honestly did not believe there was any danger. But those crews were sampling clouds that had blown halfway around the world from test sites in the US and the USSR. The 82 Wing crews would be flying through the atomic cloud within hours of the test, a couple of hundred miles from Ground Zero.

Flying Officer RS Webster, DFM, rear gunner on Lincoln A73-55, did not remember much of Gale's talks, but he did remember that 'we were given a lecture by a scientist about radioactive rays some time before the test, and were jokingly informed that if we were contaminated we may become sterile'.[30] That might not seem like a laughing matter, but the boffins constantly joked about the prospect of sterility with the servicemen, who could not tell whether they were supposed to take the warnings seriously.

Meanwhile, on the tarmac, the ground crew were busy bolting filter canisters to the aircraft. The cylindrical canisters were 12 inches long and 8 inches wide, each containing a mesh filter lined with special paper designed to catch radioactive dust. Two canisters were bolted under each wing. At the end of an air-sampling sortie, the filters would be removed and the paper burnt in a special oven. The ashes would then be tested for radioactivity.

Gale also took measures to test for fallout in Broome, applying a special paint to the roof of a nearby building and fitting a filter to the downpipe to catch any radioactive rain that might fall after the blast. His colleague, Crooks, did the same thing in Cairns, Rockhampton, Brisbane and Suva in Fiji.

Finally, at a late stage of proceedings, each aircraft was given a beta-gamma monitor, which Warrant Officer Ray Turner, signaller on A73-51, remembered as a 'small white box which had a meter on it'.[31] According to Gale, the monitor was added when it was suggested 'that it would assist the aircrews in their search for the cloud to have an instrument in the aircraft which would indicate whether there was radioactivity present'.[32] That seems like a fairly obvious point in retrospect. Following installation, Gale held a special briefing, showing the aircrafts' signallers how to use the equipment. The airmen were ordered to take readings every 10 minutes and record the observations in a special log.

•

One other outfit was extremely busy during Phase Two: West Australian Newspapers Limited.

Ever since the voyage of the *Thelma* – in which several press men had sailed to the Montebellos to confirm the presence of the atomic test site – Jim Macartney, Managing Editor of WA Newspapers, had been planning his company's coverage of the test. 'It's going to happen in our own paddock and we are going to cover it for the world, without any outside help', he proclaimed.[33] But the British and Australian governments were not making it easy. Both Churchill and Menzies had announced that no press correspondents, photographers, radio commentators or unofficial observers would be permitted to attend the tests. Another layer of official secrecy was added when, at the urging of the Brits, the Australian Government introduced an official system of Defence Notices (or D-Notices) similar to the one used in the UK. Under the D-Notice system, news organisations agreed not to publish or broadcast any information that the government deemed detrimental to national security. It was essentially voluntary censorship. The first few Australian D-Notices covered topics like experimental military equipment, the Woomera Rocket Range and troop movements in Korea. D-Notice No 8 covered atomic tests.

On Wednesday 2 July, Acting Prime Minister Arthur Fadden asked the leading east coast newspaper associations to attend the inaugural meeting of the Defence, Press and Broadcasting Committee at Victoria Barracks in Melbourne in 12 days' time. The purpose of the meeting, to be chaired by Defence Minister Philip McBride, was to establish the exact procedures of the D-Notice system and discuss any concerns about the prohibited topics.

No one thought to invite WA Newspapers.

When Jim Macartney got wind of the omission, he was incensed. Repeated efforts to wangle an invitation went nowhere. Four days before the meeting, Macartney fired off a blistering 232-word telegram to Prime Minister Robert Menzies:

WE WERE INFORMED LAST WEEK THAT A MEETING OF PRESS AND BROADCASTING PEOPLE WAS TO BE HELD NEXT MONDAY IN MELBOURNE TO DISCUSS SECURITY MATTERS STOP THESE MATTERS ARE FOR OBVIOUS REASONS GIVING US GREAT CONCERN AT THE MOMENT STOP WE HAVE EXCHANGED TELEGRAMS WITH SIR ARTHUR FADDEN AND NOW WE HAVE A MESSAGE FROM MR MCBRIDE SAYING WE CAN NOT BE REPRESENTED AT THE MEETING STOP THIS WOULD MEAN THAT THERE WOULD BE NO WEST AUSTRALIAN REPRESENTATION WHATEVER AT THE MEETING BECAUSE NEITHER OF THE ONLY TWO DAILY NEWSPAPERS HERE IS A MEMBER OF THE A N P A OR THE A N C STOP NORMALLY WE ARE CONTENT TO BE REPRESENTED AT

DISCUSSIONS WITH THE GOVERNMENT OF COMMON NEWSPAPER INTERESTS BY MR WILLIAMS OF THE MELBOURNE HERALD BUT ON THIS OCCASION SPECIAL CONSIDERATIONS OF WHICH YOU ARE AWARE MAKE IT IMPORTANT THAT WE SHOULD SEND OUR OWN REPRESENTATIVE STOP WE HAVE ACCORDINGLY MADE ARRANGEMENTS FOR OUR EDITOR MR ERNEST DE BURGH TO TRAVEL TO MELBOURNE FOR THE MEETING ON MONDAY AND HOPE IN THE MEANTIME TO RECEIVE YOUR APPROVAL OF HIS ATTENDANCE STOP FAILURE TO ADMIT HIM WOULD MEAN THAT THE DAILY PRESS IN WESTERN AUSTRALIA WAS TOTALLY EXCLUDED FROM DISCUSSION OF MATTERS OF NATIONAL IMPORTANCE WHICH SHOULD CONCERN ALL THE PEOPLE OF AUSTRALIA ... MACARTNEY MANAGING EDITOR WEST AUSTRALIAN[34]

No one spoke to Robert Gordon Menzies that way – especially not some jumped-up Western Australian newspaperman. There was no telling what he would do. As Ernest de Burgh winged his way across the country, Macartney and his staff waited anxiously for Menzies's reply. Finally, one day before the meeting, it arrived:

MACARTNEY, WEST AUSTRALIAN PERTH
YOUR TELEGRAM RE MEETING MONDAY STOP MEETING NOT DESIGNED TO REPRESENT EVERYBODY AT FIRST MEETING STOP NEWSPAPER ASSOCIATIONS BEING CALLED TOGETHER IN FIRST INSTANCE TO WORK OUT WAYS AND MEANS OF COVERING GROUND BUT WOULD BE PLEASED WEST AUSTRALIAN REPRESENTATIVE

## PRESENT IF POSSIBLE MAKE JOURNEY IN TIME
## R G MENZIES[35]

Incredibly, Macartney's gambit had worked: the managing editor of WA Newspapers had faced down the prime minister of Australia. The following day, Ernest de Burgh was admitted to the inaugural meeting of the Defence, Press and Broadcasting Committee.

The upshot of that meeting, and subsequent negotiations, was that *The West Australian* and the *Daily News* were allowed to cover the test from the mainland, as long as their reporters and photographers remained outside the prohibited zone. Macartney's plan was to send up a second expedition, much larger than the first, to keep a lookout from a suitable point on the North West Coast. Since there would be no announcement about the time and date of the blast, the press men needed to be equipped for a long stay – possibly as long as three months. This was an expensive proposition, but the enormous cost of the expedition could be offset by selling the stories and pictures to newspapers around the world.

Early in August, *Daily News* reporter Jack Coulter flew back to Onslow to reconnoitre the nearby coastline. Armed with a map, a compass and his wartime training as an artillery officer, Coulter investigated dozens of sites with fellow *Thelma* crew member Billy Clark as his local guide. He eventually chose Mount Potter, a 300-foot peak in a line of hills called Rough Range, about 135 miles north of Onslow and 55 miles from the Montebellos.

At 8.30 a.m. on Saturday 16 August, a convoy of four vehicles – a Ford V8 flatbed truck, a Land Rover with a trailer on the back, a Jeep and a Holden sedan – left Perth and headed north. Between them, the vehicles were carrying almost 7 tons of equipment, including cameras, generators, tents, Army surplus field telephones, rolls of cable, and an ingenious portable prefabricated darkroom.

The expedition, which initially comprised nine men, was led once again by *The West Australian*'s intrepid circulation manager, Jack Nicoll. Following an epic 900-mile slog, they arrived at Mount Potter on 22 August and set up base camp at a nearby billabong, immediately dubbed Burton's Billabong in honour of chief photographer and senior expedition member Doug Burton.[36] The water was too brackish to drink, but could still be used for washing. Drinking water was carted from a sheep tank 6 miles away.

Prior to departure, WA Newspapers had negotiated for the Postmaster-General's Department (PMG) to install a temporary post office at Mount Potter. The flatbed truck was parked under the telegraph line, which ran right past the billabong, and a PMG linesman from Roebourne installed two Morse keys under a tarpaulin on the back of the truck and patched them into the telegraph line. Once the linesman was finished, the truck was officially designated the Mount Potter Telegraph Station, and two of the state's fastest telegraphists, Ted Rodgers and Roy Buchanan, were flown up from Perth to man the keys.

Other members of the expedition bashed a trail from the base camp to the hill in four-wheel drives, laying telephone cable as they went. Mount Potter was too steep and rocky to drive up, so instead they hacked a footpath through the spinifex on the side of the hill and dug footholds among the rocks. Over the next two days they lugged 2 tons of equipment up the hill, each man doing ten trips a day.

At the top of the hill, dubbed Nick's Nob in honour of expedition leader Jack Nicoll, the darkroom was put together and the field telephone was linked with the post office at the main campsite. Since there was no shade, the press men strung up tarpaulins around the darkroom, but these were soon torn to shreds by the wind. The ironstone ground was so hard that it was impossible to dig postholes; instead, gelignite was used. The cameras were then mounted on wooden stands: two long-lens cameras dubbed Long Toms, with lenses 160 and 120 inches long, believed to be the biggest in the world at the time; a 35-mm robot camera with a 20-inch lens; and a 16-mm camera gun. The Long Toms were designed and built by physicist and photographer Bill Mangini, WA Newspapers' 'secret weapon', with the assistance of Doug Burton and Harold Rudinger.[37] All three men were at Mount Potter, aiming their cameras at the precise point on the horizon beyond which the Montebellos lay, some 55 miles off.

One week after arrival, the observation post was fully operational, and the long vigil commenced. Armed with field glasses, the press men took turns scanning the horizon for signs of the blast. Each shift was an endurance test. The wind constantly blew at 40 miles per hour and sometimes gusted up to 60 miles per hour. Dust stung the eyes and damaged camera equipment. Men suffered headaches because of the gale and could not sleep. In desperation, they carted tons of ironstone rocks up the hill and built a waist-high windbreak to shelter behind.

They lived like that for six weeks, eating tinned food and sleeping in cots and sleeping bags, with no female companionship except for a few pin-up girls stuck up on the Long Toms. For those who had been in the services – which was most of them – it was just like being back in the war.

One day not long after camp was established, a Dakota swooped down out of the sky, pinpointing the observation post and the nearby base camp. It was 86 Wing Detachment, keeping a close eye on the press men while out on patrol. A Dakota appeared nearly every day after that, often buzzing by at frighteningly low altitudes. To stick it up the nosy airmen, the press men arranged painted stones on the hilltop spelling 'TOP SECRET: KEEP OUT'.[38]

It soon became obvious that two teams were needed to cover the test – one at Mount Potter and one at Onslow – so more men were sent up from Perth. Eventually, the total expedition numbered 17 men, including one ringer: Lionel 'Bill' Hudson, a correspondent for AAP–Reuters with a sideline shooting news footage for American television. Four men were sent into Onslow, and the rest remained on duty at Mount Potter.

The Onslow team comprised reporters Norm Milne and Jack Coulter and photographers Owen Williams and Phil Martin. Naturally, they set up headquarters at the pub, which was christened the Bleedin' Beadon.[39] Life in Onslow was a lot easier than it was at Mount Potter. The Onslow team spent their days watching the horizon from a beach shack with uninterrupted views and noting the movements of military ships and aircraft. At night, they kept a lookout from the pub's verandah and interrogated unwary servicemen.

During the long wait, Coulter and Milne filed stories full of local colour. One Wednesday morning, a huge bomb appeared on the front steps of the pub, complete with what appeared to be a lit fuse. It was an old sea mine with the words 'A-BOMB – STAND CLEAR' painted on the side.[40] After Onslow Police, ASIO and Royal Navy bomb disposal experts descended on the scene, local pranksters Cliff Ross and Bill Rooney were forced to confess to the hoax. Luckily for them, the bomb had long since been disabled. A few days later, it disappeared just as mysteriously as it had arrived. In its place was a sign saying: 'THE A-BOMB HAS GONE OFF'.[41]

This prank was soon topped by an even more dramatic effort. At 2.00 a.m. one morning, the whole town was awakened by a deafening blast. The press men dashed outside to check the horizon for signs of a radioactive glow, while Naval vessels in the bay furiously signalled one another to see if there had been an accident. Daylight revealed the cause of the explosion: a few sticks of gelignite in a 44-gallon drum half-buried on the beach near town. The culprits, who really should have known better, were the airmen from 86 Wing Detachment. Sick and tired of waiting for the real bomb to go off, they had taken matters into their own hands and staged an unauthorised rehearsal. The dangerous stunt probably did little to endear them to their Base Commander, Squadron Leader Leo Britt.

By mid-September, it had become clear from troop movements in Onslow that the test was drawing near. Round-the-clock watches were set at Mount Potter, Onslow and Newspaper House in Perth. For 24 hours a day, the press men watched and waited for the bomb to go off.

•

Meanwhile, Task Force scientists in the Montebellos had been conducting rehearsals since the beginning of the month.

First, there was the large-scale telemetry and communications test, followed ten days later by the general scientific rehearsal. A few things went wrong here and there – the vaunted Kerr-cell cameras played up, and various apparatuses that worked perfectly in laboratory conditions broke down when exposed to the elements – but all in all, everything went about as well as could be expected.

The next test was the big one: the full-scale operational rehearsal scheduled for 18 to 19 September. Delayed by a day due to rough seas, the full rehearsal ultimately went ahead in conditions so good that they were deemed unrealistic.[42] Over two days, each and every scientist and serviceman in the Task Force practised the role allotted to him, with sailors and marines transporting teams of boffins to various sites to activate and check their gadgets before evacuating each area in stages. Once all ships had withdrawn to a safe distance, the countdown commenced, and the control room team went through the motions of detonating the weapon.

There was no explosion, but the rehearsal was a lot more realistic than almost anyone realised.

On the morning of R–1 (the day the 48-hour rehearsal commenced), an RAF Sunderland flying boat alighted on the lagoon with some very important cargo on board: the radioactive core and its back-up.

Encased in special protective canisters, the cores had travelled from England to Singapore in an RAF Hastings transport aircraft, then on to the Montebellos in the Sunderland, bypassing the Australian mainland for security reasons. The itinerary had been worked out by Wing Commander John Rowlands, the RAF science officer who had discovered the criticality risk in the original weapon design. He accompanied the cores to the Montebellos, and would be in charge of assembling the weapon as Assistant Director of the User Interests Division.

The scientist tasked with carrying the primary core was Bill Moyce of HER. Moyce was a tall explosives expert from South London with big ears and a dry sense of humour who had been in charge of assembling the cores back at Aldermaston in the UK. In the event of a crash in the ocean, his instructions were to place the core in a cork container with a bag of dye attached so that it could possibly be recovered. If it looked like they were going to crash on land, he was supposed to bail out by parachute while clutching the canister to his chest. 'I used to wonder how I was supposed to hold it', he later recalled. 'We never went through any rehearsal.'[43] Luckily, he never found out.

With the arrival of the core, Dr Tyte made the astonishingly risky decision to incorporate it into the operational rehearsal. On his orders, the real core was loaded into the real weapon, significantly raising the stakes of the rehearsal and introducing the possibility of a deadly criticality incident where there had not been one before. In yet another sign of the ongoing deterioration of relations between Dr Tyte and Admiral Torlesse, the Technical Director apparently neglected to inform the Task Force Commander of the change of plans. The two men's petty squabbles were now becoming downright dangerous.

Under the close supervision of Moyce, Wing Commander Rowlands fitted the core onto the end of the cartridge and ratcheted it down into the weapon. All around the compartments, neutron counters had been set up to warn of impending criticality. Although a number of tests had been conducted at Aldermaston, this was the first time the core had been lowered into a real high-explosive sphere, and the scene in the weapon room was incredibly tense.

'What's all this ticking?' asked a bemused Lieutenant Commander Peter Draisey, captain of the *Plym*, who was watching from the doorway.

'If that goes "Bzzzzt" you won't be 'ere anymore', replied Moyce.[44]

# 10.

# D-DAY

On Sunday 21 September, a sleepy day in Onslow, a big four-engine RAF Hastings landed on the airstrip outside town. After local Customs and quarantine personnel boarded the aircraft, five well-dressed men disembarked and climbed into the back of an enclosed truck that whisked them off through town and towards the ocean. It was an offence for vehicles to drive on the jetty, but instead of stopping the truck drove straight on, finally pulling up at the landing stage. The men were then hustled aboard a Naval pinnace for the short trip to frigate HMAS *Hawkesbury*, which was anchored some way off in the bay.

Known as one of the finest ships in the fleet, the *Hawkesbury* was looking spick and span, with every surface scrubbed and shined to within an inch of its life. Lined up on deck, nervously waiting to greet the new arrivals, were Lieutenant Commander RJ Scrivenor and his officers. As the highest-ranking visitor came up the ship's side, his smiling visage immediately put the Naval officers at ease. It was William Penney, Chief Superintendent of HER, along with four special guests: Dr OM Solandt, Chairman of the Canadian Defence Research Board; Professor Ernest Titterton, Chair of Nuclear Physics at the Australian National University (ANU); Professor Leslie Martin, Australia's Defence Scientific Adviser; and

Mr Alan Butement, Chief Scientist for Australia's Department of Supply.

The five VIPs were quickly ushered below and away from the long lenses of the press photographers on shore. As soon as they were safely stowed away, the captain gave the order to weigh and proceed for the Montebellos. It was a smooth operation, and all involved congratulated themselves on its success, believing that Penney and his companions had successfully evaded the attentions of the press.

They were wrong. The press men from WA Newspapers had suspected that something was up as soon as the *Hawkesbury* appeared in the offing and a scheduled cricket match between the Army and the Town was cancelled. When asked for comment, the security men, Major Kingwell and Jack Clowes, were vague and noncommittal, but something about their behaviour seemed 'a little too casual' to Norm Milne and his mates.[1] Knowing that Penney was due to arrive any day, they set up a stakeout. Two men were stationed on the first-storey verandah of the hotel, watching the only street in and out of town. Two other men borrowed some fishing gear and strolled out along the jetty, casting their lines near the landing, while a fifth walked down the beach and waded out onto a reef to keep an eye on the *Hawkesbury* from the seaward side.

The so-called fishermen were photographers who had deliberately ditched their cameras to make sure they weren't kicked off the jetty by security men. As Milne later explained, 'the main object of the operation was to discover whether Dr Penney arrived – not to get pictures'.[2] Now they could only watch in frustration as Penney and several other world-famous scientists strolled right past them. 'Here was one of the biggest news pictures of the year right before their eyes and in good daylight and they could do nothing about it!' wrote Milne.[3] But the sacrifice was worth it: despite a battle with the censors, news of Penney's arrival hit the press within hours.

Penney's travel plans were so secret that MI5 had booked airline tickets to Australia for him and other top atomic officials for November in an attempt to mislead the press about the target date. The plan, dubbed Operation Spoofer, very nearly worked when *The West Australian*'s man in London, Basil Atkinson, got wind of the bookings and started writing up a story. He had almost finished when he realised that he had come across the 'top secret' information a little too easily; there was something 'fishy' about it, so he put the story in a drawer and never finished it.[4]

Atkinson's journalistic instincts had been right. In reality, Penney had flown into Darwin in an RAF Hastings on Saturday 13 September before flying on to Woomera. Given the many difficulties the Task Force had experienced in the Montebellos, he was hoping to find a mainland site to conduct more atomic tests as soon as next year. With the help of a laconic Aussie bushman named Len Beadell, he found one: a large claypan on the north-western outskirts of the rocket range, marked by a fossilised emu footprint. Officially designated X200, the site would come to be known as Emu Field.

Penney's VIP guests were the only official observers invited to witness the blast. Because the Brits wanted to keep numbers down to the bare minimum, all four men had been asked to muck in and earn their keep.

Dr Solandt had travelled to Australia with Dr Penney as an observer for the Canadian Government, which also contributed a number of working scientists to the HER team. A bespectacled physiologist, Solandt had studied the effects of atom bombs on the human body at Hiroshima and Nagasaki, and become interested in the civil defence side of atomic warfare – the effort to protect civilians from the full impact of the blast and the ensuing radiation. In the Montebellos, he would investigate the efficacy of structures like bomb shelters and concrete bunkers.

The other three men all represented the Australian Government in one capacity or another. To the surprise of many commentators, Australia's most eminent nuclear physicist, Mark Oliphant, Foundation Director of the Research School of Physical Sciences at ANU, had not been invited. The 50-year-old South Australian physicist had played a crucial role in the birth of the atom bomb – he had supervised the groundbreaking theoretical work of Otto Frisch and Rudolf Peierls, served on the MAUD Committee, which led to the creation of Tube Alloys, and helped design the machine that enriched the uranium for the Hiroshima bomb at the Berkeley Lab in California – but since then he had been declared persona non grata by the US and UK governments. Oliphant was openly critical of the atomic policies of both nations, and had been known to give away valuable secrets in the name of open scientific inquiry. The Americans suspected him of being a Communist, which he almost certainly was not, but in 1952 suspicion alone was enough to get you blacklisted in Washington and London.

Awkwardly, one of Oliphant's subordinates at ANU was invited to the Montebellos in his place. Professor Ernest Titterton was a 36-year-old physicist from Staffordshire, England, who had recently immigrated to Australia to become Chair of Nuclear Physics at ANU. Like Penney, Titterton had played an important role in the Manhattan Project, triggering the Trinity test in New Mexico in July 1945 (the world's first atom-bomb test) and then conducting both countdowns for Operation Crossroads at Bikini Atoll in 1946. Following his return to England, Titterton joined the newly established Atomic Energy Research Establishment (AERE), occasionally visiting HER to consult on the weapon's firing system, before taking up his post at ANU.

An arrogant man, Titterton was an enthusiastic advocate of atomic weapons, as demonstrated in an opinion piece published in the lead-up to the test:

The slogans 'Ban the A-Bomb' and 'Ban the H-Bomb' can be seen on walls in most large cities in the world. The people who write them are either idealists who misunderstand the position or propagandists who have an ulterior motive ... It is not atomic weapons which we have to ban, but war itself. All wars are horrible and wasteful of lives and material, whatever weapons are employed. Far from deprecating the capability of the Western Allies to manufacture atomic weapons it is a matter for satisfaction that it is these nations, with their love of freedom and democracy and the high value they place on human lives, which have in their custody the majority of these weapons of mass destruction.[5]

Despite their different personalities, Penney and Titterton were good friends from their days at Los Alamos. Penney had even offered Titterton the role of Technical Director for Operation Hurricane before offering it to Dr Tyte, but he had been forced to turn it down, having already accepted the job at ANU. Still keen for his assistance, Penney then asked Titterton if he would consider taking a few weeks' leave to help the Telemetry and Communications Division in the Montebellos. The official request went through Prime Minister Robert Menzies, who called Titterton into his office in Canberra for a chat one day. As Titterton later recalled: 'The brief given to me by the Prime Minister was: in view of your experience, which is unique in Australia, of three nuclear weapons tests around the world, I would be glad if you would be prepared to go to the Monte Bellos to lend whatever help you can to Dr Penney's team – as he was then – and at the same time to – well, essentially stick your oar in to make as certain as it is humanly possible to be certain that there will be no adverse effects on the Australian people, flora and fauna, and in particular aborigines.'[6] Since Titterton had never seen a mushroom cloud he didn't like, he jumped at the chance.

Employed by neither government, Titterton's role at the Montebellos was unique and ambiguous. By contrast, Leslie Martin and Alan Butement were the Australian Government's top military scientists. The 51-year-old Martin was a silver-haired physicist from Footscray, Victoria, who served as both Defence Scientific Adviser and Professor of Physics at Melbourne University. The 48-year-old Butement was a moustachioed radar expert, born in New Zealand and schooled in England, who oversaw Woomera Rocket Range as Chief Scientist for the Department of Supply. Both men had assisted Penney on the Woomera reconnaissance.

Despite their obvious qualifications, Martin and Butement were lucky to be invited to the Montebellos, and were only there because the Australian Government had more or less begged for their inclusion. Many of the British planners wanted them out, most notably Lord Cherwell, Churchill's infamously snobbish scientific adviser, who tried to limit the number of invitations for the colonials by citing 'lack of accommodation' as an excuse.[7] Penney, on the other hand, recognised the importance of keeping the Australians onside, and argued for including both Martin and Butement. After much toing and froing, both men were invited at the last possible minute, in a remarkably ungracious fashion. Martin's official invitation arrived only one month before the target date. The letter from the UK High Commission in Canberra tactlessly emphasised his low security clearance (he would receive no access to the weapon itself or any weapon design and efficiency data) and insisted that he earn his keep by assisting the Meteorological Division with cloud-tracking duties and the Radiological Hazard Division with health-monitoring duties. To top it off, the British diplomats also stated that they 'assume that Professor Martin is appropriately covered by the *Official Secrets Act*', which made it sound like they had no idea who he was, even though he had just returned from official talks in London.[8]

William Penney, father of the British bomb. (Alamy)

Rear Admiral Arthur Torlesse, DSO, RN, Commander of the 4th Task Force. (© Imperial War Museums (GOV 5636))

**Boom defence vessel HMAS *Karangi* of the Epicure reconnaissance.**
(Australian War Memorial)

**Onslow, Western Australia, nearest port to the Montebellos.** (© West Australian
Newspapers Limited)

**The Montebello Islands.** (© West Australian Newspapers Limited)

Escort carrier HMS *Campania*, headquarters ship for Operation Hurricane, entering Fremantle Harbour in July 1952. (© West Australian Newspapers Limited)

Frigate HMS *Plym*, target vessel for Operation Hurricane, on arrival in Fremantle Harbour. The (unarmed) bomb is in her forward hold. (© West Australian Newspapers Limited)

The *Thelma* en route to the Montebellos. (© West Australian Newspapers Limited)

The crew of the *Thelma*. From left to right: Harold Rudinger (photographer), Jack Coulter (reporter), Jack Nicoll (expedition leader) and Norm Milne (reporter). (© West Australian Newspapers Limited)

*Top*: RAAF Dakotas at Onslow, Western Australia. (Australian War Memorial)

*Middle*: RAAF airmen at Onslow. From left to right: Warrant Officer Stephen Hardman (signaller), Flight Lieutenant Clarence Donnelly (pilot), Flight Lieutenant John Finlay (navigator) and Flight Lieutenant Ron Grace (pilot). (Australian War Memorial)

*Bottom*: RAAF Dakota 'beating up' the WA Newspapers observation post at Mount Potter. (Australian War Memorial)

Two of a series of photos of the developing mushroom cloud taken by HER scientists at H1, Hermite Island, 6 nautical miles south of the blast. In the second photo, the top of the cloud can be seen heading east – towards the mainland. (Australian War Memorial)

An alternative view of the cloud, taken by WA Newspapers photographers at Mount Potter, 55 miles south-east of the Montebellos, on the North West Coast. (© West Australian Newspapers Limited)

Rear Admiral Arthur Torlesse, DSO, RN, and William Penney admiring their handiwork. Penney was knighted soon afterwards. (© Imperial War Museums (A 32123))

Australian personnel coming ashore for a radiation survey during Operation Cool Off, March 1965. (© West Australian Newspapers Limited)

On Thursday 4 September, Professor Martin attended a high-level committee meeting at the Department of Defence to discuss the invitation. In what was later described as 'a ghastly unhappy scene', the committee decided that the invitation was 'an insult' and should be declined.[9] Given the generosity of the Australian Government, and the wholehearted cooperation of the Australian services, it was felt that the Defence Scientific Adviser was being treated very shabbily indeed. One committee member (probably Martin himself) was quoted as saying that 'the United Kingdom can be told to stuff their bomb up their jumpers'.[10]

The crisis was eventually averted, thanks largely to the efforts of Sir John Cockcroft. Best known as the man who 'split the atom' with Ernest Walton in 1932 (a feat for which both men later shared the Nobel Prize), the genteel Cockcroft was in Australia in his capacity as Director of AERE for talks on atomic energy research and uranium supply. He had come armed with an invitation to the Montebellos for an old Cambridge chum – Professor Martin – and was dismayed to learn that his approach had been pre-empted in such a clumsy fashion. To limit the fallout, Cockcroft met with Menzies, Martin and other senior Defence officials, emphasising the advantages of being involved in Operation Hurricane, such as access to information on blast effects, and downplaying the importance of weapon design and efficiency data. It worked, and Martin participated on more or less the same conditions outlined in the original invitation, as did Butement, whose invitation arrived even later than Martin's.

One British officer could not understand what all the fuss was about. At the height of the drama, Captain CH Hutchinson, DSO, OBE, RN, of the UK Service Liaison Staff in Melbourne, delivered a handwritten note from Cockcroft to Martin that helped turn the tide. In his subsequent report, Captain Hutchinson claimed the credit for single-handedly winning over the angry professor, observing: 'I'm afraid that I find the Australians are better at standing on their dignity than on their feet. They look for insult where none is intended, far too often.'[11]

Ironically, Hutchinson's tone-deaf comment was exactly the sort of thing that infuriated the Australians, regardless of intent.

•

After travelling overnight, HMAS *Hawkesbury* arrived in Parting Pool on the morning of Monday 22 September. The admiral's barge immediately collected the VIPs and transported them to the *Campania*, where Admiral Torlesse, Dr Tyte and their respective staffs lined up on deck to greet them.

Penney's arrival gave the weary Task Force an instant boost of morale. With his cheery face and open demeanour, the Chief Superintendent of HER projected an air of confidence and optimism, both of which were in short supply. A hands-on manager, he was famous for turning up in the lab to help out with chores that were far below his pay grade, earning him the respect and admiration of everyone at HER. As the son of a British Army sergeant major, he also got on well with servicemen of all ranks, and immediately began to heal the rift that had opened up between the service and scientific sides of the operation.

After getting settled in, Penney called a meeting of his senior staff and asked each assistant director for a status report. With only days to go before the target date, there were still plenty of technical difficulties, but most could be fixed with a little effort and ingenuity. The most alarming problem was out of the boffins' control: the weather.

Commander FL Westwater, RN, and his Meteorological Division had to ensure that no fallout reached the mainland, the command centre at H1, or the Naval vessels in the surrounding waters. The problem was that the cloud was expected to climb to 25,000 feet, and the wind invariably blew in different directions at different altitudes. They also had to pick a time with calm seas and high tides for the benefit of the Navy. Because the countdown lasted 24 hours, the conditions had to be acceptable for two straight days and be predictable 24 hours in advance.

In hopes of finding a safe window, the Meteorological Division had been poring over stacks of weather reports from all over Western Australia. In addition to the 82 Wing Detachment at Broome, reports came in from a special wind-finding station set up at Roy Hill, 300 miles east of Onslow; frigate HMAS *Culgoa*, stationed 300 miles south-west of the Montebellos as a weather ship; and the Commonwealth Bureau of Meteorology in Perth, which produced summaries of weather reports from all around Australia. Helping the Brits make sense of all this data were two Australian meteorologists attached to Westwater's team: Henry Phillpot and Harry Ashton.

Having outlined the situation, Commander Westwater concluded that there would probably only be about two days in the whole month of October when it would be possible to conduct the test safely. That meant a high chance of a costly delay or even cancellation if the necessary conditions did not appear before cyclone season commenced. A feeling of doom and gloom settled over the meeting.

Physicist JJ McEnhill described what happened next:

On examining the situation Dr Penney decided that the contamination issue might well be an exaggeration of the true hazard but that it would be possible to avoid it by judicious choice of upper wind direction for the trial. As far as obtaining such winds together with the other necessary weather conditions, he was all in favour of going ahead and planning for the first days of October. He hoped that, despite the changeable weather conditions, and the obvious difficulties of the meteorologist, all would be well. He appeared very optimistic, even although he may not have felt so. He kept reminding pessimists who hinted that the force might be locked up for weeks awaiting the forecast of a pair of suitable days that he had seen this happen before in American trials. In the period just before preparations were completed pessimism was often rife, but it had always been unwarranted and no doubt such would be the case again.[12]

Penney probably wasn't as confident as he made it sound, but his inspirational speech did the trick. The whole Task Force steamed towards a target date of 2 October, full speed ahead.

Over the following week, the scientists desperately tried to fix the last remaining technical issues. The biggest problem was the interference between the Kerr-cell cameras and the multiplication-rate apparatus at H1. Forced to choose between the two, Penney announced that if the Kerr-cell team could not get the issue sorted out, the cameras would have to go. This resulted in a desperate burst of activity from the Kerr-cell team, which tried to remedy the situation by building an aluminium cage around the cameras and screening off electrical leads.

The planners on board the *Campania* were also burning the midnight oil plotting the movements of HER staff and equipment around the islands throughout the trial and coordinating with the services. It had become painfully clear that the number of headquarters staff was much too small for an operation the size of Hurricane. Immediately beneath Dr Tyte was Charles Adams, Deputy Technical Director, who did most of the detailed scientific planning. Assisting Adams were Captain Pat Cooper, the chronically overworked Naval Liaison Officer, and Ted Marshall, Assistant Director of Technical Services. All three men had other duties that took them out of the office during the day, so most of the administration work had to be done at night. Despite the heavy workload, Adams and his team produced a comprehensive action plan for D–1 and D-Day, including work schedules, boat timetables, staff lists and contingency plans. Adams then moved straight from the *Campania* to H1 to oversee the final stages of technical preparations.

Dr Tyte remained on board the *Campania*, where relations with Admiral Torlesse were at an all-time low. At the most crucial stage of preparations, the Technical Director and the Task Force Commander were squabbling over everything under the sun and dobbing on each other to London. By the end of the month, Dr Tyte had stopped attending Torlesse's morning staff meetings altogether.

Penney's VIP guests were also based on the *Campania*, where they were divided into two distinct tiers in terms of status. As members in good standing of the atomic club, Solandt and Titterton received access to the inner circle of decision makers and a certain amount of weapon information, while the official scientific representatives of the Australian Government, Martin and Butement, were mostly sidelined and told as little as possible. To keep them busy, Penney organised tours of the outer islands, which took them far from the main hubs of activity. As John Challens, Assistant Director of the Weapon Operation Division, told Brian Cathcart in *Test of Greatness*:

> One day when we were killing time, Penney organised a shark fishing expedition with the Australian scientists, Butement and Martin. We all piled into a boat armed

with hooks and lines and landed on a beach and spent the afternoon shark fishing using the hunks of meat from these tins of stew. I think we caught one or two small sharks.[13]

•

Back in Onslow, the locals were distracted by an even bigger story than the atom bomb: Race Week.

Held in the last week of September, Onslow's horseracing carnival was the highlight of the social calendar. To the dismay of the security men, hundreds of visitors poured into town from all over the North West. The Beadon Hotel was completely booked out, and extra camp beds were set up on the verandah and even the roof. Those who missed out slept in their swags on the side of the road.

The racecourse was 7 miles out of town, with a rickety wooden grandstand and a dusty track marked with whitewashed 44-gallon drums. The races began on Thursday and finished on Saturday, in front of a raucous crowd of townspeople, servicemen, stockmen, pearl divers, miners and natives. Highlights included the Lead-Miners' Gift, the Atomic Town Maiden Burst and the spectacular Native Stockmen's Race, which featured Aboriginal stockmen dressed in colourful shirts, jeans, elastic-sided boots and broad-brimmed hats on specially trained stock horses. (Due to a local ordinance, these expert horsemen were barred from Onslow after sunset, and were forced to stay at the native camp 3 miles out of town – an all too common arrangement in Western Australia at that time.) The main event, with a prize of 25 guineas, was the Onslow Cup. Held on Saturday afternoon, the big race was won by odds-on favourite Bungarra, which left the field in a cloud of dust.

Almost as important as the races were the surrounding festivities. The pub was packed from morning to night all week long, except for when the races were on and the racecourse bar was packed instead. A staggering amount of alcohol was consumed over the course of the week, including 700 gallons of draught beer, 32 cases of bottled beer and three dozen bottles of champagne.[14] There were dances and parties every night, culminating with the Race Ball on Saturday night, when the ladies of Onslow showed off their best new ball gowns, ordered by catalogue from department stores in Perth and delivered by State Ships. The ball went on well into the night, the last dancers finally staggering home about 3.00 a.m.

By Sunday afternoon, the main street of Onslow, which had been so crowded the day before, was practically deserted. Even the bay was empty, the Naval ships and lighters having slipped out under the cover of darkness. With race week done and dusted for another year, all eyes turned towards the northern horizon. Surely, the locals thought, it must be any day now ...

•

On Saturday 27 September, a powerful Australian fleet under the flag of Rear Admiral Jack Eaton, DSO, DSC, RN, arrived off Parting Pool.

Admiral Eaton was a 49-year-old Southern Rhodesian on loan to the RAN as Flag Officer Commanding the Australian Fleet. As presently constituted, his fleet comprised the aircraft carrier and flagship HMAS *Sydney* (III), destroyer HMAS *Tobruk* and three frigates: HMA Ships *Shoalhaven*, *Macquarie* and *Murchison*. The fleet's task was to provide a beefed-up security screen for the Task Force and take over air patrol duties from the RAAF. The mission was codenamed Operation Crusher.

The Australian Fleet's journey to the Montebellos had been quite eventful. In late August, the *Sydney* and the *Tobruk* left Sydney to conduct a series of air exercises off the Solomon

Islands. The *Sydney*, under the command of Captain HJ Buchanan, DSO, was carrying the Sea Fury fighter-bombers of 805 Squadron and Firefly fighters of 817 Squadron. The aircraft conducted daily navigation exercises and regularly rehearsed air-to-surface strikes and anti-aircraft manoeuvres. The *Tobruk*, under Commander Jack Mesley, DSC, served as rescue destroyer during take-offs and landings, steaming in close with men and boats ready to respond in case of emergency.

The exercises were not without risks. On Tuesday 2 September, Captain Buchanan reported:

> Navex sorties were continued, and this time were enlivened by an accident on landing when a Firefly, in a fast approach, flew over both barriers and hit a second Firefly in the deck park. The Observer of the second Firefly was still in the cockpit and had the unusual experience of having the tail of the aircraft cut cleanly off a few inches behind him by the propeller of the first machine. Fortunately he was unharmed.[15]

The next weekend, the flagship stopped in at HMAS *Tarangau* at Manus Island, New Guinea, to bring on board eight aircraft that had staged up from Nowra, New South Wales. (Today, *Tarangau* is better known as Manus Island Detention Centre.) Although the new arrivals all landed safely on the flight deck, one of the *Sydney*'s Sea Furies developed engine trouble while acting as a radio link over the Bismarck Sea. With oil pressure failing, the pilot was forced to land, wheels up, on a deserted airstrip at Point Gloucester, New Britain. He was rescued by boat before a salvage party went ashore to dismantle the aircraft and retrieve all the movable fittings. The airframe was left for the NOIC North Eastern Area to deal with.

Following a series of official functions and buffet suppers, the *Sydney* and the *Tobruk* left *Tarangau* to rendezvous with the 1st Frigate Squadron off Port Moresby. The Frigate Squadron was under the command of Captain Sam Beattie, VC, RN, of the *Shoalhaven*, a 44-year-old Welshman revered for his actions during the 1942 raid on St Nazaire, France. As captain of the obsolete destroyer HMS *Campbeltown*, Beattie had rammed his ship, loaded with explosives, into a German shipyard's dry dock. The subsequent explosion destroyed the dock, and Beattie, who was captured by the Germans, was awarded the Victoria Cross. Beattie was often asked what it was like to ram a dry dock with a floating bomb under a hail of German bullets. A man of few words, he usually replied: 'I suppose one did experience a considerable jar.'[16]

Travelling in company with the 1st Frigate Squadron was the British submarine HMS *Thorough*, which had been playing the role of Soviet submarine in the squadron's anti-submarine exercises. At the rendezvous, Beattie's squadron came under Eaton's flag and all ships combined for a joint air and surface anti-submarine exercise. The *Thorough* admirably demonstrated her strike capabilities and evasive techniques before heading off on an independent cruise, while the Australian ships proceeded for Darwin.

On Thursday 18 September, the Australian Fleet anchored in company off Booby Island in the Torres Strait, and Admiral Eaton invited his commanding officers to a meeting on board the flagship: Captain Buchanan, Captain Beattie, Commander Mesley, Lieutenant Commander Arthur Chapman of the *Macquarie*, and Lieutenant Commander Colin Thompson of the *Murchison*. Only now were the captains officially briefed on Operation Crusher and the precise roles their ships were to play in the atomic trial. Luncheon followed.

Three days later, the Australian Fleet arrived in Darwin for the first time since the Second World War. It was a grand occasion, with hundreds of locals waving from shore and practically every boat in Darwin sailing out to meet the fleet. To return the hospitality, a lavish cocktail party was held on the *Sydney*'s flight deck, with 150 guests, including local dignitaries, high-ranking officers from all three services and their wives, all of whom enjoyed a spectacular view of the sunset over Darwin Harbour.

The intensive training programme continued en route from Darwin to the Montebellos, until 2330 IK (Item King time) on Friday 26 September, when the fleet struck trouble. Approaching the islands on the normal shipping route, the *Sydney*'s echo sounder showed depths of 40 fathoms (240 feet) and gradually shoaling (or getting shallower). When the soundings suddenly dropped to 10 fathoms (60 feet), an alarmed Captain Buchanan ordered the helmsman to reverse course. The entire ship's company held its collective breath as the 15,000-ton aircraft carrier made a laborious turn, scraping over a horrifyingly shallow patch of 5 fathoms (30 feet) with only a few feet to spare. After another near miss, the entire fleet changed course to approach the islands from the north.

When the *Sydney* finally arrived off Parting Pool, Admiral Torlesse greeted Admiral Eaton by flying over and landing on the flight deck in a Dragonfly helicopter, impressing all on board. But the goodwill was short-lived. For security reasons, the Task Force Commander refused to tell the Australian admiral the target date or any other useful information about the trial. According to Admiral Torlesse's paranoid logic, the Flag Officer Commanding the Australian Fleet, the most senior sea-going officer in the RAN, *the man in command of security patrols for the test itself*, was a security risk simply because he was Australian. Admiral Eaton (who was not even Australian!) was understandably 'disgusted' by the official British attitude towards him and his adopted service.[17] The RAN had contributed warships, aircraft and thousands of men to the combined effort, undertaking tedious and often dangerous work for the benefit of the British Empire. Eaton's own fleet had been drilling for four weeks straight, his officers and men repeatedly risking their lives, and the Royal Navy's response was to impugn their loyalty? It was outrageous.

Despite the infuriating snub, Operation Crusher commenced immediately. Taking off from the deck of the *Sydney*, and supported by the *Tobruk*, flights of six to eight Sea Furies and six to eight Fireflies conducted daily air patrols around the prohibited area (except on Sundays). The single-seat Sea Furies were equipped with 20-mm cannons and 500-pound bombs, the two-seat Fireflies with 20-mm cannons and 60-pound semi-armour-piercing rockets. Down below, the frigates conducted nonstop surface patrols. The *Murchison* covered the area to the west of the islands (Patrol Able), the *Shoalhaven* the east (Patrol Baker), and the *Macquarie* the north (Patrol Charlie). Any Soviet submarine or Asian fishing boat trying to reach the Montebellos would have to get by a determined Australian frigate armed with 4-inch guns, Bofors guns, 20-mm Oerlikons, depth charges and a Hedgehog (a spiky-looking anti-submarine weapon which flung a barrage of mortars into the sea).

Admiral Torlesse could rest easy; thanks to the Australian Fleet, the Montebello Islands were pretty damn secure.

•

On Tuesday 30 September, the Task Force was buzzing with excitement. If everything went according to plan, the following day would be designated D–1 and the trial would commence. So it was with impeccable timing that a member of the *Culgoa*'s company began complaining of severe abdominal pains. The frigate, under the command of Lieutenant Commander Graham Wright, was stationed some

300 miles south-west of the islands as a weather ship, but when the rating was diagnosed with acute appendicitis she was ordered to proceed to Geraldton 'with all despatch'.[18] With the *Macquarie* filling in as weather ship, the *Culgoa* steamed off at top speed, securing to Geraldton Wharf at midnight and landing the agonised rating in 20 minutes flat, before racing back to her station.

By the morning of Wednesday 1 October, the shore camps had been run down and all three landing ships – HM Ships *Zeebrugge*, *Narvik* and *Tracker* – had joined the *Campania* in Parting Pool, leaving poor old HMS *Plym* alone in the lagoon.

At 0630 IK, Admiral Torlesse and Dr Tyte convened a frosty meeting to decide whether to announce D–1 Day. Alas, the weather reports were unpromising, so the signal 'Charlie Oboe' ('Called Off') was sent out, and the entire Task Force went to stand-by.[19] The announcement was met with audible groans from scientists and servicemen alike, and the feeling of doom and gloom returned. Many of the boffins were worried about the effect an extended delay would have on their equipment. It would not be long before the finicky machines started breaking down due to the effects of heat, moisture, wind and sand. For some teams, it would mean going right back to square one and starting all over again.

The next day brought better news. At 0630 IK on Thursday 2 October, Torlesse and Tyte met once again and found that the promising conditions developing overnight had eventuated. Wind and tide were in their favour. At 0645 IK, the signal 'Tare Dog' ('Today is D–1 Day') was sent out.[20] The starting gun had sounded.

For the sake of clarity, the two-day countdown was divided into seven distinct stages. Phase Mercury was the final preparation for the trial on land sites. The endless rehearsals now paid off, as a small armada of boats and landing craft transported dozens of scientists to sites all around the islands.

From the jetties and landings they dashed off to their individual stations, checking every instrument and switching on every battery. Once fully operational, the status of each device was reported back to H1 and the *Campania*, where progress was charted on boards and checked against the schedule. T2 was evacuated, along with all the remote sites, while all non-necessary luggage and gear were removed from H1, ready for evacuation the following day. Before each departure, a roll call was held to make sure that no one was left behind. Then it was back in the boats for the last return trip to H1, the *Campania* or the LSTs, as the case may be. The seas got rougher as the day wore on, and the lubberly boffins were tossed from stem to stern and drenched with spray, but no one wanted to call off the test because of rough seas, so no one did.

Most of the larger boats and landing craft were now ordered to make their way to the Lowendal Islands, about 12 nautical miles south of the Montebellos, which had been chosen as the safe anchorage from which the *Campania* and most of the other ships would witness the test. Due to rough seas, six of the *Campania*'s pinnaces were weather-bound for much of the day, eventually making a successful dash for the Lowendals during a break in the weather. Two landing craft heading for the Lowendals were turned back because of rough weather and told to spend the night at Claret Bay. Their crews would be much closer to the blast than they would have liked.

There was one more hitch when the LCMs transporting the sappers and Land Rovers from Trimouille to Hermite could not enter Stephenson Channel because the tide was too low; the Royal Marines were forced to go the long way around to drop off their passengers and cargo at Rum Cove, on the seaward side of Hermite, before proceeding to nearby Claret Bay for the night. They would return to Rum Cove in the morning to complete the evacuation of H1.

During the morning, the Australian Fleet was ordered to clear the danger area, and HMA Ships *Murchison*, *Shoalhaven* and *Hawkesbury* were sent to the Mary Anne Passage to commence new patrols designed to ensure the safety of inshore shipping. The *Murchison* patrolled the western end of the passage from Airlie Island to North Sandy Island (Patrol Dog); the *Shoalhaven* patrolled the eastern end around Legendre Island (Patrol Easy); and the *Hawkesbury* patrolled the middle of the passage, from Sholl Island right up to the edge of the danger area (Patrol X-Ray).[21]

By the evening of D–1, the Montebello Islands had been evacuated, except for H1 and the *Plym*, where a skeleton crew remained with the weapon room team. At 1830 IK, following another favourable weather forecast, Phase Mercury was declared over and Phase Venus commenced. The ships now moved from stand-by positions to safe positions: the *Campania* and the *Zeebrugge* left Parting Pool and headed for the Lowendals, while the *Tracker* and the *Narvik* shifted to the preliminary withdrawal position, 4 nautical miles south of Trimouille, to wait for the last evacuees from the *Plym*.

By now, the *Plym* had been stripped to bare essentials, with many of her parts claimed as souvenirs. The remaining crew was so small that the ship's captain, Lieutenant Commander, Peter Draisey, cooked dinner. John Challens, Assistant Director of the Weapon Operation Division, remembered it as 'a most awful concoction of tins and things that he had found around the ship'.[22] To make matters worse, the skipper insisted on doing the dishes in case the test was cancelled and they all had to come back and do it again.

Over at H1, the camp was now double its usual size, with over 60 scientists, sailors, sappers and marines looking for somewhere to sleep. Extra tents were set up, and the marines were ordered to sleep in their landing craft yet again. 'It was cold and windy in the camp that evening and conditions superficially did not seem to be suitable for the trial', wrote McEnhill.[23] Dr Butterfield had been sent over from the *Campania* so there would be a doctor on hand if anything went wrong. There were no medical emergencies that night, but Butterfield did treat a few scientists for nerves. Many were on duty all through the night. Late in the evening, there was a short lecture on the effects that would be experienced by those at H1 when the weapon was detonated. It was supposed to be reassuring, but whether it had the intended effect is doubtful. 'Afterwards, those who could, turned in before midnight for some sleep. The night was very windy and tent flaps smacked so loudly that conditions seemed to be worse than they had ever been at H1', wrote McEnhill.[24]

At 0030 IK on D-Day, Dr Tyte and Admiral Torlesse once again examined the weather forecast. It remained favourable, so Phase Venus was declared over and Phase Mars commenced. This was the loading of the weapon. In the *Plym*, Wing Commander Rowlands removed the cases containing the radioactive components from a safe and placed them in a glove box in the weapon room. While Bill Moyce studied the neutron counter for any sign of trouble, Rowlands put his hands in the gloves and opened the containers. The nickel-plated initiator was placed in the indentation in the centre of one of the gold-plated plutonium hemispheres. The two halves were then fitted together – carefully – and the gleaming golden ball was attached to the end of the cartridge with a metal claw known as the gauntlet.[25] The tension in the weapon room was almost unbearable as the cylindrical cartridge, which was about 2 foot 6 inches long, was hoisted above the device and lowered into the chamber – carefully, *very* carefully – by Rowlands's RAF team. Moyce relayed every step by radio back to Deputy Technical Director Charles Adams at H1, where the running commentary was recorded for diagnostic purposes in case anything went wrong.

At 0200 IK, after 90 minutes of suspense, the cartridge was fitted home and the aluminium cover was shut tight. Phase Mars was declared over and Phase Jupiter commenced. This was the 'detting', or the fitting of the detonators, for which Challens was in charge.[26] He and his team placed 32 detonators around the circumference of the weapon, each one attached to four different cables connecting the device to two separate firing systems, with built-in redundancy. The process took two hours, and when it was done the device looked like something out of *War of the Worlds*: a gleaming aluminium ball constructed from geometric shapes, 5 feet in diameter, suspended about 2 feet above the deck, with 128 cables springing from equidistant points around the surface and snaking around the deck of the weapon room.

At 0400 IK, Phase Jupiter was declared over and Phase Neptune commenced. This was the testing of the firing system and the telemetry connections between the *Plym* and H1, which continued until about 0600 IK. About 15 minutes later, Phase Saturn commenced when two parties led by Lieutenant Commander Draisey left the *Plym* in harbour launches for the *Tracker* and the *Narvik*. The party bound for the health ship included the RAF team and most of the scientists, including Moyce, while the party bound for the *Narvik* included most of the *Plym*'s remaining crew. The seas were still rough, the boats were small, it was dark and cold, and the boffins did not have much fun, but they made it safely to the LSTs. Once the passengers were on board, the boats were hoisted and the ships weighed anchor and moved off to their safe positions, the *Narvik* joining the *Campania* and the *Zeebrugge* at the Lowendals, while the *Tracker* took up her station as health ship somewhat closer to the bomb, about 10 nautical miles south-east of Trimouille.

There were now only a few men left on board the *Plym*: John Challens; his off-sider Eddie Howse; and a small Naval team under the command of the ship's navigation officer, former patrol boat captain Lieutenant JMC Pattison. The scientists' last job was to plug in the batteries that charged up the power units. Once everything was hooked up, Challens inserted the firing key and turned it from 'SAFE' to 'FIRE'.[27] That signalled the end of Phase Saturn and the beginning of Phase Uranus: the final abandonment of the *Plym*.

At 0650 IK, Lieutenant Pattison ordered everyone into a 25-foot motor cutter and headed for Hermite. As they roared off into the lagoon, everyone turned back for one last look at the doomed frigate, which was lit up like a Christmas tree in the early morning darkness. For the Navy men, it was an emotional moment. The *Plym* had been their home for many months. She was a good ship, not all that old, and none of them wanted to see her blown up, even (maybe especially) by British boffins.

By this stage of the operation, all the boats had seen better days, and the motor cutter was no different. With seawater streaming in from a fresh hole in the bottom, the pump was kept running for the whole trip across the lagoon. The sea was choppy, and the whole party was soon soaked with spray, but after one hour and fifteen minutes they made it safely to the jetty at H2. They were then driven up the hill by Land Rover to H1, where, alarmingly, it looked as thought the command centre was on fire.

Just before the weapon party arrived, some Naval stewards had been burning rubbish near the camp. 'Unfortunately some spinifex clumps nearby were ignited and an ugly situation threatened', explained McEnhill. 'A large area was soon on fire as the grass was tinder dry and the flames spread through it greedily. Scientific staff and Naval staff alike made a determined effort to control it because the smoke and hot air was rising directly in front of the cameras focussed on the Target Vessel.'[28]

After a desperate effort, the fire was put out and everyone returned to their stations, coughing and spluttering, clothes and faces blackened with smoke.

In the meantime, Challens had one more crucial duty to perform. He reported to Adams in the control room, where he handed over the safety key, which was inserted into the control panel. Only now, after the *Plym* had been evacuated and every last man had been accounted for, could the weapon be detonated. Once the safety key was inserted, Phase Uranus was declared over.

Phase Boreas was the final meteorological check. A weather balloon was released at H1, and to everyone's horror it showed that the wind was blowing in the wrong direction. To cancel the test now was unthinkable, so the experiment was repeated, and this time the bosses got the result they wanted. With some relief, they tossed out the first result and went with the second one. At 0845 IK, Dr Tyte gave the order to proceed.

A little earlier, at 0800 IK, Maddock had issued a time check over the radio so that everyone in the Task Force could synchronise clocks and watches. Over the following hour, all men wishing to view the test were fallen in on deck, under the control of an officer. To protect their eyes from the intense flash, the men were lined up with their backs to the islands, with no protective clothing, and the officer in charge positioned to the rear to keep a close eye on everyone. All the ships were battened down, their doors and hatches closed and heavy steel deadlights clamped down over the scuttles to protect the eyes of everyone with duties down below, such as the engine room stokers. Lieutenant Peter Bird was in charge of a group of seamen on the deck of the *Narvik*. 'The atmosphere throughout the ship was electric and it was difficult to control the impulse to turn and cast nervous glances toward the islands.'[29]

Every man in the Task Force could feel the tension, from William Penney down to the youngest National Serviceman.

At the command centre at H1, only 6 nautical miles from the target vessel, everyone was under cover, and doors had been wedged open to stop the pressure wave from blowing them open. Although no one would be looking directly at the explosion, one boffin had rigged up a pinhole camera that would allow him to watch a projection of the blast.

Down at Claret Bay, on the seaward side of the island, Lieutenant Pattison was in charge of the sailors and marines who were waiting with their landing craft. The lieutenant was armed with one of Ieuan Maddock's taxi radios – those that had proven more effective than the Navy's radios – and was tuned in to the appropriate channel. He ordered everyone to line up on the beach, facing away from the target vessel. Standing out in the open, these men were protected by nothing except the lee of H1.

By 0915 IK, everyone was in position and Maddock announced: 'Attention all stations. This is H1 control. Dog Baker has commenced. Dog Baker has commenced.'[30] The Danger Bracket had begun, which meant that the firing sequence could begin at any time in the next half-hour.

There was one more delay when the Kerr-cell cameras acted up yet again. Due to some combination of heat and humidity, the film cassettes refused to fit in the decks, but after five minutes of kicking and swearing, the boffins finally jammed them in.

Now Adams nodded to Maddock, who switched on his microphone and announced, 'Minus eight and a half minutes.'[31] The firing sequence had begun. For the next eight minutes, Maddock's cool, calm voice crackled out over the radio every 30 seconds. The countdown did not go out over the loudspeakers on the surrounding ships. Instead, the ship's captain or a designated officer relayed a running commentary from the bridge, including a warning at minus two minutes for bridge officers and other personnel on duty to turn away from the islands. For the last 30 seconds, the intervals between Maddock's announcements shrank, and the tension increased exponentially: '25 ... 20 ... 15 ... ten ... five ... four ... three ... two ... one ... NOW.'[32]

# 11

# DOUBLE DAYLIGHT

A few seconds before 0930 IK (8.00 a.m. on the mainland), HMS *Plym* was annihilated in a flash of blinding white light.

The Kerr-cell cameras first observed the fireball bursting through the frigate's hull 23-millionths of a second after the explosion. For a few frames, the ship's bows could be seen silhouetted against the fireball as it emerged from the hold. After that, she was gone.

The fireball was millions of degrees Fahrenheit – hotter than the core of the sun – and it spread at an incredible rate. After just 0.6 seconds, it was a third of a mile across. After that, the fireball contracted, but the shockwave continued to spread outwards across the lagoon. The water column shot up into the air at the same time, reaching a height of 1800 feet after just one second, at which point the mushroom cloud began to form. As a secondary effect, a tremendous wave of water about 550 feet high and two-thirds of a mile across was thrown out in all directions.[1]

At H1, the initial flash penetrated through the joins in the walls and lit up the interior of the command centre. In the control room, an unfazed Maddock kept counting upwards. At three seconds, scientists charged outside to man their high-speed cine-cameras and still cameras, swapping plates as fast as they could. What they captured was a dark, roiling cloud towering thousands of feet in the air. 'This was the most impressive feature of these early seconds – the vastness of the upheaval, its splendid symmetry, and the stillness', wrote an awestruck JJ McEnhill.[2]

Leading Seaman Henry Carter, a mechanic from Bedfordshire, England, was one of the last men off the *Plym*. He was now down at Rum Cove with the other sailors and marines waiting to evacuate the staff from H1. Officially, everyone at Rum Cove was supposed to be lined up on the beach with their backs to the blast, but, in 1985, Carter told the Royal Commission that he and a few others were in one of the boats.

'The signal came over the radio to prepare for count down and a black heavy canvas tarpaulin was pulled over the boat so we were now in darkness', he stated. 'We all then draped jungle green towels over our heads and I pressed the palms of my hands into my eye sockets. I was dressed in shorts and a pair of shoes.

'At zero there was a blinding electric blue light of an intensity I had not seen before or since. I pressed my hands harder to my eyes, then realised I could see the bones of my hands. It seemed that this light was passing through the tarpaulin and towel for about 10 or 12 seconds and there seemed to be two surges and two detonations with a continued rumbling and boiling sensation. My body seem [sic] first to be compressed and then billowing like a balloon.

'When the all-clear came, we removed our hands from over our eyes and towels from our heads and sunlight appeared to be coming through holes in our tarpaulin. The tarpaulin was removed and I saw the cloud rising at speed.'[3]

At the time of Operation Hurricane, Carter was a fit 30-year-old, but he soon developed a chest infection and a rash on his back that never went away. Later on, he also suffered from cataracts. Carter always suspected that these conditions were caused by radiation, but never knew what his doctors thought because he was refused access to his medical file. He died in 1998 at the age of 76.

William Penney was on the bridge of HMS *Campania* with Admiral Torlesse and his VIP guests, hoping for success. 'Suddenly there was an intense flash visible all round the horizon', he later said. 'We turned to look. The sight before our eyes was terrifying – a great greyish black cloud being hurled thousands of feet into the air and increasing in size with astonishing rapidity.'[4]

On the deck of the nearby HMS *Narvik*, Lieutenant Peter Bird stood behind his men. 'In the instant, despite a blazing tropical sun intensified by reflection from the water all around, a blinding light bathed the ships and the ocean from horizon to horizon.'[5] Everyone waited until the count of ten and then turned around. 'The sight that met our eyes as we turned was vastly more terrifying than can be appreciated from any photograph. The great, grey-black mass, just flowering at the top like a tremendous cauliflower, appeared, even at that distance, to be towering right over us.'

On HMS *Zeebrugge*, Sapper Fletcher was also struck by the brilliance of the blast. 'It's eight o'clock in the morning [sic], sunlight, broad daylight, and the whole world just lit up. Double daylight, as you might say.'[6]

After 30 seconds, the ground at H1 trembled and the command centre was hit by the blast wave, the force of which shocked even the scientists. A huge dust storm sprang up all around the islands, blocking the view of the photographers at H1. The men in the command centre scooped up records, switched off their apparatuses and prepared for evacuation. Soon, radioactive rain fell from the mushroom cloud, covering Trimouille, Bluebell, Carnation, Gardenia, Kingcup and Jonquil islands with fallout.

At this stage, the blast wave had not yet reached the Special Squadron. When it did, it was immediately followed by a second bang, alarming many of the observers. Had something gone wrong? Was there a second explosion? According to

Penney, the explanation was quite simple: 'The first was the direct sound wave and the second a reflection from a layer of warm air some 2 miles up.'[7] This was soon followed by a strange feeling of pressure in the ears, caused by the suction that followed the blast.

The phlegmatic Sapper Fletcher was not particularly alarmed. 'We got hit by this gush of warm or hot wind, and the ship rocked slightly ... A lot of the lads seem to think, or thought, there was a tidal wave. There was no tidal wave. The ship just rocked slightly.'[8]

Meanwhile, the cloud was growing ever higher, reaching a height of 10,000 feet after four minutes before hitting the inversion layer, which stopped its ascent. Already the mushroom shape was gone, the cloud having been warped and twisted into a giant Z by the contrary winds at different altitudes. The top portion of the cloud, between 10,000 and 12,000 feet, was drifting east – towards the mainland.

Unconcerned by such minor matters, Admiral Torlesse dictated an emergency signal for the Admiralty. It comprised three words: 'DOUBLOON REPETITION DOUBLOON'.[9] The codeword meant that the test was successful.

According to legend, UK Prime Minister Winston Churchill drafted two cables to send to Penney upon completion of the test: one in the event of failure, which said, 'Thank you, Dr Penney'; and one in the event of success, which said, 'Well done, Sir William'. Sadly, this tale seems to be apocryphal. The real reply said:

> Congratulations on your successful achievement. Please convey to those concerned at Montebello and at home the thanks of Her Majesty's Government for all their toil and skill which have carried this great enterprise to fruition.[10]

Penney was knighted soon after.

•

There were many Australian ships in the North West that day, scattered all around the Montebellos at various distances from the blast. Their exact positions are disputed to this day.

Not too far off was the frigate HMAS *Hawkesbury*, officially on patrol about 20 nautical miles east-south-east of the islands. At the beginning of the firing sequence, Lieutenant Commander Scrivenor cleared the lower decks so everyone could witness the historic moment:

> Eight minutes later, there was a brilliant orange flash, followed by a boiling cloud of smoke, dust and water, shooting up into the sky with dramatic speed. The typical 'mushroom' was soon distorted by the high winds in the upper levels. The blast of the explosion was felt 2 minutes and 16 seconds later.[11]

Able Seaman Vince Douglas was a 23-year-old boatswain's yeoman (or ship's rigger) on the *Hawkesbury*. A former shearer and kangaroo shooter from Rockhampton, Queensland, Douglas told the Royal Commission that the frigate was much closer – about 9 nautical miles from the blast. 'At the time of the explosion I was standing next to the ship's funnel. I remember seeing a flash, I turned around and heard a roar like a train approaching in a tunnel. Then a tremendous crack like a whip-lash passed directly overhead. I saw a mushroom cloud and the aftermath of a terrific explosion. There was black and white smoke, orange and red flames ascending through the centre of the mushroom.'[12]

Many other members of the ship's company have insisted over the years that the *Hawkesbury* was closer than 20 nautical miles.

HMAS *Koala*, now under the command of Lieutenant Commander Dick Taudevin, DSC and Bar, had returned to the

North West to continue the never-ending mooring programme. The boom defence vessel was now anchored off North Sandy Island, about 40 nautical miles south of the Montebellos, in company with MWL 251.[13]

Able Seaman Maurice Westwood, a 23-year-old boom technician from Elsternwick, Victoria, was up on deck with his crewmates. 'We were told that we were to stand with our backs towards the explosion while the detonation was occurring and we were told a few seconds after the detonation that we could turn around. We viewed the atomic cloud forming. At that time we were some forty miles from the explosion.

'Prior to the explosion we were not told of any dangers associated with it except that we should not watch the initial detonation in case our eyes were damaged. About 4 minutes after the detonation I felt a shock wave blast of air and saw a small wave form on the water which prior to the explosion was very flat and still.'[14]

Westwood and his mates were all wearing shorts and sandals, with no shirts.

At the time of the blast, HMAS *Warreen* was on her way into Onslow, where MRL 252, HMAS *Reserve* and fuel lighter SSL 563 were to be found. The *Reserve*, a Naval tug under the command of Lieutenant Commander HJ Hull, had arrived a few days earlier to tow the fuel lighter around and help service Sunderland flying boats. Later on, when she was towing SSL 563 back to Fremantle, the lighter would spring a leak and sink off Carnarvon, leading to a very uncomfortable conversation with the NOIC West Australian Area for Lieutenant Commander Hull.

Then there was Admiral Eaton's fleet. The flagship aircraft carrier HMAS *Sydney* and frigate HMAS *Macquarie* were conducting a box patrol about 60 nautical miles south-west of the islands, where both ships had been patrolling with HMAS *Tobruk* throughout the night. Admiral Eaton wrote:

From my Flagship 60 [nautical] miles to south-westward of the Monte Bellos, the initial orange flash followed by the rising radio-active smoke cloud were clearly observed. Five minutes later the noise of the explosion was heard and the shock wave rattled the windows of my bridge. By this time the cloud was estimated to be two miles high and beginning to spread with the wind. Thirty minutes later the cloud was estimated to be fifty miles long.[15]

Over on the *Macquarie*, 36-year-old Lieutenant Commander Arthur Chapman was diligently taking notes:

The smoke from this explosion was viewed at a distance of 60 [nautical] miles in fine clear weather. The sky was cloudless, the wind South Westerly force 4. The smoke rose quickly upward, billowing out in an irregular shape. There was obviously little wind in the upper atmosphere as the bearing of the peak remained steady for an hour afterwards whereas the lower parts moved to the northward. The Atomic cloud eventually spread out in a long thin line and by 1500 covered an arc of some 40 degrees. Two distinct shock waves were felt in *Macquarie* 5 minutes after the smoke was first observed. These were about a second apart and were not severe.[16]

Just before the blast, destroyer HMAS *Tobruk* had been ordered to rendezvous with frigate HMAS *Murchison* off Rosily Island, about 60 nautical miles sou'-sou'-west of the Montebellos, to exchange mail. Both ships now converged on the rendezvous point from different directions: the *Tobruk* from the north-west, the *Murchison* from the east.

Mike Rowe was a young National Serviceman on board the *Murchison*. A keen photographer, he had hatched a daring plan to capture an image of the blast with his Box Brownie camera, despite the threat of 10 years in gaol under the Commonwealth *Crimes Act* for doing so. Decades later, he told filmmaker Tom Godfrey about his scheme: 'We were told that there were to be no cameras on the deck, but I had this very small camera, and I worked out that if I undid the buttons on my fly, I could fit the camera down there and work the mechanism by putting my hands in my pockets. And seeing that I was against the rail, that's just what I did.'[17]

From below his belt, Rowe was able to capture a few crystal-clear images of the mushroom cloud billowing up above the horizon.[18] Rowe, who died of cancer in 2014, reckoned that the *Murchison* was 12 to 15 nautical miles east of the Montebellos at the time of the blast, not 60 nautical miles sou'-sou'-west as the official record states. His old shipmate Ken Palmer, who suffered from thyroid cancer, backed him up. 'There's no way Mike could have taken that photo from that distance, I reckon it was probably closer to 12 nautical miles', he told *The Daily Telegraph* in 2017, not long before he died.[19]

Like many other atomic veterans, Rowe and Palmer believed that the Australian Government had falsified the records to avoid paying compensation to men who were exposed to radiation. They had every reason to be suspicious. It is a fact that Naval logs and reports of proceedings were sometimes falsified for security reasons, or simply to avoid embarrassment. (The *Mildura*'s report for November 1951, for instance, states that the corvette was engaged in a training exercise in the Dampier Archipelago from 4 to 9 November. She was not: she was in the Montebellos, storing 5ACS's heavy equipment and preparing to tow the *Limicola* back to Fremantle.)[20] It is also a fact that countless atomic veterans were denied healthcare over the years on the basis that there was nothing in their records to say that they were exposed when they definitely were. Some National Servicemen, including members of the *Murchison*'s company, were even told that they were on other ships, thousands of miles from the blast, only for a classified document to be unclassified years later, proving that they were exactly where they said they were all along.

On the other hand, there is a wealth of evidence, including reports by Admiral Torlesse, Admiral Eaton, Commander Jack Mesley (captain of the *Tobruk*) and Lieutenant Commander Colin Thompson (captain of the *Murchison*) that the two ships were in the vicinity of Rosily Island at the time of the blast.[21] The size and shape of the cloud in Rowe's photos is also fairly consistent with shots taken from similar bearings and distances. Perhaps the old mates were simply wrong about their position. It would be an easy mistake to make after so many years, especially for ex-Nashos, who were never told anything in the first place. According to both ships' commanding officers, the *Murchison* and the *Tobruk* rendezvoused off Rosily Island at 1015 IK, just 45 minutes after the blast.[22]

Meanwhile, HMAS *Shoalhaven* was taking the order to clear the danger area very seriously indeed – Captain Beattie's frigate had left her station off Legendre Island and was steaming for Bedout Island near Port Hedland at 16 knots. At the moment the bomb was detonated, the *Shoalhaven* was over 100 miles east-nor'-east of the Montebellos and, according to the skipper, 'nothing was seen or heard' of the blast.[23] The frigate anchored off Bedout Island until after noon, when Captain Beattie received orders to rejoin the fleet. The *Shoalhaven* then weighed anchor and headed south on the inshore route – right across the path of the upper portion of the cloud, last seen drifting towards the mainland.

Able Seaman Bill Plewright was on the *Shoalhaven* that day. The 22-year-old submarine detection specialist from Bunbury, Western Australia, had already been exposed to radiation numerous times, having visited Hiroshima and Nagasaki while serving on HMAS *Bataan* in 1948, as part of the British Commonwealth Occupation Force (BCOF). Along with many of his old shipmates, Plewright had witnessed the heartbreaking sight of skeletal, radiation-burnt Japanese orphans huddled in doorways, and had drunk locally brewed beer. 'The Kirin Brewery, the biggest brewery in Japan even today, made our beer for us that we drank at HMAS *Commonwealth*, in Kure, to a Victorian recipe', he later recalled. 'But the water all came through the pipes into the Kirin Brewery which was in Hiroshima. So we're drinking irradiated water coming through hot pipes, and we're scoffing it down and thinking it's pretty good.'[24] He later suffered from bladder cancer, which he managed to beat.

During the Royal Commission into British atomic tests, Plewright alleged that the *Shoalhaven* passed right under the cloud. 'I recall that we saw the fallout cloud, which drifted directly over the ship. At the time we passed through the cloud, it was not clearly defined and was fairly ragged.'[25]

The Royal Commissioners found that the *Shoalhaven* was too far from the blast to be contaminated, but Bill Plewright was certainly exposed on many more occasions, returning to the Montebellos for a radiation survey in November 1953 and two more atomic tests in 1956. He later founded the Perth-based Australian Ex-Services Atomic Survivors Association.

There were other ships in the North West on D-Day: HMAS *Culgoa* was about 300 nautical miles south-west of the Montebellos on weather-reporting duty; HMAS *Warrego* (now under newly promoted Commander Tony Cooper) was conducting a survey in the Exmouth Gulf; the British fuel tanker RFA *Wave King* had just left the islands and was en route to rendezvous with the *Warrego* off Exmouth; and HMAS *Mildura* was en route from Onslow to Carnarvon with the unserviceable HMAS *Limicola* in tow. None of these ships were close enough for their crews to witness the blast.

With no further requirements, Admiral Eaton's fleet headed south and rendezvoused in Shark Bay, where the ships' companies spent the next seven days scraping and painting the ships' sides and scrubbing every inch of the decks in preparation for a triumphant tour of southern ports.

Over the next three weeks, the ships split up and visited Geraldton, Fremantle, Albany and Port Adelaide before rendezvousing in Victoria's Port Phillip Bay. On Thursday 30 October, HMAS *Australia*, *Wagga*, *Cootamundra*, *Colac*, *Cowra*, *Latrobe* and *Gladstone* joined the fleet and came under Admiral Eaton's flag. Despite horrendous weather, thousands of Victorians lined the shores of the bay to watch the procession, waving flags and cheering. An official welcome committee comprising the Naval Board, the Chief of General Staff, the Chief of Air Staff, the Minister for the Navy and the Minister for Defence waited on board the *Culgoa*, anchored off the south-east Melbourne suburb of Black Rock under the flag of the Naval Board. In pouring rain, the Australian Fleet proceeded into Port Melbourne in column in close order, each ship firing a 15-gun salute as she passed the *Culgoa*. To top it off, 24 of the *Sydney*'s aircraft flew by in flight formation, then turned around and flew back in anchor formation.

It was quite a scene.

Many sailors believe that the week spent cleaning and painting ships in Shark Bay amounted to a fleet-wide decontamination, and it may well be that fear of radiation motivated officers and ratings alike to scrub extra hard, but there is no evidence that any of the ships were contaminated (with the possible exception of the *Shoalhaven*). The official reason for all that hard work was the prettification of the fleet for the southern cruise and the following inspection by the Naval Board.

•

At 8.00 a.m. on D-Day, physicist and photographer Bill Mangini was on duty at the WA Newspapers observation post at Mount Potter when a flash appeared on the horizon.

'There it is', he announced matter-of-factly.[26]

Finally, after six long weeks of sleeping rough in the bush north of Onslow, the bomb had gone off. The press men had spent hours rehearsing for this moment under the strict instruction of expedition leader Jack Nicoll. Now they sprang into action. Mangini immediately flicked the switch on his cine-camera, while Doug Burton and Harold Rudinger leapt to their feet and ran to the Long Toms. They were shooting within seconds of the blast. At the same time, Dan O'Sullivan from the *Daily News* grabbed the field telephone and got the newsflash away. From the Postmaster-General (PMG) truck at Burton's Billabong, the flash went over the telegraph wires to Perth, where it was received in three minutes – over 60 seconds before the shockwave was felt at Mount Potter. From Perth, the news was relayed to Melbourne, London and New York. The Reuters office in London received word within 10 minutes of the blast – a full six minutes before the Admiralty received the official signal from the *Campania*. The Royal Navy had just been scooped by a pack of scruffy, unwashed Western Australian press men.

Back at Mount Potter, Jim Cruthers from *The West Australian* was dashing back and forth between Mangini and a chalkboard beside the field telephone, scribbling down the physicist's observations for the benefit of the men on the phone. As soon as that job was done, he scrambled down the hill and ran the mile to the base camp to begin working on his own copy.

Dan O'Sullivan and Bill Hudson were taking turns with the phone, dictating stories to Peter Barnett down in the PMG truck. Barnett was bashing out the stories on a typewriter, then handing each page over to Ted Rodgers and Roy Buchanan, the gun telegraphists, who were tapping away madly on their Morse keys. From the PMG truck, the stories travelled along the telegraph line in two directions simultaneously: the direct line south to Perth, and a more circuitous route north to Port Hedland and east to Marble Bar before heading all the way down to Perth on the inland line. Rodgers and Buchanan sent 12,000 words over the wires that day.

The photographers at Mount Potter were just as busy, taking 300 photos in the first few minutes, then dashing off to develop the negatives in the mobile darkroom. As soon as the first batch was ready, photographer Dick Long took them down the hill and jumped in the Jeep with mechanic Bob Warren. Warren tore off down the dusty track, heading for Mardie homestead, where a specially chartered aircraft was waiting to fly the negatives back to Perth. Driver Alex Laughton took the next batch into Onslow in the Land Rover for despatch on the first commercial flight south.

Over at Mardie homestead, Captain Jimmy Woods, a famous Western Australian air pioneer, had his trusty twin-engine Anson idling on the airstrip when the Jeep roared up and skidded to a halt in a cloud of dust. Dick Long handed over the negatives and Captain Woods took off so fast that co-pilot Jim Stark had to chase him down and climb aboard as the aircraft taxied down the runway.

Flying south at 4000 feet, the two aviators could see the atomic cloud stretching out like a stratus cloud along the north-west horizon for the next three and a half hours.

•

In Onslow, photographer Phil Martin was on duty at the time of the blast. A highly decorated former RAAF pilot, Martin had flown Lancaster bombers with 617 Squadron RAF (the legendary Dambusters) during the Second World War. Martin's aircraft had dropped some of the largest conventional bombs ever made, so he had seen some pretty big explosions in his time, but nothing like this.

'She's gone', he yelled.[27]

Reporter Jack Coulter and photographer Owen Williams were eating breakfast at the pub when they heard Martin's cry. Without hesitating, Williams snatched up his camera and dived headfirst through the nearest window. Executing a textbook commando roll, he came up running and was in position on the beach before the top of the mushroom cloud appeared above the horizon.

Six minutes later, Onslow was struck by a ground tremor, causing buildings to shake and windows to rattle all over town. Housewife Margaret Gazzard was in her kitchen when a cracked windowpane, which had previously been repaired with putty, came apart and shattered on the floor. At the hospital, all the doors on the verandah slammed shut, startling expectant mother Mrs Wilson of Meilga Station (mercifully, the shock did not result in an early arrival). Down the road, Nobby Clarke was harnessing his horse when it shied and broke free, bolting across the half-acre paddock and prancing in the corner until Clarke was able to catch up and soothe it.

The tension in Onslow had been so great that when the bomb finally went off, the whole town celebrated like it was New Year's Eve. There were jubilant scenes at the post office as postmaster JE Rodgers and his wife, Myrtle, danced a jig. Between Race Week and the bomb, the entire post office staff had been working nightlong shifts for 10 days. The resulting celebration caused some inconvenience for the officer in charge of the *Murchison*'s mail party, who arrived that afternoon. As the frigate's captain reported:

> This officer found that the town of Onslow had declared a
> holiday and had great difficulty in having the Post Office

opened, eventually sorting the mail with a ship's team owing to the lack of PMG interest. This attitude was undoubtedly the result of the reaction felt by the citizens on this, the afternoon of 'D' Day, and the cause for much local revelry.[28]

The party lasted all day. At the Beadon Hotel, which had not had time to restock after Race Week, the last three crates of beer disappeared in no time flat, and a week's worth of wine and spirits were consumed in a day. Once the pub was drunk dry, the party rolled on to Cliff Ross's house, where locals brought out all sorts of bottles saved for the occasion.

It was Ross who had concocted the first bomb hoax, and naturally he could not resist another prank. Some locals, especially mothers, were understandably worried about the possibility of fallout. This gave Ross an idea. Before his guests arrived, he hooked up a microphone to the radio and ran a cable into the bedroom, where he installed a co-conspirator. When the party was in full swing, the music cut out and a plummy-sounding ABC-type voice announced:

This is a warning ... an unexpected change of wind has blown the atomic dust cloud toward the mainland. All residents of Onslow are warned to evacuate their homes and head for Mardi [sic] Station where RAAF aircraft will fly them out of the area. Onslow is to be evacuated by Army transport. The explosion is the biggest known in the world and the danger to mainland residents is very serious. Navy ships in the area are heading for safety at full speed. Repeat! Here is a warning ...[29]

According to Ross's long-suffering wife, Gwyn, the announcement 'made the hair of all who heard it stand on end'.[30] Some station owners took the warning seriously and raced off in their Land Rovers before anyone could stop them, desperate to get home and evacuate their families. Others ran off to warn friends and family around town. Some of the more laconic locals shrugged and said, 'Well, if it's going to be like that, there's no particular hurry. Let's have another beer.'[31] In the end, it took several hours, and the aid of the local police, to track down all the victims of the hoax. Most of them just laughed and went back to the party.

•

Down in Perth, a special edition of the *Daily News* was rolling off the presses within an hour of the blast. The final edition contained three pages of stories from Dan O'Sullivan at Mount Potter and Jack Coulter at Onslow. But not everyone was impressed. 'The bomb, the bomb, the bomb: the ruddy thing's gone off at last', one world-weary *Daily* newsboy was heard droning.[32]

The following morning, the first dramatic photo of the mushroom cloud appeared on the front page of *The West Australian*. Six triumphant pages were dedicated to the blast, including a full-page photo spread illustrating the cloud's development over time, over a dozen articles from Cruthers and Milne, and a glowing 1100-word editorial that celebrated the test as 'indisputable proof that Britain has the material, the skill and the installations for the independent production of atomic weapons and that she will yield the initiative to none', further expressing 'profound satisfaction at an immense potential strengthening of the British Commonwealth, with a strong sense of pride in British achievement'.[33]

The British tabloids were even more triumphal. 'Today Britain is GREAT BRITAIN again', cried the *Daily Mirror*.[34] 'Britain's first atomic explosion did more than fill the Montebello sky with smoke. Overnight it restored Britain to the status of a major power', proclaimed the *Daily Express*.[35] Both newspapers used photos from Mount Potter.

The Montebello expedition was a grand success by almost any measure. Despite costing the astronomical sum of £10,000, the operation turned a tidy profit for WA Newspapers after rights to stories and pictures from Mount Potter were sold around the world. Several British agencies rated the test coverage one of the top news stories of the year. The press men even received praise from a most unlikely source: Admiral Torlesse, who sent them a telegram via the Mount Potter Post Office congratulating them on the speed and accuracy of their reporting.

Of course, the test coverage was not without flaws. With the benefit of hindsight, it seems obvious that the Australian press let down the public by voluntarily submitting to self-censorship and parroting the government line. For this, the press men of WA Newspapers can perhaps be forgiven. Unlike today's journalists, almost everyone involved in the Montebello expedition was a returned serviceman (even *The West Australian*'s esteemed editor, Ernest de Burgh, was a veteran of the First World War who had been gassed at Amiens). Based on hard-won experience, many of them truly believed that the bomb was a necessary evil in the fight against Communism. It is unsurprising that they would draw the line between national interest and public interest in a different place than journalists of later generations would.

Harder to forgive in retrospect is the press's condescending attitude towards the Aboriginal peoples of the North West, who were generally portrayed as backwards and superstitious. In the lead-up to the test, several Australian newspapers published cartoons of stereotypically 'primitive' Aboriginals being spooked by the blast. 'Natives at a sheep station near Roebourne were alarmed by the sudden thunder-clap that "hit their ears" while the sky above was clear', reported *The*

*West Australian.* 'Several of them said that they feared they were going deaf.'[36] The *Daily News* used racist terms to report that Aboriginal people at Mardie Station 'went scuttling up windmills and tanks to see the spectacle'.[37]

History would show that Aboriginal Australians were right to worry about the effects of nuclear tests.

# 12.

# THE AFTERMATH

Phase Three of Operation Hurricane – the re-entry and recovery of scientific records – began as soon as the weapon was detonated.

As Task Force Commander, it was Admiral Torlesse who had the uneasy responsibility of sending men back into the contaminated area. The admiral was under no illusions about the dangers of radiation. Back when he was first named Task Force Commander, he wrote:

> Radiological safety must be one of the chief concerns of the Naval Commander but, equally evidently, some degree of risk must be run by some people if we are to achieve the full purpose of the trial ...
>
> As Naval Commander I must expect to have to order or approve the acceptance of some degree of risk. This is a customary Service obligation, but it is performed in the knowledge that the Admiralty accept liability for those killed or injured on duty. I want to be certain that the same applies to all who take part in Operation 'Hurricane' whether or not they are volunteers for any or all of their duty.[1]

Realising that certain tasks carried extra risk, especially the initial re-entry sorties, Torlesse asked High Explosive Research

(HER) in the UK whether it was possible to set two levels of permissible dosage: 'a general standard and a special (once only) standard for volunteers'.[2]

To find an answer for Torlesse, Chief Superintendent of HER Dr William Penney and his colleagues looked to the existing recommendations set by the International Commission on Radiological Protection and UK Medical Research Council, which had already established two levels of permissible dosage for the general public and civil defence workers who might be called upon to respond in the event of an atomic attack.

In the 1950s, gamma and X-rays were measured in roentgens, an old-fashioned unit of radiation exposure that measured the level of gamma or X-ray radiation in the air. All forms of radiation could be measured in roentgen-equivalent-physical (rep), a unit of absorbed dose that measured the effect of radiation on tissue by comparing it to the effect of 1 roentgen of gamma or X-rays. For Operation Hurricane, total figures representing exposure to all forms of radiation were expressed in rep, but because the boffins tended to focus on the dangers of gamma radiation, most figures bandied about were in roentgens.

After a number of adjustments, Penney came back with not two but three different dosage levels for Operation Hurricane.[3] The lowest was the 'normal working rate' of 0.3 rep per day, which included a maximum gamma component of 0.1 roentgens per day. The normal working rate applied to all personnel involved in the operation. The next level up was the 'lower integrated dose' of 15 rep, which had a maximum gamma component of 3 roentgens. The lower integrated dose only applied to personnel whose tasks were deemed 'necessary for the smooth running of the operation' and required the authorisation of a health escort. Anyone who received the lower integrated dose would be barred from re-entering the contaminated area for the rest of the operation. The highest level was the 'higher integrated dose' of 50 rep, with a maximum gamma component of 10 roentgens, which was only to be used 'in cases of extreme urgency' and required the authorisation of the Task Force Commander. Anyone who received the higher integrated dose would be banned from further exposure for at least a year.

These levels were in line with the accepted international standards of the time. There was just one problem with that: there is no such thing as a safe level of exposure to ionising radiation. Ionising radiation causes two different types of effects on the human body: non-stochastic and stochastic effects. Non-stochastic effects are the obvious ones that appear more or less immediately, like radiation burns and radiation poisoning. They occur over a certain threshold of exposure and increase in severity according to dose. Stochastic effects are the not-so-obvious ones that crop up years or even decades later, like cancer and genetic disorders. They increase in probability, but not severity, according to dose. As Dr Elizabeth Tynan, author of *Atomic Thunder: The Maralinga Story*, explains:

> There is no threshold, meaning in effect that if a given number of people are exposed to any amount of ionising radiation, the probability is that a statistically predictable number of them will suffer cancer or genetic damage. There is no safe dose; any exposure may cause risk of serious illness.[4]

At the time of Operation Hurricane that fact was not yet fully understood, but even if it had been, the test would still have gone ahead. Britain's top priority was to become an atomic power, not look after the radiological health and safety of sailors and sappers. As Admiral Torlesse said, some men would have to take some risks for the greater good.

•

The first men to re-enter the contaminated area were the helicopter crews.

Two hours after the blast, two Dragonflies took off from the flight deck of HMS *Campania* and headed for the Montebello Islands. Their task was to retrieve a radioactive water sample from as close to Ground Zero as possible. The mission was so dangerous that Admiral Torlesse had authorised the use of the higher integrated dose for both crews. Each officer was equipped with protective clothing, a respirator, a film badge and a personal dosimeter, and the helicopters were fitted with dose rate meters capable of taking readings up to the deadly level of 300 roentgens. All throughout the Task Force, scientists, sailors, sappers and marines watched in admiration as the helicopter crews headed straight for Ground Zero.

While the back-up helicopter hovered above, the lead helicopter, flown by Lieutenant Commander Denis Stanley, DFC, and Senior Commissioned Observer Jackie Lambert, DSM, swooped in over the lagoon at an altitude of just 30 feet. What they found was a hellscape. The cloud, which had been torn apart by the contrary winds, now sprawled ominously over miles of sky to the north of Trimouille. All around the islands, black smoke billowed into the air from scrub fires set off by the fireball. The sand on the once pristine beach near Ground Zero was black and the surrounding sand dunes had been levelled. Where the *Plym* had been moored, there was now a giant crater in the seabed, 1000 feet across and 20 feet deep with a raised rim all the way around. Eerily, the shape of the crater conformed roughly to the outline of the *Plym*.

Lieutenant Commander Stanley took the Dragonfly in as close as he could get to Ground Zero, stopping only when the dose rate reached 14 roentgens per hour – the maximum level he and Lambert were permitted to receive. Dangling beneath the helicopter at the end of a 20-foot line was a small metal canister about the size of a milk bottle. It was Lambert's job to lower the canister into the water, unstopper it by compressing a grip on the end of the line, and restopper it by releasing the grip once it was full. The fliers had practised this routine almost every day for six weeks, getting their time down to 60 seconds flat, but now it was the real thing. As the Dragonfly hovered 20 feet above the water, it took Lambert 105 nerve-racking seconds to fill the canister.

'We were being very careful', he later explained.[5]

Once the canister was stoppered, Stanley pulled up and left the area at speed. With the sample dangling from the end of the line, the Dragonfly flew over to the landing ship tank HMS *Zeebrugge*, home of the Radiochemical Division. The sample was carefully lowered onto a canvas sheet spread out on deck and bundled down to the lab for investigation. Later on D-Day, after a few more samples were delivered, the *Zeebrugge* moved out of the area and anchored off North Sandy Island, 40 nautical miles south, where the radiochemists could analyse the samples in peace and quiet, away from any background radiation.

Lieutenant Commander Stanley and Observer Lambert were both awarded MBEs for their roles in Operation Hurricane, and deservedly so – they were undoubtedly two of the gutsiest men in the whole Task Force. Thanks to their protective clothing, and their coolness under pressure, both men were able to limit their exposure to under 5 roentgens. That was less than half what they were permitted to receive, but still a significant dose – equivalent to about 30 years of normal background radiation. Luckily, neither of them keeled over from acute radiation poisoning. Denis Stanley was still flying recreationally in his 80s, and died in 2009 at the age of 88. Jackie Lambert did not live as long, dying at 61 in 1971. Whether exposure was a factor in either man's death is unknown.

While the helicopters were still in the air, HMS *Tracker* moved into position about 5 miles south-east of Hermite. As health ship, the *Tracker* was now the most important ship in the Task Force. All re-entrants would pass through the landing ship tank before and after each sortie into the contaminated area, first for briefings and preparation, then for radiation monitoring and decontamination.

Lieutenant Colonel Alec Walkling, Assistant Director of the Radiological Hazard Division, was in charge of health control. Walkling was a gruff, no-nonsense Royal Artillery officer attached to HER. His division was based on a specially installed halfdeck in the LST's tank space, which was divided into clean and dirty areas. The clean side was now full of activity as the first survey teams prepared to re-enter the contaminated area. In the control room, a large map of Trimouille sat alongside a bank of meters recording dose rates from remote-control gamma flux-meters on the islands. On the other side of the compartment, survey teams and boat crews were briefed on their tasks and given preliminary isodose contour maps drawn up from the data received from the islands. (Isodose maps resemble topographical maps, but instead of levels of elevation, the contour lines show levels of contamination.) The re-entrants were also introduced to the health escorts who were to accompany them. Health escorts were responsible for the radiological safety of survey teams, and were equipped with radiac devices, wristwatches and walkie-talkies. It was up to them to make sure no one exceeded the maximum permissible dose or broke the rules by eating, drinking or smoking, thus exposing them to the risk of ingesting alpha particles. HER's preference was for all tasks to be completed before the re-entrants exceeded the normal working rate, but, if that plan failed, health escorts had the power to authorise the use of the lower integrated dose.

Following the briefing, the survey teams and boat crews passed through a series of compartments to collect different items of protective clothing and equipment. Each man was given a gas mask, two dosimeters and a gamma film badge.

The dosimeters were set to measure different integrated dose ranges, enabling the men to keep track of how much radiation they were receiving in real time. The film badges were developed later, providing the scientists with a more precise measurement of the men's exposure. Since beta radiation was also a concern, one person per party was given three beta film badges to wear at various places on the body.

The re-entrants now came to the clean change room, where they stripped down to underwear and socks before being weighed. With the help of Naval ratings, they donned their protective clothing: a pair of overalls that zipped up at the back, rubber boots, rubber gloves, a neckerchief and a floppy bush hat. The gamma film badges were pinned on the outside of the protective suit, clipped to the waist or chest; the beta film badges were worn inside the suit, near the chest, waist and leg. The men did not have to wear the gas mask until they reached the contaminated area, but then they had to keep it on until they left. Finally, the re-entrants went up on deck to the embarkation space to wait for the boats, milling about awkwardly while the sailors gawked at them in their strange get-up and made facetious comments.

The first groups to go in were three water survey teams tasked with tracking the spread of contaminated water and ascertaining the safest routes to the recovery areas. Teams of two, each comprising a Royal Navy officer and a scientist, boarded specially modified motor pinnaces fitted with enclosed metal canopies to protect passengers and crew from fallout. Entry was via a small hatch on top, just large enough for two men to stick their heads out at once. Under the canopy, the boat was stiflingly hot. Once the survey teams were squared away, the boat crews, who were also dressed in protective clothing, cast off and headed for the contaminated area.

The wind had dropped right away over the course of the morning, and the seas were calm and flat. As the boats approached the islands, they found that the surface of the sea was littered with hundreds of dead fish and other sea creatures. It was a terrible scene that seared itself into the minds of all who saw it. Those creatures not vaporised by the blast or killed by the shockwave were slowly poisoned by radiation. The Montebello Islands had always been a fisherman's paradise, but not anymore. From D-Day onwards, all fishing was banned, except for scientific purposes. The fish were too 'hot' to eat.

The seawater was hot as well. The survey teams found only a slight increase above background levels in the section of the lagoon south of Trimouille, but that was because wind and tide were moving north. From the southern end of Trimouille onwards, they found increasing contamination and considerable turbulence involving stirred-up sand and seaweed. One boat tried to make it through to Gladstone Beach at the north end of the island, but found it too hot and was forced to turn back. Outside the lagoon, to the north of Trimouille, another team encountered water measuring 25 milliroentgens per hour.[6] For the purposes of Operation Hurricane, contaminated water was defined as 'that in which the measured radiation intensity in the water exceeds 0.1 mr [milliroentgens] per hour'.[7] The water north of Trimouille was 250 times that level.

Despite these findings, the boffins were not overly concerned about the state of the water. DJ Savage, leader of the Radiological Hazard Division team in charge of contamination sampling, concluded 'that the level of activity in the sea over ground zero on the afternoon of D-Day was such that it would have been quite safe to drink after distillation'.[8]

No one was silly enough to drink water from Ground Zero on D-Day, but just about everyone drank water distilled from the surrounding area in the days and weeks ahead. The ships' orders were to stop distilling when the dose rate in the water exceeded 0.1 milliroentgens per hour, but, as long as the readings were lower than that, the distillers kept on running. As Lieutenant Colonel Walkling explained: 'To have insisted on no distillation unless the measured concentration was zero would have proved impossible, partly because of the difficulties of reliable measurement and more particularly because the spread of water born [sic] contamination was so extensive that, without some completely external supply of drinking water, the operation of re-entry could not have been successfully carried out. All ships of the Force had at some time or other to operate and distill [sic] in slightly contaminated water.'[9] If only the Fortescue pipeline had worked, so fresh water could have been sourced from the mainland.

The fourth team to enter the contaminated area was the first land survey team, and it was led by an Australian officer: Squadron Leader AD Thomas, RAAF, Scientific Adviser to the Chief of Air Staff. A 31-year-old radio expert from Sydney, New South Wales, Thomas was one of just two Australian officers permitted to participate in the recovery process. (The other was Brigadier AW Wardell, MC, Director of Civil Defence.) The airman had been attached to HER for the past month, training with radiac instruments and conducting exercises on Trimouille. It was Penney who gave him the honour of leading the first shore party. As Thomas later recalled: 'Dr Penney as he then was said to me, "Well, it is your country Thomas and we have been occupying it for a while, and made a bit of a mess here. Perhaps you might like to repossess it and lead the first party ashore." So it was a sort of a joke, you see, so I said all right, and I went in.'[10]

Squadron Leader Thomas and two British officers clambered into a boat and headed for T1 near the south-east corner of Trimouille. The boat crew tied up alongside the metal jetty, which had been twisted by the force of the blast, and Thomas ordered them to wait there. The three officers then trudged up the beach, gazing about through the lenses in their gas masks. The flags flying above the camp were half burnt, but the generator was still running and the area proved free of radioactivity. The Land Rover that had been left behind for their use was also in working order. Thomas and his team jumped in and headed for Cocoa Beach.

The landscape they traversed was covered with burning fields of spinifex and littered with debris. There were scorched aircraft components in some places, shattered concrete bunkers in others, sheets of corrugated iron from Anderson shelters lying around willy-nilly. As the team progressed, Thomas kept a close eye on his radiac device. 'We finally reached a point where there was a piece of metal from *Plym*', he later recalled. 'The meter that I had had a maximum reading of 30 roentgens per hour and as we approached the piece of *Plym* the needle went to full scale. Immediately I told the driver to turn around and get away from it quickly.'[11]

The team spent two hours trekking around the island. They confirmed the gamma flux-meters' readings, located the positions of key isodose lines, and established boundaries between clean and dirty areas. While the north of the island was heavily contaminated, the south remained relatively clean, indicating that the Meteorology Division's predictions of the cloud movement were largely correct. It was easy to spot the heavily contaminated areas because they were covered in grey fallout. At first, the scientists assumed that the mucky substance was a mixture of mud and sand thrown up from the seabed where the crater now lay, but close analysis led to a chilling realisation: it was the *Plym*. The proud frigate had been liquefied by the heat of the blast, coating parts of Trimouille and other nearby islands with a thin layer of grey metal, poisonous to the touch.

Aside from the obvious danger, Thomas also found the job to be extremely uncomfortable. It was 110 degrees Fahrenheit on Trimouille, and the protective outfits were heavy and painfully hot. Thomas's gas mask fogged up and pints of sweat pooled in his boots, sloshing around while he walked. Only once the team had returned to the pinnace and were finally able to remove their masks was there any relief.

Decontamination procedures began as soon as the boat tied up alongside the *Tracker*. Much of the ship's forecastle had been roped off as a dirty area, where the men were relieved of their instruments and records, which were put aside for monitoring. Gloves, boots and overalls were removed and placed in bins to be dealt with later. Clad in socks and underwear, Thomas and his team members padded down the companionway to the dirty waiting area below. Various parts of their bodies were monitored for alpha, beta and gamma radiation, and then they were sent to the showers to scrub all over with soap and hot water. On emerging, they were monitored again. If they still produced readings, they would be sent back to the showers as many times as necessary, but on that first day Thomas only needed one shower.

Once declared safe, the men were sent through to the clean side of the decontamination centre, where they were weighed again. To his astonishment, Thomas had lost 8 pounds in two hours on Trimouille, a figure that turned out to be about average (some of the bigger blokes lost over a stone on some sorties).[12] To replenish the fluid, the parched men were given a big drink and some salt tablets. Urine samples were also taken to test for ingested radiation.

Re-entry sorties continued throughout the day, often with hair-raising results. One helicopter conducting an aerial survey became contaminated when it flew through a cloud of black smoke over Trimouille. A rocket recovery party sent to the south end of the island to look for rockets fired through the mushroom cloud returned to find that their hands were contaminated despite the use of gloves. Luckily for them, a second shower reduced the readings to zero. Of the dozens of rockets fired, only four were found on D-Day (later on, seven more turned up). Then, at the end of the day, the health ship received a scare when the motor pinnaces came alongside and the boat crews came aboard. As the sailors stripped off their protective clothing and prepared for decontamination, the background readings on deck suddenly skyrocketed by a factor of 500.[13] Wondering if the device was faulty, the scientists checked a nearby gamma meter, which showed that readings had increased from normal background to 1 to 2 milliroentgens per hour.[14] Growing concerned, the boffins checked the sailors all over, but found no localised contamination. In fact, the contamination was spreading all over the ship. It soon became clear that a change of wind had enveloped the *Tracker* in a cloud of radioactive fallout, probably from the spinifex fires on Trimouille. Lieutenant Commander RL Caple, the ship's commanding officer, gave orders to depart the area with all despatch, and the ship soon steamed clear, but some residual contamination remained overnight.

By the end of D-Day, a picture of the islands was beginning to develop, and it was not very pretty. 'The general situation is that the whole of Trimouille, Alpha Island, North West Island and all islands between must be considered dirty for purposes of re-entry', reported Lieutenant Colonel Walkling. 'Hermite is almost certainly clean and priority will be given tomorrow to confirmation of this over as large an area as possible so that clean operations can begin ...'[15]

The following day, bad weather limited activity to a survey of the bottom half of Hermite, and the *Tracker* was contaminated again. This time, the health ship wandered into a patch of radioactive seawater, causing a sudden rise in radiation levels in the main water intake. The distillers and one engine were shut down immediately, but not before the saltwater circulation system had become contaminated. It was half an hour before the *Tracker* steamed clear.

Over on the *Campania*, Admiral Torlesse was unhappy with how things were progressing. Clearly, he had been right to worry about the radiological safety of the thousands of men under his command. Torlesse and Penney were due to fly to England in a few days to make their reports and pose for the press, but the admiral did not feel that he could in good conscience abandon the Task Force. After sharing his concerns with Penney, he sent a signal to London:

> Contamination over the greater part of Trimouille and northern half of the lagoon is extensive and severe. Limited experience so far indicates that large-scale recovery of records and examination of test equipment on Trimouille will involve much contamination of personnel and boats and possibly some very responsible decisions. We are not dealing with exactly calculable risks. In circumstances and in view of explicit responsibility of the Naval Commander for safety, I could not advise my leaving Monte Bello with Penney on D+5 Day, or the absence of at least fourteen days which this journey would entail. Dr Penney concurs.[16]

After some debate among the bigwigs in London, Torlesse was given permission to remain with the Task Force; Commander Derek Willan, captain of HMS *Narvik*, went back to London in his place.

•

While the Royal Navy Task Force continued to operate on Item King or IK time (GMT + 0930) in the Montebellos, RAAF units on the mainland were still using How or H time (GMT + 0800), adding an unnecessary element of confusion to proceedings. This bizarre arrangement was another symptom of the decision to separate the air-sampling programme from the main operation in the islands. Given the importance of clear communication while planning and executing something as dangerous as an atomic test, it was never repeated on any subsequent trials.

For Group Captain Geoff Hartnell, 82 Wing Detachment Commander and Base Commander Broome, D-Day began early in the morning with orders to stand by for operations from HMS *Campania*. Then: nothing. The control room did not hear anything else until news of the blast was broadcast on the ABC. The airmen could only shake their heads at the lack of communication from the *Campania*.

Expecting orders to go up at any moment, Group Captain Hartnell and his staff used the most recent wind data to devise a comprehensive search pattern with three aircraft intercepting the cloud and two more conducting a sweep downwind of the Montebellos. The aircrews were alerted and brought to readiness. Then, at 1100 H, the detachment received a signal advising that a search would not be required until approximately 2000 H, and further advising that the cloud had topped out at a height of 10,000 to 12,000 feet.

This was not what Hartnell was expecting to hear. Throughout the build-up, he had been working on the assumption that the air-sampling sorties would be conducted between 15,000 and 25,000 feet. His airmen had made no wind-finding sorties at all below that height. So while most of the aircrews were stood down, one Lincoln was sent up to check the wind south of Broome.

The aircraft returned seven hours later, having discovered an alarming amount of wind shear: at 12,000 feet, the winds were westerly, but, down at 10,000 feet, they swung right around to a southerly. 'This meant that the cloud we would be searching for would have been subjected to both westerly and southerly winds for unknown periods', noted Hartnell.[17] The original plan was scrapped, and the Detachment Commander and his staff came up with a new search pattern, factoring in both winds. 'This left a gap in the centre but it was felt that if the two search area [sic] gave negative results it provided an obvious or fairly certain area for the second attempt.'[18]

Hartnell's detachment finally received orders from the *Campania* at 2115 H, asking them to begin searching for the cloud at 2000 H – 75 minutes earlier! The coded signal, which had originally been sent at 1637 H, had taken almost five hours to reach Broome in an intelligible form. 'It is not very nice to have to blame the ship but undoubtedly this is where the fault lay', reported Hartnell. 'In the first place the cypher would not crack, in the second place the operator in the ship was atrocious. Thus the signal was received, and the ship requested to repeat back many times. In the end there were about four old and experienced operators at BROOME, both service and civil trying to take down the message. Eventually it was proved conclusively that the signal itself was wrong and so the whole thing had to be referred back to the originator.'[19] Luckily, the aircrews had all remained at the campsite rather than wandering off around town. All five aircraft were in the air a little over an hour later, with Group Captain Hartnell leading the way in Lincoln A73-52.

Flying Officer ED McHardie, a 34-year-old ex-soldier from Brisbane, Queensland, was the captain of Lincoln A73-41. 'Prior to the flight we had not been given any specific instructions about flying through radioactive areas, nor had the effects of radioactivity been discussed. We were not told not to eat or smoke during the flight nor were we issued with dosimeters or film badges. I do not recall ever having seen a dosimeter, or film badge …'[20] It was night, so the navigators used the stars and the dead-reckoning computer to navigate. On reaching the search area, the aircraft split up. 'Each aircraft was given a separate sector to fly. The sector was covered by flying a straight course for a nominated distance then turning at [a] right angle for a shorter distance then turning another ninety degrees to parallel the first course and so on.'[21]

Each Lincoln had been fitted with two canisters under each wing to collect radioactive air samples. In the tail of the aircraft, the signallers were operating beta-gamma monitors that were supposed to tell them when they were in the cloud. Warrant Officer Ray Turner was a signaller in Lincoln A73-51, which flew two separate air-sampling sorties out of Broome. 'It is fair to say that we didn't really know what was going on. The whole thing was "hush hush" and we really were not given a serious briefing about what we were all about. My job on those two flights was to be the radio operator and meter monitorer [sic] and in my task of monitoring that meter I was assisted by a second wireless operator who was also performing that task. At no time during those flights did I notice the needle flicker on the meter. Prior to the flight I recall being told how to operate the meter, I was told how to switch it on and take readings but, as I indicated earlier, no readings were recorded.'[22]

Sergeant William Bovill was one of the navigators in Turner's aircraft. 'We were told that that device was there to detect radioactivity and when we detected radioactivity we would locate the cloud. Tube was supposed to light up when radiation was detected. However, the equipment simply did not work.'[23]

Turner and Bovill were right. The British scientist in charge of the operation, Hubert Gale, admitted that the monitors did not work properly in his 1985 statement to the Royal Commission. 'I cannot recall the reason for this, but I believe it was something to do with a deficiency in the internal battery supplies', he wrote.[24]

Whatever the cause for the stuff-up, it meant that no one realised they had entered the cloud, when, in fact, all five Lincolns had. Since the aircraft were flying at 10,000 feet, the aircrews were not on oxygen. They were breathing in the radioactive air that permeated the unpressurised aircraft. Over the course of the eight-hour-long flights, they drank water from canteens and ate in-flight rations, further exposing themselves to the risk of ingestion. The crews then returned to Broome early the next morning in a dejected state, thinking they had failed to locate the cloud.

Leading Aircraftman Colin Bird, a 27-year-old engine fitter from Brisbane, Queensland, was a senior member of the ground crew. Bird was another serviceman who had been exposed repeatedly while visiting Hiroshima with the British Commonwealth Occupation Force (BCOF) in 1946 and 1947. He was now in charge of removing the filter canisters from the Lincoln bombers. 'Dressed only in shorts and a hat, I would stand on a ladder underneath the wing of the Lincoln Bomber, unbolt the cannisters from the wings, and hand them down to another RAAF ground staff member ... I did not wear any safety clothing such as gloves, face mask, or what was referred to as a "moon suit" ...

'Once removed the "filter cannisters" were placed in a military vehicle which was commanded by British scientists who were dressed in fully protective clothing, known as "moon suits". We were instructed that the reason why British scientists were wearing fully protective clothing was that they were working in dust free areas or clean rooms. As a result, they could not come in contact with the planes. When entering a dust free area or clean room, the British scientists would discard their fully protective suits, leaving it outside the clean room and this suit would then be burned.'25

The official explanation for the use of so-called moon suits by British scientists may well have been legitimate, but it was not a good look when Bird and his mates were standing around in shorts and boots. The glaring discrepancy between the levels of protection afforded boffins and servicemen would be repeated time and again throughout the atomic testing programme, leading many servicemen to believe they were seen as expendable.

About half an hour later, Gale emerged from the laboratory grinning like a Cheshire cat. The young boffin told Group Captain Hartnell that the cloud had been found after all. 'Subsequently it was found that samples of almost the same intensity had been collected by each and every aircraft and the smile on Mr Gale's face was worth a night's hard work', reported Hartnell.[26] With an abundance of riches for Gale to work with, no more sorties were required on D+1, and the tired crews were sent to bed.

Meanwhile, the ground crew had already begun servicing the contaminated aircraft. When aeroplanes fly through an atomic cloud, radioactive particles land on their skins and become lodged in the seams between panels and around the doors and windows. The power plants become particularly dirty, with particles sticking to the greasy engine parts like glue. The Lincolns were not decontaminated in any way before the ground crew began working on them, because no one knew they were contaminated. At some point or another, Gale apparently checked the aircraft for contamination. Improbably, he found them all to be clean, but since he was using one of the same devices that failed to register any radiation in the cloud, his results must be regarded as dubious at best. Ultimately, the ground crew spent hours refuelling the aircraft and servicing the engines, putting them at as much risk of exposure as the aircrew.

Over the next few days, 82 Wing Detachment was asked to conduct a number of follow-up sorties. On D+2, three aircraft conducted a low-level search at 500 feet in an area 700 miles west of Broome, and although one aircraft was forced to return to base with mechanical difficulties, all three returned with positive samples. The following day, one final search was conducted at 9000 feet in an area between Broome and the Montebellos, yielding faint readings.

During the same period, the first samples were packaged up and sent on for analysis. Two sets were sent to Darwin for forwarding on to Harwell, and another set went to Melbourne for the Radiochemical Division team at Melbourne University.

Flying Officer Owen Jones of Lincoln A73-55 was a signaller on the Melbourne flight. 'All the pads from the various planes and operations after the explosion on 3 October were collected together and packaged roughly. To the best of my recollection the pads were wrapped with paper making a large parcel of the size of a box about 3 feet in diameter. The parcel was placed in our aeroplane through the back door and no special protective cover was placed around it. We flew our Lincoln containing the parcel from Broome to Laverton in Victoria on 4 October 1952. The flying time was 9 hours 20 minutes. We wore no protective clothing being dressed in ordinary RAAF flying gear. When we arrived at Laverton it took another 2 hours before the parcel was removed because we were waiting for someone with sufficient authority to give us a discharge for it.'[27]

When Jones eventually returned home to Amberley in Queensland he handed his flying suit to his wife, who put it in with the family washing.

The 82 Wing Detachment's exposure could have been worse. The samples from all five aircraft on the D-Day sorties produced gamma readings of about 0.5 milliroentgens per hour, while the later samples were considerably weaker.[28] For an average eight-hour flight, that meant each crew member received a maximum gamma dose of about 4 milliroentgens – well below the daily working rate all personnel were permitted to receive – but there was also the significant risk of ingestion of alpha particles from all that time spent eating, drinking and smoking in a contaminated aircraft.

The RAAF would not realise it had a problem on its hands until after the next atomic test – Totem 1, the first of two tests conducted during Operation Totem at Emu Field, South Australia, in 1953 – when many of the same aircraft and aircrews spent hours flying through a visible reddish-brown dust cloud that rolled all the way across the desert from South Australia to North Queensland. Once the Lincolns entered the cloud, the radiation monitors (which were actually working this time) went right off-scale and stayed there. When Lincoln A73-47 returned to Woomera, pilot Flight Lieutenant Douglas Buchan, AFC, was so concerned about the level of contamination that he ordered ground crew not to approach the aircraft until it had been checked by British scientists. The boffins found that the sample canisters were too hot to touch for the next 12 hours, and recommended isolating A73-47 and any other contaminated aircraft on a distant part of the runway for the same length of time.

Despite the fact that Buchan and his crew were not wearing any film badges or dosimeters, the Brits somehow came up with an estimated dose of 0.3 roentgens per man – an extremely suspicious finding that just happened to equate to the exact amount each serviceman was allowed to receive.

Warrant Officer William Turner was a 30-year-old signaller in Lincoln A73-52, which turned out to be even hotter than A73-47. After the flight, his crew gathered in the lab to debrief. 'Whilst we were in this scientist's room the Geiger counter started to race and the scientist went out and checked up the passageway with some of the crew and saw several people coming down the passageway carrying one of the sample canisters from one of the aircraft.' The scientists were dressed in protective suits with thick gloves and carrying the filter on the end of a long rod. 'They were told immediately to take the canister out of the building. If I recall correctly, he screamed at them, "Get that f—g thing out of here".'[29]

Pilot Officer Andy Stapleton was the 22-year-old captain of Lincoln A73-25, flying out of Richmond, New South Wales.

Stapleton's crew spent so long flying around in the cloud that they eventually became lost somewhere over the Queensland outback. After 12 hours in the air, they landed at RAAF Williamtown near Newcastle, New South Wales, with so little fuel in the tank that two of their engines cut out before they taxied to a stop. No one at Williamtown knew what to do with them, so they were ordered to remain with their aircraft, which was cordoned off by armed guards stationed 100 yards away. Stapleton's crew was eventually flown back to Richmond for the night in a Dakota, before returning the next day to refuel their own aircraft since no one at Williamtown wanted to touch it. They were accompanied by a US Air Force sergeant who went right through the Lincoln with a Geiger counter, repeatedly exclaiming 'Oh shit!'[30] When Stapleton offered the American sergeant a lift back to Richmond, he replied, 'Christ no! That bloody machine is hot, I'm not going anywhere near it.'[31]

When Air Vice Marshal Ted Daley, Director General of Medical Services, RAAF, found out about what had happened to 82 Wing, he was ropeable. The 52-year-old medical officer had raised concerns over exposure prior to Operation Hurricane, only to be told that the hazard risk to aircrews was negligible and there was no fear of aircraft becoming contaminated. Senior officers had received the same assurances prior to the beginning of Totem. It was now clear that the British scientists had let down the RAAF in a big way. 'It is fortunate that no apparent dangerous doses have been received by RAAF personnel, but this would appear to be no fault of the British Ministry of Supply', he seethed.[32]

Finally, the RAAF recognised the importance of radiological safety guidelines and decontamination procedures. Exposed aircrews were ordered to shower for an hour, and contaminated aircraft were washed down by RAAF ground crew under the direction of British scientists. For all future tests, aircrews wore protective suits, film badges and oxygen masks, and captains were equipped with dosimeters.

After Operation Totem, the 82 Wing Lincolns returned to base at RAAF Amberley in Queensland. Eight aircraft were still contaminated to some extent or another; by far the most heavily contaminated were A73-25 (Stapleton's aircraft), A73-47 (Buchan's aircraft) and A73-52 (Turner's aircraft).[33] In each case, most of the contamination was in the power plants, where the engines and radiators got gummed up with radioactive particles. Oily or greasy sections of the airframe were also badly affected. Luckily for the aircrews, most of the interiors were relatively clean.

Under the direction of British scientists, the ground crew began decontaminating the Lincolns. 'I, along with other ground staff, were ordered to wash the planes using high pressure steam hoses', recalled Colin Bird, the engine fitter in charge of removing filters at Broome. 'This task was carried out by standing underneath the plane spraying the high-pressure steam hose upwards … Whilst standing beneath the Lincoln Bomber, spraying upwards with the hot steam hose, I would be completely saturated with the highly contaminated water which was running off the Lincoln Bomber.'[34]

For protection, Bird and his mates were given normal white overalls, which were discarded before showering at smoko, lunch and knock-off time. They also wore film badges to measure their exposure, but, according to Bird, the badges did not arrive until long after they had begun work on the Lincolns.

Colin Bird soon developed a painful condition diagnosed as 'tropical ear'.[35] A foul yellow discharge ran from his ears all day every day, plus he experienced vomiting, headaches, dizziness and convulsions. Years later, a cancerous growth was detected behind his right ear, and then he was diagnosed with cancer of the throat. The cancer spread right through the right side of his neck, his right shoulder and his upper torso.

Bird underwent operations and radiation treatment and fought for compensation for years, but, in 1988, the High Court ruled that 'he would have to show that his cancer had been caused by his exposure to radioactive material' to receive compensation.[36] Since there was no difference between cancer that was caused by radiation and cancer that was not, that was basically impossible.

Colin Bird died of cancer in 1995 at the age of 70.

Despite all the hard work by Bird and his mates, four aircraft remained contaminated at the end of 1953: Lincolns A73-25, A73-47, A73-52 and A73-54.[37] The hot aircraft were towed to an isolated area of the air base, where they were roped off and painted with black crosses to indicate that they were off limits. The warnings did not stop overzealous ground crew from cannibalising them for spare parts.

In 1954, the RAAF drew up official procedures for the protection of air and ground crews, the decontamination of aircraft, and the disposal of radioactive waste, before building a specialised decontamination facility at RAAF Amberley. The No 3 Aircraft Depot (3AD) Decontamination Centre was a fenced-off compound consisting of a small brick workshop, which was divided into clean and dirty areas, and a saucer-shaped concrete hardstand big enough to accommodate one aircraft at a time. The whole thing was designed so that the toxic run-off from the decontamination process would drain into a large tank, where it could be pumped into an evaporator and reduced to a manageable quantity for disposal. The evaporator did not work properly, though, and it took months of experimentation with different additives to stop the run-off foaming up, shooting out of the exhaust stack, and covering the nearby countryside. Heavy rain also caused the underground sump to overflow.

Sergeant Noel Freeman of Cottesloe, Western Australia, was the non-commissioned officer in charge of the small team that worked on the contaminated Lincolns. 'Each aircraft was towed into the saucer area where it would be completely stripped as far as possible of all components, instruments, engine parts, etc., leaving only the bare frame of the aircraft which would then be decontaminated by high pressure steam hoses which had detergent added to the water. We would climb all over the aircraft both inside and out and attempt to clean it as thoroughly as possible and many areas needed repeated cleaning to try to bring the radioactive level down to nil reading. We regularly checked the levels of radioactivity with Geiger counters to see how effective the cleaning was.

'Everything that could be removed was removed and taken inside the workshop area and cleaned there as we had to work in a closed area as much as possible. The same cleaning process would take place, i.e. the components would simply be blasted with high pressure steam and hot water hoses on the floor to get them clean and the water would be drained off into the collection well ...

'The protective clothing we were supplied with consisted of ordinary work overalls which we kept buttoned, cotton gloves, gumboots, and berets for our heads. We were initially issued with rubber gloves which we discarded shortly after since it was impossible to work in them for any length of time since they were so hot and badly affected our hands.'[38]

Sergeant Freeman and his men spent about 12 months working on the four Lincolns from 1957 to 1958. Once the airframes were finally declared free of radioactivity, they were hauled off to the tip and buried or burned (some blokes reckon they were used for target practice). Any parts that could not be decontaminated were chopped up and cemented into 44-gallon drums. Used overalls and other dirty clothes were also thrown in. The run-off – a toxic mixture of radioactive water and industrial-strength chemicals – was distilled in the evaporator, sealed in 44-gallon drums, and loaded onto a Lincoln bomber that took off and flew out over the Coral Sea. At a designated point off the Sunshine Coast, north of Brisbane, the crew opened the bomb bay doors and dumped the radioactive waste in the ocean. Drums of solid waste sank straight to the bottom, while drums of toxic sludge either burst on impact or floated on the surface until the tail gunner blew them to pieces to destroy the evidence.

This disgraceful practice was the official RAAF procedure for disposing of radioactive waste, as outlined in Air Board Orders A125/1954.[39]

•

Corporal Rex Raph was the non-commissioned officer in charge of communications at Onslow Airfield during Operation Hurricane.

'I recall that I was in my tent on the historic morning and waiting for transport to the airfield to commence duty at 8AM', he later wrote. 'First there was a rumbling sound and then the huge mushroom cloud was boiling its way up into the sky.

'On arriving at the airfield I noticed a bit of a scramble as at least two of the C47's were about to take off. I then went into the radio office expecting to be called by the two airborne aircraft. Next thing Sqn Ldr [sic] Britt was at my side and told me to broadcast an order over the radio advising the aircraft to return to base immediately. One acknowledged after a couple of calls and did return while the other either did not hear or ignored the order to return to base for some time. We could see from the verandah of the radio office that this aircraft was heading directly towards the atomic cloud. Finally my broadcast order was acknowledged and the aircraft did return and land.'[40]

The only two flights entered in 86 Wing Detachment's flight logs for D-Day were described as 'air tests' to ensure that the aircraft were serviceable for D+1.[41]

This was not the first time that the insubordinate Dakota crews had caused trouble for Squadron Leader Leo Britt, Base Commander Onslow. They had also argued with him over the control of aircraft and set off an explosion on Onslow Beach as a practical joke. The poor bloke probably couldn't wait to see the back of them.

At 0600 H the following day, Flight Lieutenant Clarence Donnelly and Flight Lieutenant Ron Grace took off in the two specially fitted Dakotas and headed for Broome at the low altitude of 500 feet to check for ground-level contamination along the North West Coast. A third Dakota, equipped with a four-wheel drive, ramps and Geiger counters, waited on the airstrip in case a follow-up survey was required.

Doug Peirson, leader of the Radiological Survey Division team, was sitting in the tail of the aircraft flown by Flight Lieutenant Donnelly, while his off-sider, Frank Hale, was in the other aircraft with Flight Lieutenant Grace. The two boffins were using sensitive radiac devices designed for geological prospecting, but calibrated to look for fallout on the mainland. Both aircraft were unpressurised and no one was wearing protective clothing, film badges or dosimeters. Peirson did not think they needed anything like that. 'No special preparations or precautions had been made with a view to entering the cloud', he later admitted. 'Had I considered that there were any hazards to myself or the air crew or the ground crew, I should have taken steps to protect them.'[42]

The flights were bumpy and uncomfortable. Dakotas were revered for their handling ability, but, at 500 feet, the warm updraughts off the rugged mountain ranges caused so much turbulence that the pilots battled to stay within 50 feet of the required altitude. Down the back of the aircraft, the boffins were forced to lie on the floor to operate their devices, the airframes rattling and shuddering all around them.

After four and a half hours of difficult flying, the Dakotas landed at Broome and the crews disembarked with some relief. Both aircraft had detected a slight rise in radiation compared to the normal background level, but Peirson considered this to be within the normal range of variation. 'The increase which we measured on the flight from Onslow to Broome was about 25% of the natural background radiation at Onslow, which made the new level at Onslow roughly the same as the pre-firing level at Broome', he explained.[43] Since the increase was detectable before, during and after the flight, Peirson attributed the rise to 'an increase in the general atmospheric radioactivity arising from the explosion' as distinct from fallout on the ground.[44] Despite the measurable increase, he decided that no ground survey was necessary.

Over on the *Campania*, Bill Penney and Admiral Torlesse were happy with Peirson's results, but, since the top portion of the cloud had last been seen heading towards the mainland, they asked him to have a look for it on the way back. This time, the two Dakotas took off at 1400 H and skirted the coastline, Donnelly's aircraft at 8000 feet, Grace's at 10,000 feet.

Flight Lieutenant Grace was flying Dakota A65-99. 'The return flight from Broome to Onslow was planned direct over the sea', he wrote in response to a 1982 Department of Health survey. 'At a point approximately halfway, Mr Hale reported high levels of Radiation being recorded by his instruments and declared that we were in the Atomic Cloud.'[45] The Dakota had flown straight into an invisible concentration of radioactive particles over the coast near Port Hedland, sending the ultra-sensitive radiac device right off the scale.

Moments earlier, the two pilots had been joking over the radio about who had the hottest aircraft, but now things were serious. Instead of flying away, Grace orbited in the cloud to obtain more data, while Hale switched over to a higher-range hand-held device to monitor the radiation levels.

As soon as the aircraft climbed above 10,000 feet, Hale began to experience difficulty breathing. According to Grace: 'I decided to descend, since the aircraft was not fitted with oxygen and Mr Hale was showing signs of distress. We were still in the cloud. During the descent we flew into clear air at approximately 8,000' and nothing more was recorded. Immediately after landing the aircraft was checked with a Geiger Counter and high readings were obtained from the leading edges of the main-planes and the tail-planes. The highest readings, however, were from the propeller blades.'[46]

The airmen were so unconcerned about these readings that they immediately headed off to the Texas Canteen at the Western Command Transit Camp to celebrate a job well done. '[Not] in all our conversation with Mr Hale and his fellow Physicist, who flew in the other aircraft, was there at any time any suggestion that we could be exposed to any risk', Grace wrote in a follow-up. 'Perhaps they didn't know either!'[47]

A few months later, Grace finished his two-year stint on active reserve and skipped his exit medical to go to the cricket. 'During a visit to a Dermatologist in Sydney during 1959/60 to have various growths removed from my nose, ears, etc., including a dark patch on one cheek, the doctor questioned me as to what I had been exposed to. We speculated on many things but at no stage did either of us think of Atomic Radiation.'[48] Grace lived for a long time after that, dying in 2008 at the age of 89, but suffered from a number of unusual skin cancers for which he suspected exposure was to blame.

While the airmen headed off to the Texas Canteen, Peirson and Hale sat down in the tail of one of the aircraft to go over their findings. 'We were both conscious that one of the planes had been slightly contaminated, but we considered that this was way below any significant radiological level', recalled Peirson. 'No steps were taken to decontaminate the aircrew, ground crew or the aircraft.'[49] By the time the scientists finished, it was already dark. They returned first thing the next morning to check the aircraft again. To their surprise, all signs of contamination had disappeared overnight, and the aircraft's radiation levels had returned to pre-operational levels. The contamination's rapid decay puzzled Peirson for years. His best guess was that the radioactive particles consisted mostly of sodium-24, a short-lived fission product, but he did not have the right equipment to test for that at the time.

According to Peirson's report, the gamma readings from the atomic cloud near Port Hedland were estimated to be 'greater than 50 times the gamma component of ground level background activity at Onslow'.[50] That sounds like a lot, but Peirson dismissed it as 'a minute dose'.[51] According to his calculations, the maximum possible gamma dose received by the men in the aircraft was just 0.1 milliroentgens – or one-thousandth the gamma component of the normal working rate.[52]

In the days after the Dakota flights, the atomic cloud continued to drift across the mainland. On the night of 5/6 September, No 10 (General Reconnaissance) Squadron RAAF obtained radioactive air samples near Townsville, Queensland, despite receiving little to no useful information from the *Campania*. Three days later, the Royal New Zealand Air Force picked up weak samples over the ocean between Norfolk Island and Fiji.[53] Hubert Gale's Queensland-based colleague, RN Crooks, also collected radioactive rainwater samples 200 times higher than normal background levels in Rockhampton and ten times higher in Brisbane.[54]

Somehow, despite incontrovertible evidence of an atomic cloud drifting across the continent and radioactive rain falling along the east coast, Peirson concluded that the coastal-monitoring survey 'showed no deposited activity' on the mainland.[55]

In February 1985, the ageing Doug Peirson appeared before the Royal Commission, and found himself being grilled by hostile Australian lawyers. Even the President of the Royal Commission, former Labor senator 'Diamond' Jim McClelland, expressed disbelief about his findings:

> Dr Peirson, you say in your statement: 'my brief was to determine whether fallout had fallen on the Australian mainland following the Monte Bello explosion at sea' ...? — Right, yes.
>
> Now, to determine that question you surveyed a minute portion of the Australian coast once and once only some 22 hours after the explosion? — That is right.
>
> Do you seriously assert that equipped you to answer the question posed in your brief? — So it was considered at the time.
>
> Do you still consider it? — Yes, in the circumstances of what I know of what happened to the clouds, yes.[56]

That was rubbish. The samples from Queensland proved that there was fallout on the mainland, albeit in small amounts. Given the low readings that Crooks had found, Peirson could have reasonably argued that the fallout was 'negligible' or 'minimal', but that is not what he said. Instead, he stuck to his guns and argued that there was 'no deposited activity' on the mainland.

The fact of the matter is that Peirson produced the results he was expected to produce. His report gave Operation Hurricane the tick of approval, and allowed Winston Churchill and Robert Menzies to assure the Australian public that the test was safe, paving the way for the UK Government to continue conducting atomic tests in Australia.

•

Back in the Montebellos, the re-entry programme was in full swing.

Over the course of Phase Three, Task Force personnel conducted a total of 940 man-sorties into the contaminated area. While it was initially hoped that most of the work could be done under the normal working rate, the health escorts soon realised it was impossible to get anything done without authorising the lower integrated dose of 15 rep or 3 roentgens per man. Adding to the difficulties for the Radiological Hazard Division, the beta badges turned out to be useless. Worn on the inside of the protective suit, they were affected by perspiration, and sometimes recorded gamma radiation as beta radiation. In the end, all the results were thrown out, and monitoring stations on the islands were used to provide a rough estimate of beta doses received by personnel. For all intents and purposes, a gamma dose of 3 roentgens was now the maximum permissible dose.

According to the Radiological Hazard team in charge of decontamination, 82 per cent of re-entrants were declared clean after one shower. Of the remaining 18 per cent, most men experienced contamination of the head, face and neck, making it clear that the bush hats and handkerchiefs were not up to the job. After the second shower, another 5 per cent were declared clean. The last 13 per cent were sent to the *Tracker*'s sick berth attendants for one or more chemical treatments. After all that, eight men still had 'slight contamination remaining' at the end of the operation.[57]

Thomas Wilson was a young sapper in 71 Field Squadron RE who was based on the *Narvik*. In 1985, he told the Royal Commission that he and a few mates had been ordered to collect samples from the islands. 'I remember we left the HMS *Narvik* in a small landing craft dressed in an overall type of uniform and a jungle green hat. Only when we reached the islands we were told to wear an old fashioned gas mask.'[58]

The sappers were also given some Geiger counters, which they had never seen before and did not know how to use. 'It was a waste of time', Wilson wrote.

The men drove around the island in an open-topped Land Rover, inspecting damage and picking up materials and foodstuffs for the scientists to examine. 'We found we had to remove the gas masks time and again as the heat was that bad it was very hard to breathe. Also we could not see because the condensation impaired our vision. My hat blew off and I was not allowed to pick it up. This left me bare headed for the rest of the tour. Also we got covered in sand and grit which was thrown up by the wheels of the Land Rover.'

Wilson and his mates were told that they were contaminated when they returned to the *Tracker*, but were not given their readings. After his first shower, Wilson was sent back to scrub with Teepol (an industrial-strength detergent), and when that didn't work he was sent to a sick berth attendant who scrubbed the contaminated areas with chemical paste and a nailbrush. When *that* didn't work, the Naval rating rubbed on more chemicals with cotton wool. 'Then I was tested again and it was found I was still contaminated. I had to go through the process again. After the decontamination I was told if ever I took ill I was to tell my doctors that I had been exposed to radiation. It was also recorded in my army pay book.'

At about the same time, the *Tracker* received two very important visitors: the Chief Superintendent of High Explosive Research and the Task Force Commander. William Penney was due to fly out on D+6, and, before he left, he and Admiral Torlesse wanted to personally inspect the effects of the blast. To the surprise and admiration of all on board, the two highest-ranking men in the Task Force joined ship on D+5, suited up, grabbed their gas masks, and boarded a boat for Trimouille, where they accompanied a shore party with orders to carry out a detailed contamination survey of T2 at Cocoa Beach, immediately opposite Ground Zero.[59]

On the basis of this experience, Penney concluded that the improvised protective suits and canopied motor pinnaces were 'unsuitable', being too hot and uncomfortable to work in. 'Neither were specially designed but were used for economy', he noted.[60] This was a startling admission, which, regrettably, was not really picked up during the Royal Commission.

Later that afternoon, a freshly scrubbed Penney sat down and met with his division heads and team leaders to hear their preliminary reports. By that time, the scientists had formed some tentative conclusions about the effectiveness of the Hurricane device and the effects of the blast. Thanks to Penney's famous toothpaste tubes (and various other measuring devices), the yield had been calculated at 20 kilotons, an estimate later revised to 25 kilotons.[61] That meant the Hurricane device was twice as powerful as the uranium bomb dropped on Hiroshima, and slightly bigger than the plutonium bomb dropped on Nagasaki. Despite the respectable result, Penney was a little disappointed: he had been hoping for a 30-kiloton yield, but the weapon was not as efficient as he would have liked.[62] Clearly, there was room for improvement.

The issue of radiation was also discussed. The fallout from Operation Hurricane had been far worse than predicted, spreading contamination all over the northern half of the group, including Alpha, North West and the top end of Trimouille. The ship-borne blast proved particularly deadly compared to an equivalent-sized airdrop, with Penney's boffins estimating that the spray from the water column and the liquefied remains of the *Plym* doubled or even quadrupled the size of the area that received a lethal gamma dose of 400 roentgens (depending on factors like the degree of protection afforded by hills and buildings).[63] From a civil defence point of view, the Hurricane blast was a nightmare.

It wasn't much fun in defence terms either. As Professor Leslie Martin, Australia's Defence Scientific Adviser, reported: 'The danger from radiation is a product of time and intensity and the accepted critical limits are such that it would be possible for a body of men to make their way through an area soon after it has been bombed. For example, at 100 R (R is the measure of radiation) 20% of men would be fairly sick but would get through with perhaps 4% or 5% killed.'[64]

It is not clear whether Professor Martin expected the sick hypothetical troops to survive in the long run, or just for long enough to do their job on the battlefield.

Later that night, there was a big party in the wardroom to see off Penney and a number of other senior staffers. 'Much liquor was drunk and many noisy and uncensorable songs were sung', admitted JJ McEnhill:

Judging by the nature and substance of some of the songs the casual listener might have gleaned the impression that perhaps the *Campania* was not a wholly popular ship with many of the men present. On closer inspection, however, he might have noted with confusion that even Naval officers of the ship joined in these raucous denouncements of the *Campania* and all her appendages. It was all a mere Wardroom frolic with perhaps a germ of real feeling prompting men to relieve themselves of some of the frustration they had felt in being cooped up for many weeks in this ship, at this remote site ...[65]

The party went on long into the night.

The following day, Penney and his chums left the Montebellos in HMAS *Hawkesbury*, taking the spare core along with them. In Onslow, Penney had his revenge on the local press men. When the frigate secured alongside the jetty, a reporter and a photographer appeared out of nowhere, clambering over crates and trucks in an effort to find the great man, but to no avail. Eventually, they gave up and returned to the pub. Later on, the press men learnt that an amused Penney had spent the time sunbathing in shorts and reading magazines up on the bridge.

Penney left Onslow in one of two RAF Hastings departing the following day, arriving at RAF Lyneham in Wiltshire, England, to a hero's welcome. This time, there was no escaping the press: Penney was mobbed. After the triumph of Operation Hurricane, the rumpled boffin with the tussled hair, round glasses and gap-toothed grin was as big a celebrity as anyone in England, except perhaps the Queen. Typically, he offered only a brief, self-effacing statement:

> The atomic test was most successful, but you will understand that I can say no more about it until I have made my report to the Government. When I have done that, I shall have a holiday. I cannot give you any details, I am afraid, about the explosion. I am very sorry but that is a closed book.[66]

Penney's VIP chums, who had returned to the Australian mainland about the same time as him, also made glowing statements to the press. On arrival in Perth, Dr Solandt proclaimed the test 'a great success' and claimed that 'everything had gone according to plan'.[67] The Canadian physiologist showed off a traditional Aboriginal 'nulla-nulla' (club) and spear presented to him by Constable Bill Connelly, Onslow's policeman. 'These will be the weapons with which the war after the next one will be fought', he joked, somewhat unfortunately.

True to form, Professor Titterton, that great cheerleader of the atomic age, described the test as 'beautifully executed'.[68] When asked if the explosion had altered the physical appearance of the islands in any way, he smirked, 'A few of the jagged points have been rounded off here and there, but the place looks very much the same as before.'[69]

Not to be outdone, Alan Butement made the bizarre and patently false claim that no animals were harmed in the test. 'One might have expected to see some dead fish floating around on the water or the bodies of other creatures on the land', he said. 'I didn't see any and I don't think any were reported.'[70]

Later on, during the Royal Commission, many, many witnesses reported seeing dead and dying fish in the Montebellos. 'I remember that after the explosion large shoals of dead fish were floating on the water around our anchorage off the atoll. The seagulls were going berserk', recalled Vince Douglas, boatswain's yeoman on the *Hawkesbury*.[71] 'When we went in to the shore on the pinnace I saw any number of dead fish and birds', said Sidney Fletcher, a Reservist on the *Campania* who crewed re-entry boats on D-Day and throughout Phase Three.[72] On the day after the blast, Maurice Pollard, quartermaster on the *Campania*, was ordered to report to the *Tracker* to get dressed in protective gear and join a sample collection party. 'We then proceeded to the outer perimeter of the explosion in 32 ft motorboats. There were four motorboats involved with three crewmembers in each. Our job was to pick up dead fish, birds and other items for examination by the Scientists.'[73]

Apparently, everyone *but* Butement saw dead fish.

Even the normally sensible Professor Martin got carried away with excitement. The silver-haired professor told reporters that the *Campania* was anchored 12 miles from Ground Zero (an important piece of intelligence from which the Soviets could estimate the maximum size of the blast), and enthusiastically re-enacted the countdown, his thrilling account climaxing with the detonation, when he said the deck of the *Campania* 'lit up with a brilliance many times greater than the brilliance of the Indian Ocean sunshine'.[74] After that, everyone breathed 'a great sigh of relief', especially the British scientists who had so much riding on the outcome. 'Most of them laughed it off with an expression of thankfulness that it wasn't a dud', chuckled Martin.

London was infuriated by Professor Martin's indiscretions. Not only had he let an atomic secret slip, he had also revealed that Penney and his boffins were not infallible – an unforgivable offence that could not go unpunished. On 18 October, the UK High Commission sent Prime Minister Menzies's office a sternly worded note, reminding the Australians that 'it has been emphasised throughout that it is of the first importance that nothing should be said about the explosion from official sources in advance of the release of the full story which would need to be carefully drawn up on the basis of Dr Penney's detailed factual report and in the light of all the relevant security considerations'.[75]

Naturally, once the carefully vetted story was released, it was extremely flattering to all concerned, with no reference to arguments between the services, personality clashes, drownings, collisions, accidental exposure of ships and aircraft, death and destruction of wildlife, or atomic clouds scudding across the continent.

At 4.30 p.m. GMT on Thursday 23 October, UK Prime Minister Winston Churchill addressed the House of Commons, revealing for the first time that the weapon had been detonated in the hold of the *Plym*:

Thousands of tons of water and of mud and rock from the sea bottom were thrown many thousands of feet into the air and a high tidal wave was caused. The effects of blast and radioactive contamination extended over a wide area. HMS *Plym* was vaporised except for some red hot fragments which were scattered over one of the islands and started fires in the dry vegetation ...

The explosion caused no casualties to the personnel of the expedition.

No animals were used in the test. Apart from some local rats which were killed, no mammals were seen in the affected area and such birds as there were had mostly been frightened away by the earlier preparations.[76]

When Penney addressed the nation on the radio a couple of weeks later, he explained in characteristically simple terms various mysteries that had baffled observers on the mainland, such as the Z-shaped cloud and the double bang. Like Churchill and Menzies, he also emphasised that the weapon would be one of peace: 'The energy and enthusiasm which have gone into the making of the new weapon stemmed from the sober hope that it would bring us nearer the day when war is universally seen to be unthinkable.'[77]

Press coverage was uniformly glowing, with some experts speculating that the Brits had leapt ahead of the Americans and were now leading the field in the nuclear arms race. But that was not the case. On 1 November 1952, just four weeks after the Hurricane test, the Americans detonated the world's first hydrogen bomb at Eniwetok Atoll in the Marshall Islands. Ivy Mike had an astonishing yield of 10.4 megatons – more than 400 times the size of the Hurricane device. This incredible leap in power and efficiency was made possible by the process of nuclear fusion, in which atoms are combined, as distinct from fission, in which atoms are split – a process which uses an atom bomb as a trigger for a much larger weapon powered by hydrogen isotopes.

For Penney and his colleagues at HER, the news must have been deflating. Ivy Mike made the Hurricane device look like a Guy Fawkes cracker by comparison. Although the UK Government did not officially make the decision to develop the hydrogen bomb for some time, Ivy Mike made it inevitable. Britain could not go back to the children's table now that it had just reclaimed its rightful place with the grown-ups. For poor old Penney, it was back to the drawing board.

•

Perhaps it was just superstitious sailor talk, but many in the Task Force could not help but notice the run of bad luck since Penney's departure.

It began almost immediately, on D+7 – one day after Penney sailed off on the *Hawkesbury*. That morning, a survey party landed at Gladstone Beach and tried to drive to nearby T4. They had gone as far as the abandoned hockey pitch, where the dose rate was 750 milliroentgens per hour, when the Land Rover broke down. The men were forced to abandon the vehicle and hotfoot it back to the beach. The following day, a second team tried and failed to restart the Land Rover, then became heavily contaminated while wading through a field of radioactive spinifex. The spiky grass repeatedly pierced their clothing, and they all required multiple showers and chemical treatments back on the *Tracker*. A big storm hit the islands immediately after that, preventing boat work for four days and causing all manner of damage: one LCA sank at its moorings, an echo-sounding boat was driven onto the rocks, and a 35-foot pinnace was plucked away and never seen again.

By this time, the spread of radioactive seawater had resulted in patches of activity up to 25 milliroentgens per hour along the high-water marks of previously clean islands. 'Slight activity was also deposited on the hulls of all the ships in the force: the area of slightly contaminated water was in fact so vast that, short of abandoning the operation, it would have been impossible to keep clear of it', reported Lieutenant Colonel Walkling. 'It was not however in any way significant as a health hazard and drinking water was never found to contain the slightest degree of contamination', he insisted.[78]

The most affected ship by far was the *Tracker*, which was required to steam in and out of the contaminated Parting Pool almost every day. The standard operating procedure was to shut the distillers while in the contaminated area and then retreat to the vicinity of the *Campania* each night to flush out the LST's systems and distil clean drinking water. This did not stop contamination from building up in the circulation system, the weed trap and the bilges, leading to elevated readings in the engine room.[79]

Chief Petty Officer Stoker Mechanic Stanley Swainston was one of the *Tracker*'s senior engineering ratings. 'During the running of the ship whilst at sea, and in harbour, my duties were to transfer oil fuel from one tank to another and to flood tanks that were empty to keep an even keel as much as possible (in other words to act as ballast)', he told the Royal Commission. 'When more fuel was taken aboard, I had to pump out the salt water which had been used to flood the tanks ...

'Just before we were ready to sail it was discovered that the condensers in the engine room were contaminated by radioactive seawater. (We were told that this was nothing to worry about!) During our journey back to England I was taken ill, with extensive vomiting, and it was found necessary to put me ashore at Colombo and taken to hospital.'[80]

After returning to England, Swainston suffered a relapse and was hospitalised again. 'On neither of my stays in hospital was I told what my illness was nor what it was due to. I retired from the Navy in '54, supposedly 100% fit, but I can honestly say I was never as well as I had been previous to this experience.'[81]

Shortly after Swainston retired, doctors discovered a patch on his lung. He had also become impotent. Swainston suspected that both conditions were caused by the radioactivity in the *Tracker*'s engine room.

One effect of the heavy weather in mid-October was to flush out much of the contaminated water in the lagoon. The radioactive seawater had lingered far longer than expected, despite the normal working of the tides. It now dispersed throughout the Indian Ocean, flowing south on the Leeuwin Current past major ports like Carnarvon, Geraldton and Fremantle. Along the way, radioactive particles settled on the seabed, burrowed in seaweed, and entered the food chain through ingestion by fish and shellfish.

•

During the same period, 180 Engineer Regiment was conducting a clean-up operation on Hermite Island when disaster struck.

On D+10, Sapper Frank Furlong was clearing rubbish when his bulldozer turned over on him, pinning him to the ground. Cries went up immediately, work halted, and men came running in from everywhere to try and free him, but it was no use: Furlong was dead.

Furlong's mates were gutted, his bosses saddened and frustrated. The Royal Engineers had been in the Montebello Islands for six months, and by all reports had done an impeccable job. They had survived storms, heatstroke, an atomic explosion and a radioactive mushroom cloud without a major incident, only to lose one of their own in a freak mishap just weeks before departure.

The Army's attempts to contact Furlong's family failed, and no one could figure out what to do with his remains. Should the poor fellow be buried at sea, since the operation was under Naval command? Should he be taken to the mainland and buried in Onslow? Or should he be returned to the UK and buried on home soil? In the end, he was laid to rest in a lonely grave on Hermite, not far from where he died. It was a decision made for the sake of expediency, and it did not impress his mates, who responded by building the best grave they could. It was lined with Oregon timber, reinforced with corrugated iron, and topped with a concrete slab 8 feet long by 4 feet wide and 6 inches thick. On the solid rock headstone was a brass plaque with the inscription: '1884763 Sapper F Furlong, Royal Engineers, 13 Oct 1952'.

Strangely enough, it would not be Furlong's final resting place. Thirteen months later, during a follow-up radiation survey carried out by HMA Ships *Karangi*, *Fremantle* and *Junee*, Furlong's remains would be exhumed by two undertakers from Perth and re-interred in Onslow Cemetery.

To this day, Sapper Furlong's new grave is visited by nuclear veterans and their families as they travel through the North West.

•

With cyclone season about to begin, the Task Force was under pressure to wrap up operations and depart the islands by the end of October.

From D+13, recovery operations wound down and salvage operations commenced. Sailors and marines went ashore each day to bring back whatever equipment was still intact, while sappers dismantled structures they had painstakingly built. Those that could not be dismantled, such as concrete bunkers, were destroyed to avoid leaving valuable data for Soviet spies. Demolitions commenced on D+16, and almost ended in disaster when one of the *Campania*'s Dragonfly helicopters seemed to appear out of nowhere, inadvertently hovering right over an explosive charge moments after the fuse had been lit. 'The Commander of the *Campania* [Commander Bromley] was taking his last chance of seeing the site from the air on that day', explained McEnhill. 'The demolition party now at a safe distance waved frantically to the occupants of the helicopter, to move them off, but the Commander, knowing nothing of the advancing fuze below him, waved cheerily back.

Fortunately the pilot decided then to fly off and the explosion took place when they were at a safe distance.'[82]

With so little time available, the Task Force did not even attempt a proper clean-up. Radioactive rubbish was left strewn all over Trimouille Island. The metallic grey fallout covering the northern half of the archipelago was left untreated. On the *Tracker*, contaminated suits, gloves and boots were cemented into 44-gallon drums and dumped overboard in deep water, away from the islands. All in all, the health ship dumped 75 drums of radioactive waste off the North West Coast.[83] On the *Zeebrugge*, the large quantity of liquid waste left over from the Radiochemical Division's experiments was also sealed in 44-gallon drums. Petty Officer Graham Mabbutt, a 21-year-old rating from Devonshire, England, was in charge of winching the steel drums up from the laboratory on the tank deck and out over the side. 'There were 20 to 30 drums in all and to my certain knowledge six to eight of them were seeping badly', he told the Royal Commission. 'There was a problem in that the davit would not swing properly because it was too small and the drums would catch in the scuppers. I then had to step forward and manually shove the drum clear of the ship's side. I did this because I was in charge of the operation. I remember getting splashed over the arms and legs by the seeping liquids from these drums. I can clearly remember a scientist who was observing these operations saying when he saw me being splashed "one day you may live to regret that". This raised a laugh among the ratings present as it was taken to mean that it might affect my ability to have children.'[84]

Mabbutt later developed a nervous disorder and a skin condition – which the doctors blamed on his nervous disorder.

•

There is considerable confusion about the precise movements and activities of HMAS *Koala* during the month of October 1952, due in no small part to the mysterious disappearance of the ship's logs for that period, but what we do know is quite alarming.

The *Koala* was now under the command of Lieutenant Commander Dick Taudevin, DSC and Bar, a 35-year-old British expatriate who had been one of the youngest destroyer captains in the Second World War. According to Taudevin, the *Koala* was the last ship to leave the lagoon before the test, and the first ship to go back in after the water was declared 'clean' on 19 October.[85]

The *Koala*'s first job was to recover a six-boat trot mooring about a half a mile south of Ground Zero. For Able Seaman Sandy Brennan, a 26-year-old diver from Moonee Ponds, Victoria, and Able Seaman Bill Smith, a 25-year-old diver from Campbelltown, South Australia, that meant immersing themselves in water that until recently had been considered too dirty for boat work. Plunging in regardless, the two men attached grapnel hooks to the mooring gear, which was winched on board and stowed in the lower hold.

'Our main diving gear was shallow gear which only included a type of gas mask which was air driven by a hand pump, shorts and a woollen jumper', recalled Smith. 'The deep diving set was very heavy and cumbersome and we only had a small ladder which was made to take light weights ... our skin was very much in contact with the contaminated water and the diving gear in those days was very primitive ... with no wet suits at all ... water came into our mouth and was swallowed during the course of the dives. This was unavoidable.'[86]

On the evening of 30 October, when the Task Force was preparing for departure, the *Koala* was given another unenviable task: raising the LCA that had sunk during the storm after D-Day. This time, the divers were sent down to put lifting wires around the 8-ton landing craft, which was then lifted to the surface, stowed on the forecastle, and taken to the *Tracker* to be checked for radioactivity.

Unsurprisingly, the LCA was hot.

So hot that Lieutenant Commander Caple, captain of the *Tracker*, wanted nothing to do with it.

At this late stage of proceedings, it was far easier to pretend that the landing craft had never been salvaged than go through the rigmarole of attempting to decontaminate it. The decision was made to dump it in deep water as soon as possible.[87]

As Smith recalled, a British scientist also checked the men involved in the recovery operation and found that they too were contaminated. 'He made us bath [sic] many times (about 8 or 10) and we had to scrub ourselves well each time. He said we had no right to be in the water and that "there had been a mess-up along the line" with us being told to dive when we definitely should not have been.'[88]

The following day, Squadron Leader AD Thomas – who had led the first shore party after D-Day – was briefed about the stuff-up and ordered to check the *Koala* for radiation. The Australian airman went right through the ship, deck by deck, compartment by compartment, with a radiac device. 'I found that the boom area and the hoisting gear of the vessel were contaminated with radioactive sand, mud and seaweed and I also found that the contamination had spread because the fine weather and wind had caused the sand and mud to dry resulting in this being moved around the ship', he later wrote.[89] The sailors had walked through the radioactive mud and sand and traipsed it all around the ship. The boom area was highly contaminated, and so was the carpet in the skipper's cabin. At least one rating had managed to get his bunk dirty. Fortunately, the galley showed no signs of contamination.

Overall, Thomas was not too concerned. The highest readings he had recorded were in the milliroentgen range, so the crew's gamma dose was unlikely to be dangerous, but he was still concerned about the risk of sailors ingesting alpha particles while eating, or wiping their noses and mouths. On Lieutenant Commander Taudevin's orders, a party of ratings was detailed to decontaminate the ship under Thomas's direction. The men were dressed in protective clothing and instructed in decontamination procedures, but not given masks because Thomas did not believe there was much risk of ingestion from the decontamination process. As the Royal Navy ships departed the Montebello Islands one by one, the ratings scrubbed every inch of the *Koala* with the industrial-strength detergent Teepol. Many items that proved impossible to clean were wrapped in canvas with lumps of concrete or iron and thrown overboard. The write-off list included the moorings recovered from the lagoon and the skipper's carpet.

Sandy Brennan was one of the men in the decontamination party. 'We were issued with protective clothing for cleaning out the lower hold of the ship. But it was so hot below decks that we could not stand the heat and removed parts of our clothing while we worked ... The lower hold of the ship was scrubbed over and over again. Whether we got it properly cleaned I can't remember but doubt it as the mooring left a lot of barnicles [sic] which were very hard to remove.'[90] Brennan admitted that they were told not to remove their clothing, but did it anyway. It was just too hot.

At least one member of the ship's company received a heavy dose of radiation: the ship's cat. When Squadron Leader Thomas monitored the feline, the needle went crazy. 'I was concerned because he had probably licked himself clean and I had no way of knowing what contamination he had taken on his tongue and ingested. However I understand that he lived a long time.'[91]

The decontamination of *Koala* took 48 hours of almost nonstop work with very little sleep. When the boom defence vessel was finally declared clean, Lieutenant Commander Taudevin gave the order to weigh anchor and proceed for the mainland. The *Koala* was one of the very last ships to leave the islands at the end of Phase Three.

•

Twelve months later, Lieutenant Commander Taudevin returned to the Montebellos as captain of the *Karangi*, along with many of the same ratings, for a radiation survey with the *Fremantle* and the *Junee*. While British scientists surveyed the islands, the *Karangi*'s company surveyed the lagoon and the surrounding waters. They began by monitoring the remaining fourth-class mooring buoy in Bunsen Channel, which was still reading 2 milliroentgens per hour. That mooring buoy was used by all three ships throughout the week and recovered by the *Karangi* at the end of the survey. The sandy mooring components dredged up from the bottom showed readings of 8 milliroentgens; 'vigorous hosing' reduced the intensity by half. The components were then 'scraped' until the readings were reduced to the 'acceptable' level of 0.1 milliroentgens.[92]

Next, the *Karangi* carried out a slow sweep over Ground Zero, taking soundings of the bomb crater. Since the ageing boom defence vessel was not equipped with echo-sounding facilities, soundings were taken the old-fashioned way, with hand-leads lowered either side of the forecastle. When the sandy leads were hauled on board, they turned up readings of 1 milliroentgen per hour on average. At the end of the first day, the ship's company caught a 12-foot shark, portions of which were given to the scientists for testing, and 50 pounds of smaller fisher with a seine net and line. The fish showed readings of up to 2 milliroentgens per hour, but after they were washed all traces of radioactivity disappeared and the men were allowed to eat them. The ship's company kept fishing all through the week. 'Most excellent fishing results were obtained in the Islands, many hundredweight of fish being taken – sufficient to include regularly in the menu for a fortnight, still leaving a balance for everyone to take home on return', reported Taudevin.[93] So the men's families ate the fish too.

Over the course of a week, the *Karangi* recovered 80 tons of moorings from the lagoon and Parting Pool, including the contaminated boat trot dumped by the *Koala* in October 1952. This time, no trace of radioactivity was found, and the moorings were dutifully broken down and stowed on board.

For reasons known only to Lieutenant Commander Taudevin, the *Karangi* then returned to Ground Zero to creep for the remains of the *Plym*'s moorings. On the first few passes, they recorded a number of snags but failed to bring anything to the surface. Then: success! 'On the sixth and final creep ... a piece of *Plym*'s plating was recovered', reported Taudevin. 'This measured approximately 4' x 4' and showed a reading of 15 mr. The plate was twisted: on one side rusty: well preserved grey paint was observed on the other side. After being photographed and inspected by the scientists, this plate was later dumped in a disused part of the Lagoon.'[94]

Meanwhile, the leadsmen, who had been steadily reporting 4½ to 5 fathoms, suddenly reported a shallow patch of 15 to 16 feet. Peering over the side, Taudevin spotted a small uncharted shoal, which he suspected was in fact wreckage of the *Plym*. To find out for sure, he ordered the ship's divers to investigate.

The following day, Able Seaman Alex Donald, a 23-year-old diver from Subiaco, Western Australia, and Able Seaman Jack Dodds, a 21-year-old diver from Victor Harbour, South Australia, inspected the shoal at close quarters, running their hands over the contaminated seabed. 'When we came out of the water, we had a Royal Navy lieutenant commander there, who had a Geiger counter, and he put it over us', Donald later recalled. 'We were using Salvus gear, to be quite frank, in shallow water, and the equipment was ditched over the side, and we were both placed in the shower and scrubbed mercilessly for about half an hour.'[95]

To the captain's surprise, the divers reported that the feature was a reef made of coral and rock, rising from a depth of 30 feet to within 12 feet of the surface at low tide. So it was not part of the *Plym* after all.

Dick Taudevin retired from the Navy in 1957. In later years, when the press began to examine the high incidence of cancer and other long-term health effects associated with atomic tests, he grew depressed. As captain of the *Koala* and then the *Karangi*, he had taken his ship into contaminated waters time and again, exposing his men to danger by ordering them to dredge up red-hot moorings and landing craft and even pieces of the *Plym*. It was all so senseless.

Taudevin's wife, Sheila, had been an officer in the Women's Royal Naval Service, and knew the Navy inside and out. She later told the Royal Commission: 'He expressed to me the thought that he felt that his ship and his company were being put in a very tricky situation. He told me that he felt very unhappy about it.'[96]

On 12 November 1979, Dick Taudevin committed suicide. He was 62.

# 13.

# STANDARD OPERATING PROCEDURE

As early as 1951, British officials had realised that parts of the Montebello Islands would remain dangerously radioactive for months after Operation Hurricane. The contaminated islands would not only be hazardous for fishermen and scavengers, they would also present tempting targets for Soviet spies hoping to gather data about the design of the weapon and the size of the blast. Consequently, the Hurricane Executive in London and the Hurricane Panel in Melbourne arranged for an Australian unit comprising members from all three services to remain in the islands for a period of up to three months. During that time, the Joint Services Training Unit (JSTU) would conduct security patrols and learn radiological safety, radiation detection and decontamination techniques. For members of the JSTU, Operation Hurricane would be the atomic equivalent of a live-fire training exercise.[1]

The original plan was to base the JSTU on Hermite Island, which was expected to remain uncontaminated, with HMAS *Warreen* in support. By the middle of Phase Three, the Task Force had gained valuable experience in re-entry and decontamination procedures and it had become clear that, for logistical reasons, it would be more convenient to base the unit on a ship than on an island on the far side of the lagoon. The *Warreen* was too small for the job, so, instead, HMAS *Hawkesbury* was ordered to stay behind to support the JSTU and patrol the islands in the wake of the Task Force's departure. The announcement was greeted with dismay among the *Hawkesbury*'s company, who had already been in the Montebellos for months by this stage. To soften the blow, the frigate was sent back to Fremantle for a week's leave before embarking the training unit.

In late October, members of the JSTU arrived at HMAS *Leeuwin* in Fremantle from units all over Australia. The officer in charge was Lieutenant AA Andrews, Head of the RAN Atomic, Biological and Chemical Defence (ABCD) School at HMAS *Penguin* in Sydney. A 50-year-old former gunner from North London, Andrews had no experience with atomic theory prior to 1951, when he was sent back to England for three months of training, but he took radiological safety extremely seriously, 'even at the expense of personal popularity', as he himself admitted.[2] Two of Andrews's petty officer instructors from the ABCD School were attached to the JSTU as instructors. The rest of the unit comprised 12 trainees from all three services and three unsuspecting other ranks roped in to act as camp stewards. None of the trainees had any idea what they were in for. Most of them had volunteered for a 'secret mission', assuming it would be some sort of derring-do in Malaya or Korea. Once they discovered they were going to the Montebellos, it was too late to back out.

Before leaving Fremantle, all members of the unit were given an introduction to radiation theory and protective equipment. They were also outfitted with two sets of kit, in case one became contaminated.

On Monday 27 October, the ragtag unit embarked in the *Hawkesbury* and set off for the Montebellos. Also on board was Surgeon Lieutenant JR McNeill, a 29-year-old Scottish expat on loan to the *Hawkesbury* to supervise the unit's health and safety.

Throughout the three-day voyage, the trainees received daily lectures on radiation theory and the use of radiac devices, although it appears that some men (namely the Air Force officers) missed some or all of the lectures due to seasickness.[3]

The *Hawkesbury* arrived in Parting Pool just as the Task Force was preparing to depart. Before the *Campania* weighed anchor, Squadron Leader AD Thomas – now Australia's most experienced atomic serviceman by far – transferred to the *Hawkesbury* to supervise the JSTU and conduct follow-up investigations for HER. Not for the first time during Operation Hurricane, security requirements meant that communication regarding chain of command was somewhat lacking; no one seemed to know who was supposed to be in charge of the JSTU. According to Admiral Torlesse, Squadron Leader Thomas was in overall command, but the Australian airman, perhaps being diplomatic, described himself as an adviser to Lieutenant Andrews. For his part, Lieutenant Andrews was 100 per cent sure that he was in charge, no matter what anyone else said. 'In general, the whole hearted co-operation of Squadron Leader Thomas was most valuable even though the presence of this officer had not been communicated to the officer in charge of the Training Unit', he wrote in a rather passive aggressive section of his report.[4]

In the end, the senior officers from all three services – Lieutenant Commander RJ Scrivenor, RAN, captain of the *Hawkesbury*; Major Frank Vincent, Royal Australian Engineers (RAE), senior Army officer in the JSTU; and Squadron Leader Thomas, RAAF, Scientific Adviser to the Chief of Air Staff – got together to decide that, yes, the punctilious Lieutenant Andrews was indeed in command of the training unit.

The next few days were spent establishing a health control centre in the lee of a cliff on South East Island. Aside from a few locally purchased items, most of the unit's stores and equipment were provided by the Brits, including a motorboat, motor pinnace, protective clothing, radiac instruments and tents. A volunteer shore party from the *Hawkesbury* helped establish and run the camp, which included a Nissen hut that served as both a lecture room and a monitoring centre. Of the officers present, only Squadron Leader Thomas had actually seen a decontamination centre operating under live conditions, so there was a certain amount of trial and error involved during the set-up process. In fact, the situation descended into farce at times, with the *Hawkesbury*'s ratings displaying the patience of Job as they were repeatedly ordered to dismantle and shift structures and equipment they had only just assembled.

Since classroom facilities were limited, Lieutenant Andrews decided to cut the theoretical section of the course down to one day in order to get to practical exercises as soon as possible. According to Andrews, most of the trainees were 'keen and interested', but there were exceptions.[5]

Flying Officer JE Nicholls, a 32-year-old veteran of Borneo and Occupied Japan from Peterborough, South Australia, and Flying Officer Keith Peck, a 30-year-old National Service instructor from Kempsey, New South Wales, were distinctly unimpressed with Lieutenant Andrews and his course.[6] The airmen had missed some or all of the preliminary lectures in the *Hawkesbury* due to seasickness, and received only one full day of theory in the islands. Neither of them rated Lieutenant Andrews at all. According to Peck: 'We both formed the impression that he knew little more than we did since he seemed to be reading from the instruction manual as he was attempting to explain to us some pieces of equipment nobody could really understand.'[7] The airmen may have been more forgiving if not for Andrews's pedantic demeanour, which they found to be insufferable.

Lieutenant Graham Jenkinson was a 29-year-old RAE officer from Mareeba in Far North Queensland. Unlike the airmen, he had no problems with the course. He described the training as 'very thorough' and 'very intensive ... both theoretical and practical'.[8] Regarding Lieutenant Andrews, he was diplomatic: 'His competence I have a high respect for. His knowledge, well, okay, he was like the rest of us ... He was probably seeing instruments for the first time that had come out from England and were not possibly available ... but I think he picked them up very quickly and was able to instruct us in them. He was a very good instructor.'[9]

Many years later, during the Royal Commission, Australian lawyers gently quizzed the elderly Andrews on his familiarity with the unit's instruments. His replies were emphatic:

> Did you have any trouble using the monitoring equipment yourself? — None whatsoever.
>
> Had you used it before? — Yes, of course, on the training course in England.
>
> Was there any equipment with which you were not familiar? — No.[10]

Appropriately trained or not, the JSTU began conducting practical exercises on Trimouille on Thursday 6 November, beginning with a preliminary reconnaissance by Lieutenant Andrews's two staffers, Petty Officer LD Monaghan and Petty Officer SR Leal. Once the senior ratings had established that the island was safe enough to visit, Lieutenant Andrews sent in small teams to take turns conducting familiarisation, monitoring and plotting exercises. Each sortie began at the base on South East Island, where unit members were briefed on the day's exercise and kitted up in protective gear. At first, they wore overalls, rubber boots, rubber gloves, respirators, neckerchiefs, bush hats, film badges and dosimeters, but, later on, the hats and sweat rags were replaced with white anti-flash hoods that gave the head and neck extra protection from radiation.

There were two paths leading down to the boat landing: a clean path and a dirty path. Both were made of bituminised material that could be rolled up and burnt when it got too dirty. On the way into the contaminated area, unit members took the clean path; on the way back, the dirty one.

Leading Seaman TK Peters usually coxswained the motorboat. A 21-year-old Naval rating from Euroa, Victoria, Peters had a quirky sense of humour and was valued for his ability to keep up morale. Most days, he took the motorboat across the narrow channel to T1, where a Royal Navy Land Rover had been left for the JSTU. Despite the earlier salvage operation, the landscape was still littered with debris: shattered concrete bunkers, twisted scaffolding, bent sheets of corrugated iron. At the other end of the island, near Gladstone Beach, there was a rubbish tip full of radioactive material abandoned by the Brits.

According to Keith Peck, no one could get the gamma monitors to agree with each other at first: 'Lieutenant Andrews could not understand what was going on and eventually I managed to work out that the devices had to be calibrated before being used. The means of doing this was to use a radioactive source which was locked up in the Captain's safe. After getting access to this we were at least able to calibrate the instruments every time and then they worked fairly well.'[11]

Once the trainees had familiarised themselves with the equipment and the surroundings, they began working on tasks for Squadron Leader Thomas, including an updated isodose map of Trimouille. Teams spread out around the contaminated zone, working their way in from the areas with the lowest readings to the hotter ones, while avoiding the worst spots, like Main Beach, immediately north of Ground

Zero. By comparing the new isodose map with the earlier ones produced during Phase Three, the scientists back in the UK could chart the rate of decay of the radioactive contamination of the Montebello Islands.

The men were also told to note any objects that gave particularly high readings. Their instructions were to approach close enough to identify the object without touching it, then report it to Squadron Leader Thomas. Most objects were pieces of debris, dead or dying animals, or long-term samples deliberately left behind by the British scientists. The hottest objects of all were pieces of the *Plym*. Squadron Leader Thomas then advised the trainees whether or not to collect the items for further study. Selected items were placed in plastic bags and taken back to base for despatch to the *Hawkesbury*. Fish and water samples from the surrounding sea were also collected, along with readings of the nearby moorings.

By now it was cyclone season again, so the weather was getting more and more humid, and the suits more and more uncomfortable. During the Royal Commission, Keith Peck alleged that trainees stopped wearing respirators in the contaminated area. 'While we initially wore the gas masks we found that after a few days we developed severe heat rashes because of them and from then on we removed them and did not wear them again during my entire stay in the vicinity of the Monte Bellos. In fact after getting the rash we didn't even bother taking the gas masks ashore and simply left them in our quarters.'[12]

Both AA Andrews and Graham Jenkinson, who topped the course, and was subsequently made a team leader, denied that allegation. Both men were adamant that respirators were to remain on at all times in the contaminated area. 'Because we were keenly aware of the radiation hazard from dust, respirators were not removed during re-entry – notwithstanding that they were intensely uncomfortable and filled up with sweat', stated Jenkinson.[13] But both men were forced to concede that some personnel could have disobeyed orders while out of eyeshot. As Andrews said: 'You get idiots everywhere, do you not ... we do in the Navy anyway.'[14]

The average sortie lasted about three hours, and then, when the job was done, the men returned to South East Island for decontamination. Warrant Officer Max Jellie, a 33-year-old sapper from Brisbane, Queensland, described the process: 'As soon as a person arrived from a contaminated area they would be checked with a Geiger counter, they would have to take off their clothes which consisted of double breasted overalls with zippers down both sides, the overalls would fit inside and outside of rubber boots, rubber gloves covering the forearms and a standard service respirator which had filters which was attached to your chest and a mask which covered the whole face and which was held down by straps. There was also a RAAF type slouch hat and sweat rags would be placed around the back of the neck and under the chin. The clothes were checked and placed in 44 gallon drums – there being separate drums for each article of clothing. The clothes were then washed in copper boilers. After undressing, you would be checked with a Geiger counter and required to take a shower. The Geiger counter usually registered a reading and the usual "hot spot" was at the back of the head where contamination collected to the hair. To my knowledge this was the only area where contamination was found on any of the personnel involved. After showering, another check was made with a Geiger counter and quite often people would have to take further showers and scrub the back of their neck to remove the contamination. It was not unusual to have to shower up to six times.'[15]

The showers used seawater, which Peck alleged was still radioactive: 'We knew from time to time the water would become radioactive because the ships would suddenly signal to us that they were leaving the area for a short while because the water had become radioactive. They would then steam off for some miles and then return later when the water was safe.'[16] But according to Andrews the water was tested and 'showed no signs of radioactivity'.[17]

At the end of the day, the decontaminated personnel were ordered to drink their daily allowance of two bottles of beer to replace their lost fluids, then returned to the *Hawkesbury* for the night. Film badges and dosimeter readings were given to Squadron Leader Thomas for observation, but, because there was no darkroom in the *Hawkesbury*, the film badges could not be processed until Thomas got to RAAF Pearce. In the meantime, he and Surgeon Lieutenant McNeill used the unreliable dosimeter readings to keep track of the trainees' exposure. Since the unit was not subject to the Hurricane Trial Orders, exposure limits were not strictly enforced. Instead, the officers in charge simply tried to keep exposure levels as low as possible without stopping personnel from doing their jobs.

According to Graham Jenkinson, the trainees tried to keep to a 'desirable' dose of 0.1 roentgens per day or 0.5 roentgens per week: 'It was a safety limit which we were expected to come to and I think the critical word is desirable. It was desirable that we keep to .1 per day. If we did not, well ... we had a job to do, we were doing it. We were prepared to have it a little bit either side.'[18]

Max Jellie was similarly philosophical: 'We believed we were taking a calculated risk to complete the job. We were over-irradiated on five or six separate occasions and accepted over-exposure as an almost standard operating procedure.'[19]

The training programme wrapped up on Friday 14 November, after which the JSTU spent a couple of days surveying a few of the smaller islands before conducting a radiation-monitoring course for 11 ratings from the *Hawkesbury*, culminating with a visit to Trimouille. Towards the end of this period, the unit started to run out of film badges, so team leaders wore badges, while other team members made do with dosimeters. The situation was far from ideal, but, as Graham Jenkinson recalled: 'We thought it was the best thing to do; if there was only a short number, it was better to at least have a reading for one member of the party, and it more or less confirmed the reading of the dosimeters and the dose rate meters anyway. So, we worked without protection because we had the dosimeters.'[20]

Overall, Lieutenant Andrews was happy with the results of the training programme, especially the isodose map of Trimouille, which he noted was 'done remarkably well', in his opinion 'rather better than the original'.[21] By far the most impressive students were the engineers, who claimed the top three spots in the class, led by Lieutenant Jenkinson (Major Vincent was not assessed). Undoubtedly, the sappers' experience with reading and plotting maps and navigating difficult terrain gave them a distinct advantage over the sailors and airmen.

With a small unit of officers and men from all three services working in such a dangerous, high-pressure situation, it was inevitable that some tensions would arise. Over the course of the month, relations between the Naval instructors and Air Force trainees went from bad to worse. Flying Officer Nicholls in particular became so fed up with Lieutenant Andrews and his petty officers that he eventually stopped cooperating altogether, leading to an awkward atmosphere in the health control centre and especially the *Hawkesbury*'s wardroom. The situation reached crisis point after a particularly dirty sortie, when Petty Officer Monaghan instructed Nicholls to return to the showers for a second wash. Sick and tired of being ordered around by pushy sailors, Nicholls refused point blank, and was reported for his efforts. Even his fellow Air Force officer, Squadron Leader Thomas, could not defend his behaviour. 'In fact, he refuses to take any further interest in our activities and has become an embarrassment to me due to his uncompromising attitude and unwillingness to assist myself and others', he wrote in a scathing report to Air Commodore Hely.[22]

It was Nicholls himself who came up with the solution when he asked to be returned to his unit. Lieutenant Andrews was happy to be rid of him, and both Squadron Leader Thomas and Lieutenant Commander Scrivenor were forced to agree that his early departure would be best for all concerned. Nicholls was sent packing on the next flight back to Perth.[23]

He was not the only one to go home earlier than expected. By late November, Lieutenant Commander Scrivenor had come to the conclusion that the JSTU was bigger than it needed to be to conduct the remaining security patrols, so, on his recommendation, the unit was reduced to a team of six sappers and five volunteers from the *Hawkesbury*. The rest of the unit was despatched by air from Onslow over the course of eight days, from 24 November to 1 December.

During the Royal Commission, Keith Peck alleged that he was medically evacuated during this period, with symptoms including diarrhoea, hair loss and sore eyes – symptoms that sounded a lot like radiation sickness. He was backed up, at least partially, by Squadron Leader Thomas and Petty Officer Monaghan, who both remembered him being sick, but could not say for sure whether radiation was the cause. Unfortunately for Peck, there was no mention of his evacuation in the *Hawkesbury*'s log, Surgeon Lieutenant McNeill's medical records, or the JSTU training report.

After trying to get hold of his medical file for years, Peck received a bizarre and contradictory statement from the Department of Defence, which concluded:

The operational report of the Unit does not record any medical evacuation of Flt Lt Peck and there is no endorsement on his personal files as to any exposure to radioactivity. However, his medical documents indicate that he suffered from radiation sickness and underwent specialist treatment, including weekly blood counts.[24]

The fact is that Keith Peck was exposed to radioactivity, just as the other members of the JSTU were. According to the official report compiled by Squadron Leader Thomas from relatively reliable film-badge readings, Peck received a total gamma dose of 1.16 roentgens during his time in the Montebellos.[25] That was equivalent to about eight years of normal background radiation – and about average for members of the JSTU. But evidence supplied by Graham Jenkinson in the form of a signal to the *Hawkesbury* from the health control centre on South East Island showed that Peck had gone without a film badge on at least one occasion, meaning that his actual dose was *at least* 1.16 roentgens – plus double that in beta radiation and whatever alpha dose he may have accrued if he did indeed remove his mask in the contaminated area.[26] The reason no such figures appear in Peck's medical records is security. Like everything else to do with Operation Hurricane, Thomas's report was so classified that it was only seen by the top brass. It never made its way into Peck's file.

For years after Operation Hurricane, Peck underwent weekly blood counts, experienced neck and shoulder pains attributed to 'no specific injury', and suffered from bouts of 'high temperature and listlessness' that sent him to bed for weeks at a time.[27] For treatment, he was given blood transfusions and a large bottle of iron tonic, which he was told to drink three times a day to build up his red blood cells. He eventually recovered physically, but his marriage suffered and so did his work. He ended up getting divorced and leaving the Air Force.

Keith Peck died in 2008 at the age of 85.

•

By early December, the JSTU had been reduced to a small security team of six sappers and five sailors from HMAS *Hawkesbury*.

Whenever the frigate was out of the area to collect mail or provisions, the men were left on South East Island with a pinnace and a radio. Lieutenant Commander Scrivenor described their experience in rather grisly detail:

> Although South East Island was nick-named 'Day-dream Island' by the more hardened campers, it was certainly no 'picnic' ashore. Apart from the shortage of fresh water, and the sand being driven by a persistent wind, hordes of nocturnal black rats swarmed from the rocks and over-ran the camp. At first there was much slaughter among the invaders; but before long, the campers gave up the struggle and prepared for a nightly siege behind galvanised iron barricades.[28]

As team leader, Lieutenant Jenkinson re-entered the contaminated area almost every day. He was later given a similar job at Emu Field, and returned to the Montebellos for the follow-up survey in November 1953. According to his own records, based on meticulously recorded dosimeter measurements, and backed up by official film-badge records, Jenkinson received a total dose of 15.97 roentgens in thirteen months.[29] As he later told the Royal Commission: 'Why I am interested in that, why I maintained that record, is that I understand that that calculated in another form in relation to .1 roentgens per year is that I received the equivalent of 160 years normal dosage.'[30]

Jenkinson retired from the Army in 1958, and went on to become President of the Townsville Chamber of Commerce.

For his many contributions to the community, he was named Queenslander of the Year, 1992, and awarded a Member of the Order of Australia.

Graham Jenkinson died in 2007 at the age of 84, following a long illness.[31]

•

Members of the *Hawkesbury*'s company were also exposed to the threat of radiation for an extended period of time.

In Phase Three, the *Hawkesbury* was tasked with ferrying personnel from the Montebellos to Onslow and recovering fallout samples from the dan buoys around the islands. After the Task Force's departure, the frigate remained on hand to patrol the islands and support the JSTU. Throughout November, the ship sailed around the contaminated test site, watching for unauthorised vessels and individuals attempting to remove radioactive material or photograph the crater in the lagoon.

In their haste to depart, the Brits had left behind loads of valuable equipment. Early in December, Captain F Bryce Morris, NOIC West Australian Area, ordered the *Hawkesbury* to recover as much as possible for the benefit of the rapacious Naval Stores Depot at Fremantle. Over the next few weeks, members of the ship's company salvaged 30 tons of gear from the islands, including generator sets, charging boards and batteries, all under the watchful eye of Squadron Leader Thomas. The industrious sailors wore normal working rig, and were equipped with film badges, but not dosimeters, which were only available for members of the security party. There was also a Geiger counter in the ship's sick bay. 'This was situated amid-ships on the port side', recalled Able Seaman Vince Douglas, the former shearer and kangaroo shooter from Rockhampton, Queensland. 'The main passage-way to the f'ocsle [sic] messes passed directly outside the sick-bay, and I can vividly recall that the geiger counter was making a load [sic] clicking noise the whole time. It was quiet [sic] audible from the passage-way, even with the door shut. This didn't concern us because we were told by Doctor Penny [sic] and boffins that everything would be alright.

'I recall an occasion after the explosion when the ship's company were mustered on the quarter-deck to be addressed by Doctor Penny [sic] who said: "You will be alright, although for about nine months you will probably be sterile, but after that you'll come back better than ever."

'I and some of my shipmates proved that theory wrong by fathering children within a year.'[32]

In mid-December, the *Hawkesbury* and the remaining members of the security party returned to Fremantle for Christmas leave. Before the frigate left the Montebellos, members of the ship's company put up warning signs in multiple languages on beaches all around the islands. The authorities in Onslow were briefed about the ongoing threat of radiation, and the RAAF was asked to conduct aerial patrols in the ship's absence.

At the last moment, Lieutenant Commander Scrivenor also decided to embark the Royal Navy Land Rover that had been used on Trimouille ever since D-Day. Unsurprisingly, the vehicle was red hot, reading 2000 counts per second (roughly 20 milliroentgens per hour), despite having been washed down by the Radiological Hazard Division prior to the Task Force's departure.[33]

Under the supervision of Lieutenant Andrews, the Land Rover was washed down again and prepared for loading, a task that called for considerable ingenuity in the absence of cranes and landing craft. Unfazed, the *Hawkesbury*'s sailors improvised a raft from several lengths of 2-inch steel pipe and 44-gallon drums. First, they connected three sides of the frame, lashed it to the drums, and floated it out into 3 feet of water. Next, they fitted two support beams across the raft and draped a large tarpaulin over it. Using pierced-steel planks as a ramp, the sailors drove the Land Rover up onto the raft, wrapped it in the tarp, and lashed it in position. The final section of the raft was then floated out and secured in place. The Land Rover was towed by pinnace to the ship in Parting Pool, hoisted inboard by the aft davit, and stowed aft of the ship's funnel.

Able Seaman Douglas helped build the raft and load the Land Rover onto the *Hawkesbury*. During the subsequent voyage to Fremantle, it was so hot below deck that he slung his hammock from the Land Rover to one of the ship's stanchions, but an officer ordered him to move his hammock and keep away from the Land Rover because it was 'hot'.[34]

At Fremantle, the radioactive Land Rover was driven up the road to HMAS *Leeuwin*, the Naval base at Point Preston in East Fremantle. Engine Room Artificer (Fourth Class) George Smith, a 27-year-old British expat from Yorkshire, was one of two senior stoker ratings ordered to decontaminate it. 'The officer who instructed us to decontaminate the vehicle said that the British had been unable to do it, but we would give it a go and see if we could', Smith later recalled.[35] The two stokers were given overalls, gloves, boots and a Geiger counter to check for radiation. They spent weeks cleaning the Land Rover with water and various types of degreasers and detergents. 'After a few days, we stopped using the gloves because they were too hot and uncomfortable, but I think we continued using the overalls and footwear. During the course of the decontamination, we would become soaked in the runoff water. There was no special area designated for the decontamination and we simply parked the vehicle on some open ground, about 100 yards from the Swan River and did the decontamination there. The waste water just ran and soaked away into the ground.'[36]

Despite the stokers' best efforts, the Land Rover remained radioactive and was fenced off in an area behind the workshop. When the November 1953 radiation survey was planned, Captain Morris, NOIC West Australian Area, proposed sending it back up to the Montebellos to avoid contaminating a second vehicle, but that idea was firmly vetoed by Captain Bill Saxby, the Royal Engineer in charge of the survey. ('Vehicle is not repetition not safe to maintain or repair except under expert advice', he signalled unambiguously.)[37] Instead, another Land Rover was purchased from the Department of Supply and sent up on board HMAS *Karangi*. When it came back three weeks later, it was found to be reading 60 counts per second (approximately 0.6 milliroentgens per hour).[38]

*Leeuwin* was now stuck with two radioactive Land Rovers. Under the instruction of Lieutenant AA Andrews, who had returned to Western Australia to supervise the November 1953 survey, the vehicles were decontaminated in a process similar to the one used on radioactive Lincolns at RAAF Amberley.

Norm Cunningham was a 19-year-old plumber's apprentice and National Serviceman from Subiaco, Western Australia, who was walking by the workshop one day when he saw some ratings working on one of the Land Rovers. 'I noticed a large hole dug about 20 ft x 20 ft x 6 ft deep with a Land Rover ute in the centre of the hole', he later wrote. 'The Land Rover was being dismantled, piece by piece, and placed on racks, in the bottom of the hole. There were air hoses and sand blasting machines on each side of the hole with fire hoses at either end ...

'The Navy engineers were dismounting the Land Rover piece by piece in special overall suits. All the radioactive soil or mud would be buried when the Land Rover was dismembered.

'The body, motor, gearbox, mudguards and petrol tank were in the hole; each section that was removed was then sandblasted, washed and checked for radiation before being removed from the hole and stored inside the Engineers workshop, ready to be assembled.

'The tyres were one thing they could not delouse. I do not know what happened to them.

'The engineers had Geiger counters, checking each section of the Land Rover, as it was disassembled.

'The Engineer asked the new National Service Personnel, was there anybody that could solder as they had a hole in the petrol tank that had to be repaired before it could be refitted in the vehicle. Not knowing the problems with Radioactivity I volunteered to solder up the petrol tank.

'The engineers had soldering irons, solder and spirits of salts to do the repairs, they assured me the petrol tank was not radioactive, they ran the Geiger counter over the petrol tank it did not squeak.

'I spent about two hours repairing and soldering up the hole in the tank and testing it for leaks.'[39]

The vehicle Cunningham worked on was green, which means it was probably the Department of Supply Land Rover, as Royal Navy Land Rovers were usually blue.

Lieutenant Andrews declared the Department of Supply Land Rover clean in December 1953, but recommended that it be checked from time to time in case it should somehow become 're-activated'.[40] It was eventually shipped back to Naval Stores Sydney by HMAS *Sydney* in June 1954.[41]

No one knows what happened to the Royal Navy Land Rover. Many old salts believe it was buried on the grounds of *Leeuwin*. Others believe it was dumped at sea. There is also a rumour that it sat in the Naval Stores Building in Shuffrey Street, Fremantle, for years before being offloaded.

The 'Radioactive Land Rover' (often referred to as the 'Radioactive Jeep') has since become the stuff of legend in Fremantle. The RAN moved to HMAS *Stirling* at Garden Island in the 1980s, and HMAS *Leeuwin* was given to the Army and renamed Leeuwin Barracks. When Defence announced plans to sell off the valuable riverfront property in 2015, all the old rumours about the radioactive Land Rover resurfaced. Responding to a series of pointed questions from the *Fremantle Herald*, the Department of Defence checked the site with a 'ground-penetrating radar', but failed to locate any metal objects as big as a Land Rover.[42] A 2018 environmental assessment by an independent consultant found 'minor contamination including the presence of asbestos and fuel residue', but no evidence of radioactivity.[43]

That is where Defence would like matters to rest, but, on closer examination, the surveys were much too superficial to prove anything conclusively. The company hired to conduct the 2015 ground-penetrating radar survey only examined a small area, 25 metres by 25 metres, half of which was covered with a concrete slab and cricket nets. 'Without the removal of the existing structures (concrete slab, cricket nets, scrap metal pile) and conducting an intrusive investigation it will not be possible to determine the exact nature of the anomalies found during the survey and if an unknown quantity of anomalies lay beneath the structures', the report concluded.[44] Many ex-sailors believe they were looking in the wrong place, anyway.

The 2018 environmental study was conducted by a separate firm, which wrote off the story of the radioactive Land Rover as an 'unsubstantiated anecdote', and failed to check the grounds for radioactive waste, despite the existence of multiple documents proving that two radioactive vehicles had been decontaminated at *Leeuwin*.[45] Even if the Royal Navy Land Rover was eventually offloaded, as seems likely, the threat of radioactive runoff soaking into the water table and flowing into the Swan River over time should have been taken more seriously.

•

HMAS *Hawkesbury* spent Christmas 1952 at Fremantle. It was a welcome respite for the ship's company, but their ordeal was far from over. Early in the new year, the frigate was ordered to return to the Montebellos for one last patrol.

By this time, the ship's company was completely fed up with life in the islands. 'Generally speaking, I recall that tour of duty as one of the worst experiences of my naval career', wrote Able Seaman Douglas. 'Aboard the *Hawkesbury* we lived like animals. Our rations were drawn from a cold store at HMAS *Onslow* [sic] which was equipped with World War II vintage refrigerators. In the result the food spoiled soon after we got it aboard ship. Also it was believed that the cold store was pilfered by civilians ashore so that we never got the best stuff anyway.'[46] That was an outrageous allegation – which may well have been true. Nor'-westers are a resourceful bunch.

Able Seaman Douglas had more reason than most to be annoyed: he was due to be married in Brisbane, and he and his fiancée were forced to postpone the wedding numerous times as the *Hawkesbury* was kept on station.

After salvaging another 20 tons of stores and equipment, the frigate finally weighed anchor and left the Montebellos for good on Thursday 15 January 1953. The ship's company was relieved to see the last of the barren, blasted, Goddam Isles. The British sailors' nickname for the place had never seemed so appropriate.

All the *Hawkesbury*'s efforts were not in vain. Partly in recognition of her outstanding contribution to Operation Hurricane, the spiffy frigate was awarded the Gloucester Cup – the annual award for the finest ship in the Royal Australian Navy – for 1952.

Vince Douglas was eventually married on 6 February 1953. The Queenslander was hoping for some extra leave for a long honeymoon to compensate for the hardship station. He did not get it. In the years that followed, he developed skin lesions on his face, chest and forearms that never went away. He eventually suffered a nervous breakdown and was discharged 'PUNS' ('Permanently Unfit for Naval Service') in 1964.[47]

Vince Douglas died in 2004 at the age of 75.

# EPILOGUE

With HMAS *Hawkesbury*'s departure from the Montebello Islands, Operation Hurricane finally drew to a close.

All in all, the atom bomb and its trial had cost British taxpayers somewhere between £100 million and £200 million – a bargain compared to the United States' astronomically expensive Manhattan Project. Australia's not-insignificant contribution amounted to precisely £201,662 (a figure which includes a write-off of £247 for Army tents loaned to the Navy and accidentally blown up on D-Day).[1]

But the true cost of Operation Hurricane was much higher than that. The test destroyed the environment of the once pristine Montebello Islands, leaving the remote archipelago too contaminated for human visitors and the surrounding waters full of dead and dying fish. Despite the best efforts of the British and Australian meteorologists, part of the radioactive cloud had drifted right across the mainland, from Port Hedland on the west coast to Townsville on the east, dropping fallout who knows where in between, because no one bothered to look for it. By far the most likely to be affected were the 4583 Aboriginal people living in and around the North West at the time.

When British scientists returned to the Montebellos for a follow-up survey in November 1953, they found the islands 'still highly radioactive' and 'unlikely to change for ten years or more'.[2] So much for former UK Prime Minister Clement Attlee's optimistic prediction of three years. Since the islands were clearly too dangerous to enter without protective clothing, the ban on visitation was extended indefinitely.

Worst of all, the scientific and political success of the trial opened the door for the long-term testing programme that followed. From 1953 to 1963, 11 more atomic tests were conducted on Australian soil, including nine on the mainland. The Atomic Weapons Research Establishment (AWRE), as HER was now called, tinkered constantly with the design of the radioactive core and the bomb casings to produce the most powerful, efficient and economical bombs possible, spreading fallout over half the country in the process. The dark legacy of this programme continues to this day.

The first series to follow Hurricane was Operation Totem. In October 1953, AWRE conducted a comparative trial of two weapons containing different ratios of plutonium-239 (the top-grade material used in the Hurricane device) and plutonium-240 (a cheaper alternative) at Emu Field, South Australia. The bombs were detonated on 120-foot towers in the middle of the desert, using relatively small quantities of the radioactive ingredients to keep the blasts smaller and more economical. Totem 1, detonated on 15 October, had an estimated yield of 10 kilotons; Totem 2, detonated 12 days later, 8 kilotons.[3] Fallout spread over surrounding missions, stations and native camps, and was subsequently tracked as far as Townsville.

The British scientists did not like Emu Field very much. It was a tad warm, and rather sandy, and did it really have to be *so very isolated*? Even before Totem was over, another reconnaissance party set out, hoping to find a more convenient location for a permanent proving ground. They eventually found one: an 'open undulating salt bush area' on the eastern edge of the Nullarbor Plain, 100 miles south of Emu Field and 40 miles north of the Transcontinental Railway Line.[4]

It was Alan Butement, Chief Scientist for the Department of Supply, who gave the site its now infamous name. Maralinga is an Aboriginal word for thunder, but the name did not come from the language of the Anangu peoples of the Western Desert. It was a Yolngu word from Arnhem Land in the Northern Territory. It had nothing to do with the place or its traditional owners.

In 1956, during the lead-up to the Melbourne Olympics, AWRE conducted four atomic tests at Maralinga. The series, codenamed Operation Buffalo, tested variations of Britain's first two deliverable atom bombs: Blue Danube, a potentially powerful strategic bomb so big it could only be carried by heavy V-bombers (Vulcans, Victors and Valiants); and Red Beard, a smaller tactical weapon able to be deployed by lighter aircraft.

The first test, held on 27 September, was a tower shot featuring a Red Beard warhead with a 15-kiloton yield. The weather was not quite right that day, but there had already been a long delay and the press men in attendance were growing restless, so they went ahead and did it anyway. The cloud rose much higher than expected and spread fallout all over the eastern states.

The second test was a ground burst featuring a reduced capacity 1.5-kiloton Blue Danube described by one commentator as a 'nuclear landmine'.[5] The test left a giant crater in the desert floor, 140 feet across and 70 feet deep. Despite the smaller cloud, fallout still reached the east coast.

The third test was Britain's first ever airdrop. On 11 October, a Valiant bomber from No 49 Squadron RAF flew over Maralinga and dropped a reduced capacity 3-kiloton Blue Danube that detonated at 500 feet. Pilot Squadron Leader Ted Flavell and bomb aimer Flight Lieutenant Eric Stacey were awarded Air Force Crosses for gallantry. Fallout was detected in Adelaide, Melbourne, Sydney and Hobart.

The fourth and final test was another tower shot, featuring a 15-kiloton Red Beard device detonated at five minutes after midnight. Why was it detonated in the middle of the night? Because the day before was a Sunday, and the Australian Government had banned atomic tests on Sundays for religious reasons.

The following year, AWRE conducted one more series of atom-bomb tests at Maralinga. Operation Antler was originally supposed to comprise five tests but was eventually reduced to three: two tower shots (1 and 6 kilotons respectively) and a balloon burst (a 25-kiloton weapon detonated while hanging from balloons 1000 feet in the air).

In addition to the atomic tests, AWRE also conducted almost 600 top-secret minor trials at Emu Field and Maralinga between 1953 and 1963. Planned and executed with little to no oversight from the Australian Government, the minor trials were tests of individual bomb components and mad experiments to see what would happen if an atom bomb was accidentally blown up in a plane crash or set on fire in a warehouse. The Vixen B trials involved the detonation of multiple dummy warheads containing real live plutonium. The resulting explosions left millions of fragments of plutonium – one of the most dangerous substances on Earth – scattered around the desert. Other trials added sprinklings of toxic beryllium and radioactive polonium to the red dust. If anything, the minor trials were even worse for the environment than the atomic tests.

When the Brits finally left Maralinga, they conducted a couple of perfunctory clean-ups, ploughed contaminated topsoil into the ground, buried radioactive waste in pits, and declared the job done. But it was not done. They had left about 20 kilograms of plutonium lying on the ground. Unfortunately, the Australian Government took them at their word and failed to check, so the true extent of Maralinga's contamination remained hidden for years.

AWRE also returned to the Montebellos for one of the most controversial trials in Australian history: Operation Mosaic (originally codenamed Operation Giraffe).

In November 1954, the Churchill Government made the official decision to develop hydrogen bombs. By this time, public opinion was turning against the bomb. The nuclear arms race was accelerating at an alarming rate; the Americans and Soviets were conducting more and more tests each year. Weapons were growing exponentially larger and becoming ever more sophisticated. To many people all around the world, nuclear Armageddon seemed the inevitable result.

If there was a single moment that turned the tide of opinion against the bomb, it was the Castle Bravo incident. On 1 March 1954, American forces detonated an experimental hydrogen bomb at Bikini Atoll. At an astonishing 15 megatons, Castle Bravo was 1000 times the size of the bomb that had destroyed Hiroshima. Fallout spread far and wide, with radioactive coral ash drifting over populated parts of the Marshall Islands and an unlucky Japanese fishing vessel called *Daigo Fukuryū Maru* (*Lucky Dragon No 5*).

When the vessel returned to port two weeks later, all 23 crew members were found to be suffering from acute radiation poisoning, with symptoms including headaches, bleeding gums, skin burns and hair loss. Six months later, 39-year-old crew member Aikichi Kuboyama died from a chronic liver condition exacerbated by exposure to radiation. The rest of the crew suffered lifelong health problems associated with radiation, many dying young.

The Castle Bravo incident sparked outrage in Japan, inspired the original *Godzilla* movie, and stoked a worldwide movement to ban nuclear tests.

For the UK Government, the timing was rather awkward. With talk of a global testing moratorium heating up, Sir William Penney, now Director of AWRE, was under intense pressure to produce a working hydrogen bomb quickly. Unfortunately for him, the political fallout over Castle Bravo caused the Australian Government to bar hydrogen-bomb tests, forcing Penney and his boffins to look elsewhere for a suitable test site. They eventually settled on two tiny atolls in the middle of the Pacific Ocean: Malden and Christmas islands in Britain's Gilbert and Ellice Islands Colony. (Christmas Island is now known as Kiritimati in modern-day Kiribati, and should not be confused with the other Christmas Island off Australia's North West Coast.)

Before heading to the Pacific, the Brits wanted to experiment with the new ingredients that powered their fusion designs. On 16 May 1955, UK Prime Minister Sir Anthony Eden sent his Australian counterpart, Robert Menzies, the following request:

> Our people here … suggested that your agreement should be sought to a programme of two firings in the Monte Bello Islands in April 1956. The experiments would consist of atomic explosions with the inclusion of light elements as a boost. It would of course be made clear in any public announcement that the explosions were atomic and not thermonuclear … The smaller of the two shots [would] be fired first and if this was completely successful the second and slightly larger shot would not then be fired. Neither would give a yield more than 2½ times greater than in the Hurricane operation.[6]

A practised diplomat, Eden was giving Menzies the soft soap. 'Light elements' was a euphemism for fusion fuel – lithium and hydrogen combined in the form of lithium deuteride – the presence of which meant the weapons could be considered hydrogen bombs. When a nervous Menzies pointed this out to the UK High Commission in Canberra, he received a condescending reply:

> Australians can be reassured. An H-bomb in normal parlance is a weapon of large yield, that is, in the megaton range, which employs the fusion reaction of light elements on a large scale. The proposed tests are not of this character but are the fission weapons used as vehicles for certain diagnostic and experimental tests ... The two rounds at Mosaic are of low yield – a few tens of kilotons – and the small amounts of light elements incorporated are solely to investigate the nature of the reaction.[7]

In layperson's terms, the Brits were saying that the Mosaic weapons were not true hydrogen bombs but souped-up atom bombs incorporating small quantities of hydrogen-bomb fuel. A less compliant government might have rejected that explanation, and prohibited the trial on the basis that it involved hydrogen-bomb fuel in any amount. The Australian Government did not.

Eden also downplayed the size of the second, larger weapon by stating that it would be no more than two and a half times the size of the 25-kiloton Hurricane blast. While it was true that Penney thought the yield would probably be 40 to 60 kilotons, it was also true that his boffins estimated its maximum possible size to be 80 kilotons – over three times the size of Hurricane.[8] Naturally, Eden (or whoever was advising him) fudged the numbers to make the weapon sound as harmless as possible.

Like Hurricane before it, Mosaic was conducted as a Royal Navy operation, with a combined task force of 15 warships, 25 aircraft and 2000 men under the command of Commodore

(Second Class) Hugh Martell, Commanding Officer of HMS *Narvik* and Operational Commander of Task Force 308. The Scientific Director was Charles Adams, bucktoothed veteran of Epicure and Hurricane.

On 16 May 1956, Mosaic's G1 was detonated on a 120-foot tower at the northern end of Trimouille. Despite an underwhelming yield of approximately 15 kilotons, the mushroom cloud climbed to 23,000 feet – far higher than predicted – where strong westerlies carried the upper section of the cloud back across the coast.

Two days after the test, patches of radioactivity were detected at Onslow Airstrip and in the surrounding bush. Low-intensity readings were later reported at air-sampling stations set up all across northern Australia. Luckily for the Menzies Government, the press did not get wind of the fallout.

Then came G2.

On 19 June, the second weapon was detonated on a 120-foot tower on Alpha Island, exploding with spectacular force. 'G1, by comparison, was like a penny squib competing with a Brock's thunderflash', reported an awestruck Commodore Martell.[9]

G2 was so big that the mushroom cloud ballooned to 45,000 feet and was clearly visible from Port Hedland, 200 miles away. The exact size of the blast is disputed to this day. The official AWRE estimate is 56 kilotons – over twice the size of any other weapon detonated in Australia – and right in line with Penney's predictions.[10] But, during the Royal Commission, Australian lawyers uncovered a report by the AWRE Blast Measurement Group estimating the yield at a whopping 98 kilotons – almost twice as big again, topping even the 80-kiloton upper limit used in safety planning.[11]

Asked to account for the discrepancy, the ageing Lord Penney (as he was by then) dismissed the higher figure as inaccurate. The Blast Measurement Group's job, he explained, was to produce a rough estimate with rudimentary devices like toothpaste tubes and diaphragm gauges as a back-up for more sophisticated methods like radiochemical analysis. 'It depends on whether you have got good instruments but suppose you have got good instruments and got good records, you cannot do it better than plus or minus 20 per cent, it might even be 30 per cent', he said.[12] Pointing to a widely scattered set of data points on the graph included in the report, the old prof suggested the results were even less accurate than that. 'What I have got to tell you (and this is a scientific point) is that a small or an error as big as that is a lot of percentage yield, a lot of percentage yield, so I would look at that and say, "Well, don't really place much weight on that."'[13]

The Royal Commissioners accepted Penney's explanation and recorded the yield as 56 kilotons, omitting the 98-kiloton estimate from their final report, but the higher figure was picked up in the media and soon took on a life of its own. As a result, there are now two competing narratives over the size of G2. In the official version, generally accepted in the UK, the weapon performed exactly as predicted, but the Blast Measurement Group failed to produce an accurate measurement because of an instrument breakdown, probably caused by difficult conditions at the site. In the unofficial version, which is more popular in Australia, the blast was much larger than expected, and the Brits covered it up to avoid a scandal.[14]

Given the established facts, both narratives are at least somewhat plausible. In the absence of further information from the UK Atomic Energy Authority, which assumed responsibility for the British atomic programme in 1954 (the Ministry of Supply was subsequently abolished), scientists and historians are obliged to take both possibilities into account. Either way, G2 was by far the biggest weapon ever detonated in Australia.

As usual, strong westerlies in the upper atmosphere carried fallout across the mainland. On D+1, radioactive rain was reported at Comet Mine near Marble Bar and civil aircraft were grounded throughout the North West. This time, there was no way to keep it out of the press. 'ATOM CLOUD MAY HAVE GONE INLAND', cried *The West Australian*.[15] Two days later, more radioactive rain was reported at Kuridala in north-west Queensland. 'ATOM RAIN FALLS NEAR CLONCURRY', shouted *The Courier-Mail*.[16]

When the controversy erupted, Australian Minister of Supply Howard Beale was in the middle of a press junket to Maralinga. Under siege from insatiable reporters who were desperate for a scoop, the accident-prone Beale rushed out several confusing and contradictory statements, initially admitting that 'some cloud containing minute particles had drifted inland' before claiming that it had miraculously 'moved safely out to sea again'.[17]

With Menzies out of the country at the time, it was left to Country Party leader and Acting Prime Minister Sir Arthur Fadden to sort out the mess. 'There is no evidence that the cloud from last week's Monte Bello atomic explosion crossed the Australian coast at any time', the veteran Queenslander confidently asserted.[18] 'I am satisfied that the whole Monte Bello operation was carried out without risk to life or property on the mainland or elsewhere.'

Fadden was being deliberately misleading. While it was true that *most* of the cloud had fallen out over the ocean, it was also true that *part* of the cloud had crossed the coast. The same thing happened after Hurricane and G1. The real problem, from the government's perspective, was that Beale had admitted it.

To account for the confusion, Fadden distinguished between 'heavy particles', which he said fell out rapidly as the mushroom cloud dispersed, and 'light particles', which remained airborne and were carried off by the wind at high altitudes. 'Such particles travel around the world generally in an easterly direction and may do so several times until they are washed down by rainfall. But the radioactivity from these particles is far below the level at which any danger to health could arise.'

That part was almost true. The highest readings after G2 were recorded at Port Hedland, Broome and Noonkanbah Station. While the readings were below the 'zero risk' level (or 'Level A') established by AWRE, they were above the recommended limit for members of the public proposed by the International Commission on Radiological Protection just three years later, in 1959. So the fallout was probably not dangerous – but it was probably not all that good for anyone either.

Just eight days after G2, the Task Force put up warning signs with 'DANGER! RADIOACTIVE – KEEP OUT' printed in six languages on all the best landing beaches around the Montebellos, fenced off the contaminated northern end of Trimouille, and sailed into the sunset.

There was no clean-up of any kind.

•

Over the next few decades, the Montebellos were largely forgotten. Officially, they remained a prohibited area. From time to time, RAN ships called in for radiation surveys and fishery patrols. Naturally, the locals ignored the ban and went fishing and treasure hunting on the islands whenever they felt like it. 'In fact I went there myself and I never had any idea it was out of bounds', said IV Blair, who salvaged yards of copper wire from the Montebellos in the early sixties.[19] He was Onslow's police sergeant at the time.

Two clean-up operations were eventually conducted. In March 1965, frigate HMAS *Diamantina*, under the command of Lieutenant Commander Peter Holloway, visited the Montebellos for Operation Cool Off. Supervised by officers trained in radiation detection, a combined works party of sailors from the *Diamantina* and soldiers from the Special Air Service Regiment spent a week replacing missing warning signs, putting up new fences around the bomb sites, fixing the fence across Trimouille, and adding a new one across the middle of Alpha.

Fourteen years later, in May 1979, a troop from 22 Construction Squadron RAE, led by Major John Quantrill, arrived in heavy landing craft HMAS *Tarakan*, under Lieutenant AJ Mapson, for Operation Capelin. The sappers spent the next 10 days camped on the beach on Trimouille, covering the bomb sites with new layers of topsoil, putting up concrete plinths to commemorate the explosions, and burying all the remaining pierced-steel planking and scattered debris. They also destroyed an old concrete bunker in danger of collapsing and replaced all the old warning signs yet again. At night, the sappers watched movies under the stars. 'It was a very relaxing couple of weeks', Quantrill later recalled.[20]

The operation was supervised by scientists from the WA State X-Ray Laboratory, who told Quantrill that ambient radiation levels in the Montebellos were 'less than you would find in Hyde Park in Sydney, with all the luminous watches'. The scientists also took hair follicles from the sappers before and after the operation to measure their exposure. 'They never told us anything', said Quantrill. 'Just told us, "We'll tell you if anything is wrong."'

Yet a radiation survey carried out by a combined team from the Australian Radiation Laboratory and WA State X-Ray Laboratory one year earlier showed that G1 Ground Zero would not return to normal background radiation levels until 2040, and G2 Ground Zero until 2060.[21] That's why the sappers had been sent up there in the first place. Once again, Australian servicemen were being kept in the dark and exposed to risks without prior knowledge or approval.

•

After Operation Mosaic, AWRE's attention shifted from Australia to the Pacific, where the British hydrogen-bomb programme was conducted.

From 1957 to 1958, nine bombs were tested at Malden and Christmas islands, including Britain's first successful hydrogen bomb, the 1.8-kiloton Grapple X, and the most powerful British weapon ever detonated, the 3-megaton Grapple Y.

Australians naturally tend to focus on the outrages of the Australian tests, but it is important to remember that most of the Pacific tests dwarfed anything that happened at the Montebellos, Emu Field and Maralinga. As usual, it was servicemen and Indigenous people – in this case Pacific Islanders – who took the brunt of it. The Grapple Task Force comprised 13,980 British soldiers, sailors and airmen, 551 New Zealand sailors, 276 Fijian soldiers and sailors, and approximately 100 Gilbertese copra plantation workers who were roped in to act as labourers.[22] Christmas Island was also home to the Gilbertese workers' wives and children, who were evacuated to nearby Fanning Island (now known as Tabueran) for the first few tests, but returned to Christmas Island before the later ones.

Following the success of Operation Grapple, the United States and the United Kingdom signed the US–UK Mutual Defence Agreement, leaving behind the postwar squabbles over atomic spies and opening a brand-new era of nuclear cooperation. In return for the use of British submarine bases and the remote Christmas Island testing facility, the Brits received access to American nuclear submarine technology and whiz-bang testing facilities in Nevada and the Pacific. It was what they had wanted all along.

•

The long-mooted global testing moratorium lasted from 1958 to 1961. After that, the nuclear arms race recommenced – and accelerated alarmingly. The Soviet Union made up for lost time by conducting 57 tests in just 65 days in late 1961, peaking with the biggest hydrogen bomb of all time – a 100-megaton device with a reduced capacity of 50 megatons detonated over Severny Island in the Russian Arctic. Nicknamed Tsar Bomba, the weapon was so powerful that the delivery aircrew was only given a 50 per cent chance of survival. (They made it!) The blast obliterated everything for hundreds of miles in every direction.

Determined not to be outdone, the United States followed up with Operation Dominic, an epic series of 31 tests over seven months in 1962, conducted mostly at Christmas Island. Approximately 300 British servicemen also participated under the codename Operation Brigadoon.

All this madness threatened to boil over during the Cuban Missile Crisis of October 1962, when the Soviet Union attempted to station nuclear missiles on the island of Cuba, just 200 miles off the Florida coast. The Americans responded to the obvious provocation with a Naval blockade, leading to the ultimate game of high-stakes brinkmanship. For 13 terrifying days, US President John F Kennedy and Soviet Premier Nikita Krushchev stared each other down from across the globe, fingers poised atop the nuclear buttons. Thankfully, cooler heads prevailed, the Soviet ships turned around, and global thermonuclear war was averted.

Chastened by how close the world had come to annihilation, the three original members of the nuclear club signed the Partial Test Ban Treaty of 1963, prohibiting atmospheric, underwater and outer space nuclear tests, but allowing underground testing to continue. (France, which had just become the fourth nuclear power, declined to sign the treaty, as did China, which soon joined the club.)

In Australia, the British atomic testing programme finally came to a close. Maralinga was quietly shuttered. The Montebellos and Emu Field had long since been abandoned. What did Australia get for all its generosity?

Nothing, really.

There was no defence agreement bringing Australia under a British nuclear umbrella, no British-built bombs for the RAAF, no technical data that would have allowed the Australian Department of Supply to build its own bomb. Robert Menzies seemed to imagine that some or all of these things would materialise at some point in time, but did nothing to make it happen. Well, almost nothing.

On 29 June 1961, Menzies broached the topic of Australia's 'nuclear capability' in a letter to UK Prime Minister Harold Macmillan, asking his fellow conservative if the UK Government would consider giving Australia either 'full manufacturing data for the production of operational weapons' or 'the supply of ready-made weapons'.[23] But Menzies's request came about 10 years too late. He and his government did not hold any cards anymore. After hemming and hawing about how to respond for six weeks, Macmillan said he was 'anxious to help' but needed to talk to the Americans first. Predictably, nothing ever came of it. If Menzies had made the same request before offering up his own country as a nuclear test site, he might have received a different answer.

Robert Menzies remains a Liberal Party icon and a hero to Australian monarchists and conservatives. When Queen Elizabeth II visited Australia in 1963, he uttered the immortal words, 'I did but see her passing by, and yet I love her till I die'. (He was standing right next to her at the time; the poor woman literally cringed.) Menzies retired three years later, after 16 years in office, a record unlikely to be beaten. In return for years of loyal service to the Crown, the Queen knighted him twice and named him Lord Warden of the Cinque Ports and

Constable of Dover Castle, ceremonial titles that came with a fancy uniform and an official residence at Walmer Castle in Kent. So perhaps it was all worth it.

•

Over the next few years, Australians mostly forgot about the atomic tests. Harold Holt, Menzies's handpicked successor as prime minister, disappeared while swimming off Cheviot Beach in Victoria. The Vietnam War, Watergate and the Dismissal happened. A younger crop of journalists came up, more subversive than their predecessors, distrustful of authority and inherently sceptical about claims of national security.

In 1976, former RAAF airman Avon Hudson blew the whistle on the contamination at Maralinga, telling the ABC and Channel 10 about buried equipment and radioactive waste contaminating the range. Brian Toohey of the *Australian Financial Review* and later the *National Times* dug up government reports supporting Hudson's allegations. The Adelaide *Advertiser* ran a big series on sick veterans and Aboriginal people. Groups like the British Nuclear Test Veterans Association, the Australian Nuclear Veterans Association, the Atomic Ex-Servicemen Association and the Australian Ex-Services Atomic Survivors Association sprang up to fight for healthcare, compensation and recognition for atomic veterans and their widows. The Malcolm Fraser Coalition Government of the late 70s and early 80s stuck to the party line, insisting that everything was fine and releasing several reports purporting to prove it, but by then no one believed the spin.

In 1983, Bob Hawke, a cocky Western Australian Rhodes scholar and former trade unionist, moved into The Lodge as Labor prime minister and announced the Royal Commission into British Nuclear Tests in Australia. To make sure that no Labor icons were accidentally embarrassed, the terms of reference were limited to 1952 onwards, leaving former PM Ben Chifley's Woomera agreement and three-point atomic programme right out of it.

The President of the Royal Commission was Justice 'Diamond' Jim McClelland, a garrulous Sydney judge and former Labor senator who liked to stick it up the Poms whenever he got the chance. The other commissioners were Jill Fitch, a health physicist from the South Australian Health Commission and member of the Australian Ionising Radiation Advisory Committee, and Dr William Jonas, a Worimi man from the mid-North Coast of New South Wales who lectured in geography at Newcastle University and later served as Aboriginal and Torres Strait Islander Social Justice Commissioner. Counsel Assisting was Peter McClellan (no relation to Jim McClelland), a methodical Sydney barrister who went on to serve as President of the Royal Commission into Institutional Responses to Child Sexual Abuse.

Beginning on 22 August 1984, the Royal Commission held hearings in Sydney, Brisbane, Melbourne, Adelaide, London, Maralinga, Marla Bore, Wallatinna, Perth and Karratha. Over 118 sitting days, 311 witnesses gave oral evidence, and a further 210 witnesses who could not be present had statements tendered into evidence on their behalf. Among those who testified were Lord Penney, who still managed to come off as likeable, even while describing his role in nuking Australia; Sir Ernest Titterton, who came off as insufferable; and Doug Peirson, who remained adamant that no fallout from Hurricane had reached the mainland, despite all evidence to the contrary.

Among the many allegations – some proven, some plausible, others debunked – several stood out as particularly shocking.

One was the so-called black mist. In the hours after Totem 1 at Emu Field, an oily black cloud rolled across the desert north-west of Ground Zero, blanketing nearby stations with fallout.

In the native camp at Wallatinna Station, 12-year-old Yankunytjatjara boy Yami Lester watched as the black mist crept through the surrounding mulga scrub. 'The old people called it "mamu" ["evil spirit"] as it looked different from anything we'd seen before. It was not like a storm coming or a dust storm or a bush fire. It was very quiet. The old people were getting woomeras and standing up trying to make that "mamu" turn the other way. As it came towards us the people were calling all the children and began digging the sand to put us in.'[24] The black mist made everyone in the camp sick, with symptoms including vomiting, diarrhoea, skin rashes and sore eyes. Not long afterwards, Lester went blind.

At nearby Mintabie, where her husband was fossicking for opal, Yankunytjatjara woman Lallie Lennon grabbed her kids and hid under a windbreak. 'It looked like a big smoke coming through the trees', recalled Lennon.[25] 'There was a smell as it came to us. It was a funny smell. It smelled like gunpowder, like something burnt.'[26] The whole family was sick for days, with vomiting and diarrhoea, and Lennon and her son Bruce developed skin conditions that never went away.

Over at Welbourn Hill, Almerta Lander, the wife of a contractor, was cooking in the camp oven outside her caravan when the black mist rolled in. 'As soon as I saw the cloud I thought it was from the bomb. It was coming from the general direction of Emu. The dust that fell was sticky. You could not wipe it off with a dry cloth like you could with ordinary dust. You had to use a damp cloth to wipe it.'[27] Soon the camp oven and the caravan were covered in the stuff.

For years, Australian authorities insisted that nothing like the black mist ever happened, dismissing it as 'a myth in the making'.[28] But, during the Royal Commission, British scientists from AWRE and the UK Meteorological Service produced detailed statistical modelling of the fallout from Totem 1. They found that 'sites reporting the "black mist" received fallout from the British test on 15 October 1953', and that it 'indeed might have had an appearance similar to that described'.[29] In other words, it happened. Whether the black mist was dangerous enough to cause Lester's loss of sight, the Royal Commissioners could not say. There was simply not enough evidence either way.

Then there was the Pom Pom incident.

In March 1957, following Operation Buffalo, Australian servicemen found an Aboriginal family camped near the crater at Marcoo, site of the 1.5-kiloton ground burst. They were Spinifex people from the heart of the desert: Charlie (Tjanyindi) Milpuddie, his wife, Edie, and their two children, Henry (Kantjari), about 11, and Rosie (Milpadi), about two. The family had spent several months travelling down an old track from the Everard Ranges near the Northern Territory border to Ooldea on the Transcontinental Railway line, not knowing that the Ooldea Aboriginal Reserve had been shut down because of the atomic tests.

The discovery of Indigenous people in the contaminated area sparked panic among the Maralinga staff. The Milpuddies were taken to a health physics caravan at nearby Pom Pom, where they were monitored, showered and scrubbed with soap, which stung their eyes. Young Henry was found to have a significant amount of contamination in his hair and on his skin, but after a couple of showers the readings came down to a 'safe' level. The rest of the family was declared clean, but Edie and Rosie were not monitored or washed too closely out of a misplaced sense of decorum on the part of the British officer in charge.

The Milpuddies were then loaded into a four-wheel drive and driven to Yalata, a depressing Lutheran mission way down south, far from their traditional lands, where Aboriginal language and culture were systematically stamped out. On arrival, Charlie's hunting dogs were shot. Edie was pregnant, but her baby was stillborn, and she later lost two more children in their infancy. Edie believed, and Anangu women still believe, that the 'poison' on the ground at Maralinga was to blame.[30] The whole family suffered from anxiety and myriad other health problems in the years ahead. Henry and Rosie both lost children of their own, and Charlie went blind before dying of heart failure and pneumonia in 1974.

The Pom Pom incident was covered up from the get-go. Colonel Dick Durance, Maralinga Range Commander, lined up everyone who had come across the Milpuddies and read them the riot act. As he later admitted: 'This would be a rather sensitive matter and we were all very guarded in anything that we had to say so that preferably it didn't get out from the range. I made this known to the men on the range that references to the incident were not to take place at all, particularly as they were under the *Defence (Special Undertakings) Act* and would remember that [they] could have great difficulties for them if they started breaking the security that was required of them in this matter.'[31]

The cover-up worked for years. Almost no one talked about the incident until numerous participants, including Edie Milpuddie, testified before the Royal Commission.

Commonwealth servicemen were also exposed time and again – sometimes deliberately. Beginning with Totem 1, RAF and RAAF aircrews flew through the mushroom clouds in specially modified Canberra bombers to collect samples. Unlike the Lincoln crews conducting cloud-tracking sorties during Hurricane and Totem, the Canberra crews wore protective suits and oxygen masks and flew pressurised aircraft with sealed-off cabins. Nevertheless, they still copped significant doses. The three British airmen in the experimental Totem 1 cloud-sampling crew received an average gamma dose of 10 roentgens – the maximum amount they were permitted to receive. Remarkably, two of the airmen lived into their nineties, while the third died in his seventies, apparently of heart disease.

During Operation Mosaic, brand new Daring Class destroyer HMS *Diana* was ordered to steam through the fallout of both clouds to test the performance of ship and crew in a realistic nuclear war scenario. Before each test, the *Diana* weighed anchor and steamed for a predetermined position, right under the predicted path of the cloud, before going to action stations and then shelter stations. The open bridge and anti-aircraft gun mountings were covered with canvas, and an elaborate system of hoses was turned on to spray the ship with seawater and prevent fallout sticking. To investigate the effect of radioactivity on the engine system, the ship steamed on one shaft and one boiler manned by four stokers in space suits, while the other engine room and boiler room were shut down to ensure they remained uncontaminated. The rest of the crew crammed into the ship's two citadels – armoured compartments akin to underground fallout bunkers – only to emerge 12 hours later, stretching and inhaling big gulps of air, after monitoring and decontamination teams declared the upper deck safe.

The pre-wetting system worked surprisingly well, reducing the level of fallout by 75 per cent compared to a section of the quarterdeck deliberately left dry.

Some officers at the Admiralty were disappointed with the *Diana*'s results. They felt that the ship and her crew were not exposed to enough radiation to represent a realistic exercise. One of their findings was that the pre-wetting system would have worked even better if it had used fresh water instead of seawater, but that was impossible because the ship could not carry enough water to keep the hoses on for 12 hours. So in the event of nuclear war, Royal Navy ships would have to be washed with contaminated seawater just as the *Diana* was.

During Operation Buffalo, hundreds of Commonwealth servicemen and officials were deliberately exposed at Maralinga. The Indoctrinee Force (a.k.a. I-Force) consisted of 283 non-technical observers, mostly officers, sent to gain experience of an atomic blast. Of the 283 men, 178 were British, 100 were Australian, and five were New Zealanders. The whole unit witnessed Buffalo 1 (the 15-kiloton tower shot) from North Base, 5 miles from Ground Zero. The men were dressed in shorts, shirts, boots and long socks. Over the next few days, small teams re-entered the contaminated area wearing space suits and film badges and accompanied by health escorts equipped with dosimeters. The indoctrinees helped recover target response items, including dummies dressed in uniforms, and were monitored and decontaminated in an experimental caravan designed for use in the field. On the way back to camp, they also passed through health control for further monitoring and decontamination (if required).

After the first test, most members of I-Force returned to their units, but about 100 remained on hand for the second test (the 1.5-kiloton ground burst). During the lead-up, they dug slit trenches 2000 yards from Ground Zero and positioned a Centurion tank nearby. When the bomb went off, 24 men were crouched in the trenches, four officers were shut in the Centurion tank, and the rest were on a witness stand 3200 yards from Ground Zero. Despite this, the British scientist in charge of I-Force, Edmund Drake Seager, insisted that 'no personnel were ever treated as "Guinea Pigs"; and, specifically, the IF [I-Force] was never so conceived'.[32] According to Drake Seager, only animals and dummies were used to study blast effects, while indoctrinees were 'positioned at distances and in locations calculated to be safe'.[33]

That was easy for him to say: he was not the one in the firing line.

On 20 November 1985, the Royal Commissioners released their report. The document ran to 615 pages plus appendices, with 201 conclusions and seven recommendations, published in three volumes. The commissioners criticised both governments and found many specific failures of planning and execution without uncovering evidence of dangerously high levels of fallout or elevated rates of mortality and morbidity in Aboriginal people and veterans. Consequently, almost everyone was disappointed.

The report did, however, contain many interesting findings. Regarding Operation Hurricane, the commissioners found that the Montebello Islands were 'not an appropriate place for atomic tests owing to the prevailing weather patterns and the limited opportunities for safe firing'.[34] They also found that there was indeed fallout on the mainland, despite Peirson's protests to the contrary, and that planners had failed to consider 'the distinctive lifestyles of Aboriginal people' in the North West. The failure to provide aircrews with appropriate instruction, protective equipment, radiation monitoring devices and decontamination facilities was deemed 'negligent'. The commissioners also concluded that the divers involved in the salvage of the sunken LCA 'were exposed to the risk of ingesting contaminated seawater in the performance of their duties'.[35] They were just as scathing in their assessments of the later trials.

The Royal Commissioners recommended reversing the burden of proof on servicemen and civilians seeking compensation for illness and injury, instead placing it on the Commonwealth. They also called for the extensive rehabilitation of all three test sites, suggesting, rather optimistically, that the UK Government should pay for it. Finally, they recommended compensating the traditional owners of Maralinga and Emu Field – the southern branch of the Pitjantjatjara people – for the loss of their lands until such time as the test sites were declared safe and returned to them.

Unsurprisingly, the UK Government initially refused to pay for the rehabilitation, arguing that they were not liable since the Australian Government had signed off on their earlier clean-ups. Only after the 1993 publication of an embarrassing report in *New Scientist*, which proved conclusively that Maralinga was still contaminated, did the Brits reluctantly agree to contribute £20 million (A$45 million) towards a proposed A$100 million clean-up of the mainland test sites.

The clean-up commenced in the late nineties, and like everything else to do with the atomic tests, it was highly controversial. The outfit that won the tender used a process called '*in situ* vitrification', which involved zapping the burial pits with so much electricity that they became underground ovens, melting the radioactive debris in temperatures of up to 2000 degrees Celsius.[36] But the machinery exploded about halfway through the operation, spraying molten lava 50 metres in every direction. Miraculously, no one was hurt. After that, the company cut its losses and capped the rest of the pits with concrete, digging up the vitrified material and burying it even deeper. Prime Minister John Howard called it 'world's best practice clean up'.[37] Nuclear engineer Alan Parkinson, who was fired from the project after criticising the process, disagreed, calling it 'a cheap and nasty solution that wouldn't be adopted in white-fella land'.[38]

Despite the operation's shortcomings, Maralinga and Emu Field were returned to the Maralinga Tjarutja Council in stages, culminating with the handover of Maralinga Village in 2009. A further A$13.5 million in compensation was paid to the council to be used for managing and monitoring the land and establishing a new community – the Oak Valley Community, 130 kilometres north-west of Maralinga.

You can go on guided tours of Maralinga now. A secure fence, hundreds of kilometres long, surrounds the range, but you can get in at the main gate if you have a permit. For safety's sake, you are not allowed out of the village without a guide. The forward area is considered safe enough to visit, but not to live on or camp on for any length of time. It probably never will be.

The Commonwealth Government handed the Montebello Islands back to the Western Australian Government in 1992. These days, charter boats from Exmouth and Dampier take groups of anglers on weeklong fishing expeditions around the islands. The archipelago's atomic history is seemingly part of the appeal, giving the adventure a frisson of danger. The coral and mangroves are growing back, and Hermite Island has been converted into a sanctuary for native wildlife transplanted from nearby Barrow Island, home of the multi-billion-dollar Gorgon gas project, but Trimouille and Alpha islands are still contaminated, with warning signs telling visitors not to stay for longer than an hour, pick up any loose debris, or camp overnight.

•

The atomic veterans had to wait decades for some semblance of justice. For years, they had been ordered not to speak about where they had been or what they had done. They were then forced to watch as their numbers dwindled at reunions, with suspiciously large numbers of once fit young men dying of cancer in their forties and fifties. In Britain and Australia, individual veterans and widows battled for compensation in court, with little success. It does not help when the government holds all the relevant service and medical records. Even when the claimants could get hold of their records, the files were often incomplete for security reasons. Veterans would be told by officious bureaucrats half their age that they were never at a test site, or had never been exposed, because the relevant documents had been removed from their files or never included in the first place. (This was a particular problem for National Servicemen in the RAN, who never officially joined the ships on which they served, but just jumped on board whenever they were ordered to.)

Many atomic veterans began to feel like they were going mad. Veterans groups provided a lifeline, helping the ageing ex-servicemen realise they were not alone, not losing their minds. But even the associations experienced little success, their demands for pensions and medals repeatedly rejected on the basis that the atomic tests did not qualify as active service, or wartime operations. (What a pity the organisations did not have access to Admiral Torlesse's papers. Way back in 1952, in the midst of an argument with Dr Tyte, he had insisted that Hurricane was 'an operation of war'.)[39] In other words, the atomic veterans would have been eligible for a pension if they had been bombed by an enemy, but, since they had been bombed by an ally, they were not.

To justify the decision to deny compensation and recognition to the atomic veterans, the UK Government frequently cited the results of a 1988 study by the UK National Radiation Protection Board and Imperial Cancer Research Fund, which examined the health outcomes of 21,000 British test participants, with follow-ups in 1993 and 2003. 'Over all the analyses, when compared with the control group, the test participant group had similar overall levels of aggregated mortality and cancer incidence', the official fact sheet stated. 'In addition, test participants and controls had, in general, a greater life expectancy than members of the general UK population. This "Healthy Worker Effect" (or "Healthy Soldier Effect") reflects the fact that a group of people who have been employed will (overall) be healthier than the general population because the general population will include the chronically sick who are unable to work.'[40]

That sort of jolly hockey sticks stuff drove the veterans up the wall. They believed that the government deliberately manipulated the statistics by including cooks and clerks and other blokes who had never been anywhere near any radiation to bring down the averages and obscure any increases in cancer or mortality rates among personnel who were actually exposed.

In 1999, Australia's Department of Veterans' Affairs commissioned a similar study of cancer and mortality rates in 16,000 Australian test participants. A panel of government and university radiation experts and health researchers conducted the study and published their findings in 2006. They found that the death rate was similar to that of the general public, but slightly higher, contradicting the cheery British findings. Significantly, the Australian experts found that death from cancer was 18 per cent higher than the general population, with much greater incidences of oral cancer, lung cancer, colorectal cancer, prostate cancer, oesophageal cancer, melanoma and leukaemia. To the dismay of Australia's atomic veterans, the experts found 'no relationship' between overall cancer incidence or mortality and exposure to ionising radiation, finding that the average test participant's dose was 'only slightly greater than the background exposure received by every Australian every year'.[41] Instead, they attributed most of the cancers to high levels of sun exposure and smoking among test participants. These findings infuriated atomic veterans, who put a lot less faith in the accuracy of AWRE's dosimetry readings than the radiation experts apparently did.

Despite the study's equivocal findings, the Australian Government made atomic veterans eligible for a DVA White Card in 2006, providing subsidised healthcare for malignant cancers – subject to strict criteria. Montebello veterans, for instance, had to be able to prove that they either came within 10 kilometres of Trimouille's Main Beach, flew through a radioactive cloud, travelled in contaminated vehicles, or worked on contaminated equipment.

The following year, the government issued a commemorative medallion for test participants, which was emphatically *not a medal*, and was not permitted to be worn as such. Many atomic veterans were insulted by the gesture. Consequently, most of the medallions are lying in bureau drawers with other useless junk.

In 2014, UK Prime Minister David Cameron announced: 'I am happy to tell the House that the Government recognise and are extremely grateful to all the service personnel who participated in the nuclear testing programme.'[42] The UK Government subsequently announced a grant of £25 million for an Aged Veterans Fund to 'alleviate suffering and increase wellbeing'. The fund was for all British military personnel, not just nuclear veterans, and it was emphasised that the payment was ex gratia in nature, and not an admission of guilt or liability on behalf of the UK Government, but the British Nuclear Test Veterans Association was invited to bid for a share of the money. The association eventually secured £6 million to create the Nuclear Community Charity Fund (NCCF). Since then, the NCCF has funded a five-year research programme into the genetic heritage of nuclear veterans and descendants at Brunel University London; the establishment of the Centre for Health Effects of Radiological and Chemical Agents; and the creation of a Care Wellbeing and Inclusion Fund to provide support for British nuclear veterans, spouses and descendants. (So far, the university has found no evidence of genetic damage in descendants of nuclear veterans, but has reported higher rates of anxiety among nuclear veterans compared to the general population.)[42]

The New Zealand and Fijian governments have also introduced funds to support Christmas Island veterans.

On Sunday 7 May 2017, Federal Liberal MP Andrew Hastie, former SAS troop commander and veteran of the conflict in Afghanistan, met with members of the Australian

Ex-Services Atomic Survivors Association in Mandurah, Western Australia. It was a bright and sunny day and, appropriately, the fellow veterans – several generations apart in age – were meeting at the stylised war memorial on the banks of the Mandurah Estuary. The federal budget was due to be handed down in two days' time, and Hastie, the local member, was there to announce that it would include A$133 million to provide atomic veterans with the DVA Gold Card, giving them access to free healthcare for life.

It was 60 years after the last atomic test, and over 30 years since the Royal Commission.

By this time, the Perth-based Australian Ex-Services Atomic Survivors Association was the last atomic veterans group still operating in Australia. Most of the old men happily posing for photos with Hastie were former sailors and National Servicemen who had served at the Montebellos in their late teens and early twenties. One of them was Jim Marlow, the 81-year-old secretary of the association, who had witnessed Mosaic's G2 from the deck of HMAS *Karangi* as a 20-year-old steward.

'As the countdown descended we were told to turn our backs to the Island, and cover our eyes with our hands,' Marlow wrote in an unpublished memoir. 'This seemed strange at first. We were given no real appreciation of possible injury, we were offered no protective clothing, remained simply in the routine dress of the day – shorts and sandals, optional "shirts off". True it is that we were given a small tag with a safety pin to attach to our shorts, called a Roentgen Tag I believe, but as we used them daily, [we] became accustomed to them, and [once] they were collected, we thought little about them. In the end we simply forgot them and what happened to them we never knew.

'I have heard of some people tell of seeing right through their hands as the explosion occurred, but I do not recall this. After the Bomb was detonated we were told to about face toward the Island again. There confronting us was a huge cloud of Black, Red, Yellow dirt, smoke and all manner of debris, whirling and twisting upward, a crown developing on top, dominated the visual, but became distorted as it rose ... Momentarily it seemed as if the world stood still, until the noise burst around us, and the wind rush competed with our posture for a few moments as it passed, before the excitement was over, and we returned to normal duty.'[44]

The *Karangi* returned to the islands the following day and re-entered the lagoon less than 48 hours after the blast.

'These men worked on the islands only four years after the first atomic test with no protective gear', said Hastie. 'Many were on [the] deck of their ships and fully exposed during a subsequent test, in very close proximity to the explosion. Of the surviving 51 members who have been surveyed, 43 per cent have had some kind of cancer. Of the 28 who have already passed on, 14 have died from cancer. This is a story of young Australians who answered their country's call during the period of national service – they served in dangerous and hazardous conditions in the Montebello Islands.'[45]

Five years later, the UK Government finally came to the same conclusion. In June 2022, Prime Minister Boris Johnson became the first British leader to meet with representatives of the British Nuclear Test Veterans Association face to face. Johnson was so moved by their harrowing stories that he promised to do something about it – and did. In one of his last acts before resigning, he ordered the government to reconsider medallic recognition for nuclear veterans. There were high hopes for an announcement timed to coincide with the 70th anniversary of Operation Hurricane, dubbed the Plutonium Jubilee, but the big day came and went with little notice in a chaotic period marked by the death of Queen Elizabeth II, the ascension of King Charles III, and the rapid resignation of Johnson's successor, Liz Truss. It fell to Truss's own successor,

Rishi Sunak, to front a gathering of 200 nuclear veterans and family members at the National Memorial Arboretum in Staffordshire, England, on 21 November 2022.

'At the height of the Cold War, often unseen and unsung, you were in the forefront of our defence', Sunak told the veterans. 'You travelled thousands of miles to the other side of the world to conduct these tests and in doing so you maintained our scientific and technological advantage in the face of the threat posed by the Soviet Union, preserving peace and ensuring the security of our country. The importance of that contribution cannot be overstated. A protective umbrella of our independent nuclear deterrent continues to keep us safe today.

'But your service deserves more. I am very pleased to announce today that His Majesty the King has decided to recognise that service formally by creating a new medal for those who served at the nuclear tests. It is a fitting tribute to the incredible contribution that you have made. It is an enduring symbol of our gratitude, so to all our nuclear test veterans, including those who are no longer with us, and all the families that have supported them, on behalf of a grateful nation, I say thank you.'[46]

Fittingly, the UK Government announced that the medal would be made available to all veterans of the British nuclear tests, including servicemen and civilians from Canada, Australia, New Zealand, Fiji and Christmas Island. Two of those men, Bill Plewright and Jim Marlow, helped me write this book. It was my honour and privilege to tell them about Sunak's announcement. There are no words for what the recognition meant to them.

Unfortunately, it was too late for most of their mates.

# ACKNOWLEDGEMENTS

This book would not have been possible without the help of a great many people. First and foremost, I would like to thank the leadership of the Australian Ex Services Atomic Survivors Association: President Rex Kaye, Founding President Bill Plewright, Secretary Jim Marlow and Treasurer Denis Flowers. Bill and Jim in particular spent hours sharing their stories of life in the Montebellos with me. Jim provided access to an unpublished manuscript by members of the association, and Bill even gave me a watch! Gentlemen, I could not have done it without you.

A warm thanks to all the other nuclear veterans and family members who spoke to me during my research: Lyn Brent, Norm Cunningham, the late Brian Emmott, Maxine Goodwin, Eric Heavens, John Quantrill, Sheryl Sutherland, Anne Trenerry and Milton Ward. I'm sorry I could not include all of your stories, but I hope you feel that this book does some justice to your experiences.

Researching the British nuclear tests would not have been possible without the dedicated historians, librarians and archivists at the National Archives of Australia (Perth and Canberra), the Australian War Memorial, the National Library of Australia, the UK National Archives, the Imperial War Museums, the State Library of Western Australia, the JS Battye Library of Western Australian History, the RAAF Association of Western Australia's Aviation Heritage Museum, the RAAF Office of Air Force History, the HMAS *Stirling* Museum, the Naval Historical Society of Australia, the Royal Australian Engineers Association and the Royal Navy Fleet Air Arm Officers Association. Special thanks to Petar Djokovic at the RAN Sea Power Centre and Jenny Kohlen from *The West Australian*, who went above and beyond to answer many, many questions.

Numerous authors, academics and experts advised me on various aspects of the trial. Thanks to: Susie Boniface, Dr Mick Broderick, Robert Drewe, Madison Hoffman, Dr Zeb Leonard, Mark Smith, Dr Elizabeth Tynan, Professor Peter Veth, Frank Walker and Dr Victor Wycoco. My dad, John Grace, also served as an invaluable in-house military adviser. Needless to say, any mistakes are mine, not theirs.

To my publisher, Sophie Hamley, and everyone else at Hachette Australia: thank you for making this book a reality. Without you, it would be just another manuscript gathering dust in a drawer.

The last five years have been challenging to say the least, and I could not have made it here without the support of my family and friends, especially: my mum, Carol Grace; my brother, Tim Grace; Bill and Peg; Jill and Jocelyn; Deryk and Linda Thomson; the Harding rent-a-crowd; the Ashfield dog walkers; the Axis of Hustle; Anne Barnetson; Pete Barr; Milly Bartlett; Leigh Berwick; MJ Birkett; Russell Brown; Hussain Currimbhoy; Katey Harris; Tiffany Hill; Adam Holland; Juliette Lovell; Reto Meier; Will Murray; Michele O'Neill; Maxine O'Shannassy; Oonagh Quigley; Morgan Quinn; Julia Pickworth; Andrew Reid; Marcus Ryan; Patrick Ryan; Tor Sagrabb; Matt Strika; Yvette Walker; Peta White; Ben Willesee and, of course, the late, great Nathan Fellows.

It was not actually my idea to write a book about Operation Hurricane. It was, in fact, my wife's idea. Bron, you are the most caring, supportive, understanding wife in the world. I don't know how you do it.

As kind as she is, Bron would never forgive me if I did not mention my writing partner, physical trainer and emotional support animal: Taya, the kelpie cross. Taya has just reminded me it is time to go for a walk.

It is always time to go for a walk.

# ENDNOTES

## PROLOGUE

1 David Wilson, *Always First: The RAAF Airfield Construction Squadrons 1942–1974*, Air Power Studies Centre, Fairbairn, 1998, p 107.
2 'Air Commodore Percival (Nobby) Lings interviewed by Ken Llewellyn about his career in the Royal Australian Air Force (RAAF)', audio recording, AWM: https://www.awm.gov.au/collection/C282960, accessed 5 May 2020.
3 Ian Hamilton, 'Cocos Drowning', RAAF Airfield Construction Squadrons Association homepage: http://raafacs.homestead.com/COCOSDROWNING. html, accessed 15 October 2018.
4 'Brisbane airman wins medal at Cocos Island', *The Courier-Mail* (Brisbane), 3 November 1952, p 1.

## 1. A BLOODY UNION JACK FLYING ON TOP OF IT

1 Depending on what you read, MAUD is either an acronym for Military Application of Uranium Detonation or an obscure reference to a woman named Maud Ray, who was the English governess of Danish physicist Niels Bohr's children.
2 Graham Farmelo, *Churchill's Bomb: A Hidden History of Science, War and Politics*, Faber & Faber, London, 2013, pp 6–7. Churchill's initial reluctance to form a nuclear alliance with the Americans seems bizarre in retrospect. Farmelo suggests that the prime minister had his hands full with other elements of the war effort, and had not yet realised the full significance of the atomic project. The fact that the US had not yet entered the war was probably another consideration. It also seems likely that Churchill and his officials believed they were much further ahead of the Americans than they really were.
3 Margaret Gowing & Lorna Arnold, *Independence and Deterrence: Britain and Atomic Energy 1945–1952; Volume 1; Policy Making*, Macmillan, London, 1974, p 6.
4 'Memorandum on the atomic bomb by the Prime Minister', 28 August 1945, TNA: CAB 130/3.
5 'No 86 Wing espionage', NAA: A2087, 5/1/AIR PART 1, p 2.
6 'No 86 Wing espionage', p 2.
7 Peter Hennessy, 'How Bevin saved Britain's bomb', *The Times* (London), 30 September 1982, p 10.
8 Brian Cathcart, *Test of Greatness: Britain's Struggle for the Atomic Bomb*, John Murray, London, 1994, p 35.
9 Cathcart, op. cit., p 35.
10 Cathcart, op. cit., p 38.
11 John S Malik, 'The yields of the Hiroshima and Nagasaki nuclear explosions', PDF, Los Alamos National Laboratory, Report No LA-08819, September 1985: https://lanl-primo.hosted.exlibrisgroup.com/permalink/f/17admmo/01LANL_ALMA2186922310003761, accessed 14 March 2023.
12 Margaret Gowing & Lorna Arnold, *Independence and Deterrence: Britain and Atomic Energy 1945–1952; Volume 2; Policy Execution*, Macmillan, London, 1974, p 457.

13 Elizabeth Tynan, *Atomic Thunder: The Maralinga Story*, NewSouth, Sydney, 2016, p 63.

## 2. DEFENCE CALL TO THE NATION

1 Frank Walker, *Maralinga: the chilling exposé of our secret nuclear shame and betrayal of our troops and country*, 2nd ed, Hachette Australia, Sydney, 2016, p 2.
2 Walker, op. cit., p 3.
3 Troy Bramston, *Robert Menzies: The Art of Politics*, Scribe, Melbourne, 2019, p 38.
4 'Australia at war – Menzies', *The Daily Telegraph* (Sydney), 4 September 1939, p 4.
5 'Poll "referendum on socialism"', *The Mercury* (Hobart), 7 December 1949, p 1.
6 '6,000 cheer Mr Menzies at Town Hall: campaign against bank plan', *The Sydney Morning Herald*, 26 August 1947, p 5.
7 George Winterton, 'The significance of the Communist Party case', *Melbourne University Law Review*, vol 18, 1992, p 640.
8 'Menzies confident in red bill challenge', *Maryborough Chronicle*, 16 September 1950, p 5.
9 'Message from Mr Attlee for Mr Menzies', 16 September 1950, NAA: A6456, R096/013.
10 AW Martin, *Robert Menzies: A Life; Volume 2; 1944–1978*, Melbourne University Press, Carlton South, 1999, p 167.
11 'Deadly, subtle aggression: Menzies' plea for plain thinking', *The Sydney Morning Herald*, 21 September 1950, p 4.

## 3. EPICURE

1 'Operation Epicure – report on reconnaissance of Monte Bello Islands', TNA: DEFE 16/412, sect III, para 1.
2 'Operation Epicure – report on reconnaissance of Monte Bello Islands', sect III, para 6.
3 'Operation Epicure – report on reconnaissance of Monte Bello Islands', sect III, para 7.
4 'Operation Epicure – report on reconnaissance of Monte Bello Islands', sect II, para 3.
5 Peter Veth, 'The Aboriginal occupation of the Montebello Islands, Northwest Australia', *Australian Aboriginal Studies*, no 2, 1993, pp 39–50; Peter Veth et al, 'Early human occupation of a maritime desert, Barrow Island, North-West Australia', *Quaternary Science Reviews*, vol 168, 15 July 2017, pp 19–29.
6 Interestingly, trailblazing anthropologist Norman Tindale claimed that the Noala people of the Pilbara coast visited Barrow and the Montebellos in more recent times, incorporating the islands into their territory, but there is little evidence to back up this claim, and, unfortunately, there are no known Noala speakers today. See: Veth, 'The Aboriginal occupation of the Montebello Islands, North West Australia'.
7 According to the vagaries of the era, Brooke's name was sometimes spelt Broock or Brookes. Similarly, the *Trial* was sometimes spelt *Tryal* or *Tryall*.
8 J Lort Stokes, *Discoveries in Australia: Volume II*, T&W Boone, London, 1846, p 207.

9   Stokes, op. cit., p 211.

10  Stokes, op. cit., p 213.

11  Myra Stanbury, 'A survey of sites associated with early pearling activities in the Monte Bello Islands, Western Australia (draft)', PDF, Department of Maritime Archaeology WA, report no 35, January 1986, p 19: http://museum. wa.gov.au/maritime-archaeology-db/maritime-reports/survey-sites-associated-early-pearling-activities-monte-bello-islands-western-austr, accessed Tuesday 7 April 2020.

12  Debbie Cameron, 'A Pearl fisher from Cheetham Hill – the Big Friday Find', Archives Plus, 21 February 2014: https://manchesterarchiveplus.wordpress. com/2014/02/21/a-pearl-fisher-from-cheetham-hill-the-big-friday-find/, accessed 22 April 2020.

13  'Operation Epicure – report on reconnaissance of Monte Bello Islands', sect I, para 9.

14  'Operation Epicure – report on reconnaissance of Monte Bello Islands', sect I, para 6.

15  'Operation Epicure – report on reconnaissance of Monte Bello Islands', intro, para 2.

16  WG Penney, 'Epicure: report on proposed site – 12 January 1951', NAA: 6455, BV1, par 15.

## 4. THE WESTERN ISLANDS

1   'Menzies's policy speech: govt. to continue to struggle to beat communism', *The Sydney Morning Herald*, 4 April 1951, p 4.

2   'Election speeches: obstruction criticized; LCP majority urged', *The Advertiser* (Adelaide), 20 April 1951, p 15; 'Mr Kekwick replies', letter to the editor, *The Examiner* (Launceston), 26 April 1951, p 2.

3   CR Attlee, cable to RG Menzies, 26 March 1951, NAA: A6456, R096/013, para 4.

4   Attlee, cable to Menzies, 26 March 1951, para 6.

5   Gowing & Arnold, *Independence and Deterrence: Vol 1*, p 337.

6   EJ Williams, letter to RG Menzies, 28 May 1951, NAA: A6456, R096/013.

7   'Operation Epicure – message from Hurricane Executive', 28 May 1951, NAA: A6456, R096/013.

8   Marsden Hordern, *A Merciful Journey: Recollections of a World War II Patrol Boat Man*, The Miegunyah Press, Carlton, 2005, p 138.

9   'Echo-sounding equipment in ships "too efficient"', *The West Australian* (Perth), 31 July 1951, p 1.

10  'The RAN prepared a new chart for the Monte Bello atomic test', NAA: A816, 3/301/539A, p 2.

11  Cathcart, *Test of Greatness*, p 158.

12  Cdr GD Tancred, 'HMAS *Warrego* – report of proceedings – August 1951', AWM: AWM78, 360/4, para 5.

13  'The RAN prepared a new chart for the Monte Bello atomic test', p 3.

14  R Adm AD Torlesse, 'Operation Hurricane – report by the Naval Commander', NAA: A6455, RC231, ch 12, para 2.

15  Ellis Glover, Royal Commission statement, NAA: A6450, 2, p 3.

16  Report on Lt Cdr AM Synnot on posting from HMAS *Lonsdale* to HMAS *Cerberus II* for exchange service, 5 May 1952, NAA: A3978, SYNNOT A M.

17 Capt AWR McNicoll, 'Department of Navy minute paper – progress report –
1.8.51 – 15.9.51', 19 September 1951, NAA: A6456, R096/013.
18 Capt AWR McNicoll, 'Department of Navy minute paper – progress report –
1.8.51 – 15.9.51'.
19 Lt Cdr J Ferguson, 'Report of proceedings – HMAS *Mildura* – September
1951', AWM: AWM78, 221/1, p 1.
20 Lorna Arnold & Mark Smith, *Britain, Australia and the Bomb: The Nuclear
Tests and Their Aftermath*, 2nd ed, Palgrave Macmillan, London, 2006, p 19.

## 5. CYCLONE SEASON

1 DW Longworth, Royal Commission testimony, NAA: A6448, 13, p 7318.
2 Admiralty, 'Chapter VIII: moorings', *Manual of Seamanship: Volume III;
BR 67 (3/51)*, Her Majesty's Stationery Office, London, 1954, pp 150–69.
May I recommend this chapter to anyone interested in learning more about
moorings?
3 Lt Cdr LN Morison, 'HMAS *Karangi* – report of proceedings on detached
duties – 20 February to 24 March 1952', AWM: AWM78, 183/3, p 1.
4 Ibid.
5 Morison, op. cit., p 2.
6 JL Symonds, *A History of British Atomic Tests in Australia*, Australian
Government Printing Service, Canberra, 1985, p 31.
7 Symonds, op. cit., pp 31–32.
8 Symonds, op. cit., p 32.
9 *Report of the Royal Commission into British Nuclear Tests in Australia:
Volume 2*, Australian Government Printing Service, Canberra, 1985, p 449.
10 'Britain's atomic progress', editorial, *The Advertiser* (Adelaide), 19 February
1952, p 2.
11 'The atomic test', editorial, *The West Australian* (Perth), 20 February 1952,
p 2.
12 'Britain's first atomic test', editorial, *The Age* (Melbourne), 19 February 1952,
p 2.
13 'Britain may test atomic weapons', *The West Australian* (Perth), 20 February
1952, p 1.
14 'Aborigines and atom bomb', *The West Australian* (Perth), 21 February 1952,
p 2 (reported speech).
15 'Aborigines and atom bomb' (reported speech).
16 Lt Cdr J Ferguson, 'HMAS *Mildura* – report of proceedings – May 1951',
AWM: AWM78, 221/1, para 19.
17 Lt Cdr J Ferguson, 'HMAS *Mildura* – report of proceedings – March 1952',
AWM: AWM78, 221/3, p 1, para 3.
18 Ferguson, 'HMAS *Mildura* – report of proceedings – March 1952', p 1, para 8.
19 Ferguson, 'HMAS *Mildura* – report of proceedings – March 1952', p 2,
para 17.
20 Ferguson, 'HMAS *Mildura* – report of proceedings – March 1952', p 2,
para 18.
21 Capt WE Hardman, 'SS *Dorrigo* – voyage report no 49', SROWA: AU WA
S1721 – cons5253 396 [v2], p 2.
22 Lt Cdr J Ferguson, 'HMAS *Mildura* – report of proceedings – April 1952',
AWM: AWM78, 221/3, pp 1–2.

23  A/Capt FB Morris, letter to Secretary, Naval Board, 29 May 1952, AWM: AWM78 221/3.
24  'Sharp attack on atom test site', *The West Australian* (Perth), 3 September 1952, p 3 (reported speech).
25  Ibid.
26  'Premier replies on atom test site', *The West Australian* (Perth), 4 September 1952, p 1 (reported speech).
27  Ibid.

## 6. THE LANDING SQUADRON

 1  'Atomic-gear ships closely guarded', *The West Australian* (Perth), 17 April 1952, p 1.
 2  Richard Murray, column, *The Sunday Times* (Perth), 20 April 1952, p 25.
 3  'Atomic explosion an "ordinary one"', *The West Australian* (Perth), 18 April 1952, p 3 (reported speech).
 4  Ibid.
 5  Ibid.
 6  'Commander Derek Willan: decorated Royal Navy officer who rescued soldiers during the "miracle of Dunkirk" and took part in the first British nuclear bomb test', obituary, *The Times* (London), 30 November 2018, p 53.
 7  'Plaque returned to HMS *Narvik*', *The West Australian* (Perth), 18 April 1952, p 3.
 8  Peter Bird, *Operation Hurricane*, 2nd ed, Square One, Worcester, 1989, p 29.
 9  'Security ban placed on atom crews', *The West Australian* (Perth), 19 April 1952, p 1.
10  'Atom ship men kept out of court', *Daily News* (Perth), 18 April 1952, p 1.
11  Ibid.
12  'Security ban said to be altered', *Daily News* (Perth), 19 April 1952, p 1.
13  'So much for security', editorial, *Daily News* (Perth), 21 April 1952, p 4.
14  'Naval head tells of "mistaken impression"', *Daily News* (Perth), 22 April 1952, p 2 (reported speech).
15  David Horner, *The Spy Catchers: The Official History of ASIO; 1949–1963; Volume 1*, Allen & Unwin, Crows Nest, 2014, p 248.
16  Jack Coulter, *By Deadline to Headline*, Access Press, Northbridge, 1997, p 102.
17  'Islands off WA for atomic tests: fleet will sail for the north today', *The West Australian* (Perth), 22 April 1952, p 1.
18  'Monte Bello landings are now prohibited', *The West Australian* (Perth), 2 May 1952, p 1.
19  'Islands off WA for atomic tests: fleet will sail for the north today'.
20  'Department of Air – minutes of conference held in room 212, N block, Air Force Headquarters at 1430 hours on 21 April 1952 (discussed RAAF aspects of Operation Hurricane)', NAA: A6456, R021/001 PART 2.
21  Symonds, *A History of British Atomic Tests in Australia*, pp 41–42.
22  Symonds, op. cit., pp 42–43.
23  Symonds, op. cit., p 41.

## 7. THE GODDAM ISLES

1 'Atomic ships sail – in deep mystery', *Daily News* (Perth), 22 April 1952, p 1.
2 Bird, *Operation Hurricane*, p 31.
3 'I or Item time' refers to the military practice of giving each time zone a letter code for clear communication, beginning with A (GMT + 0100), skipping J because it looks too similar to I (GMT + 0900), and ending with Z (GMT + 0000). In 1952, Commonwealth forces were still using the WII-era phonetic alphabet: Able, Baker, Charlie, Dog, Easy, Fox, George, How, Item, Jig, King, Love, Mike, Nan, Oboe, Peter, Queen, Roger, Sugar, Tare, Uncle, Victor, William, X-ray, Yoke and Zebra. Thus 0900 Item time equates to 0000 Zebra time.
4 Bird, op. cit., p 34.
5 Lt Col AP Smith, quoted by Air Cdre WL Hely, 'Department of Air – Operation Hurricane (letter from WL Hely, Air Commodore, Air Officer Commanding Western Area to Headquarters Eastern Area describing the work of detachments from No 86 Wing, No 82 Wing and No 5 Airfield Construction Squadron)', NAA: A6456, R021/001 PART 41, p 2.
6 'Peter George Fletcher (oral history)', audio recording, IWM: https://www.iwm.org.uk/collections/item/object/80010940, accessed 27 June 2019.
7 'Atom fleet finds the fishing good', *The West Australian*, 16 June 1952, p 6.
8 Coulter, *By Deadline to Headline*, p 105.
9 Coulter, op. cit., p 106.
10 Ibid. Writing over 40 years later, Coulter states that the press men left Perth at 2.30 a.m. on Monday 21 April, but contemporary articles by Coulter and Milne indicate that they set out 24 hours later.
11 Coulter, op. cit., p 108.
12 Ibid.
13 Coulter, op. cit., p 109. Coulter states that the *Thelma* left Onslow at 11.00 a.m. on Friday 25 April, but once again appears to be out by 24 hours.
14 Ibid.
15 Ibid.
16 Coulter, op. cit., pp 110–11.
17 'Pressmen find Montebellos like wartime beachhead', *Daily News* (Perth), April 29, p 2.
18 Symonds, *A History of British Atomic Tests in Australia*, p 63.
19 'Tremendous atom secret?' *The Sunday Times*, Perth, 14 September 1952, p 1.
20 'Under the water', letter to the editor, *Daily News* (Perth), 24 April 1952, p 4.
21 'Australian bomb tests not harmful to people', *Lithgow Mercury*, 2 May 1952, p 1.
22 Ibid.
23 Ibid.
24 Ibid.
25 *Report of the Royal Commission into British Nuclear Tests in Australia: Vol 1*, Australian Government Printing Service, Canberra, 1985, p 118.
26 *Report of the Royal Commission into British Nuclear Tests in Australia: Vol 1*, p 119.
27 'House of Commons', *The Times* (London), 15 May 1952, p 4.
28 'Bird life in Monte Bello Islands: a naturalist's fears', *The Times* (London), 23 May 1952, p 5.

29  'House of Commons', *The Times* (London), 25 July 1952, p 2.
30  Lt CF Young, 'HMAS *Koala* – report of proceedings – May 1952', AWM: AWM78, 189/2, p 1, para 13.
31  Capt T Carlin, letter to Maj F Haupt, 29 April 1952, NAA: K1214, 14/2/04.
32  'Water-supply problem overcome for Monte Bello atomic weapon test: pipe-line laid at the Fortescue River', NAA: A816, 3/301/539A, pp 3, 1.
33  RT Raph, Royal Commission statement, NAA: A6450, 4, p 4.
34  Torlesse, 'Operation Hurricane – report by the Naval Commander', ch 12, para 12.
35  Lt Col AE Walkling, 'Operation Hurricane – report of the RH Division – Team RH1 – general direction and the control of re-entry', NAA: A6455, RC250, sect 9.3.3.
36  Lt CF Young, 'HMAS *Koala* – report of proceedings – June 1952', AWM: AWM78, 189/2, p 2, para 12.
37  'Oil catches fire in an atomic ship', *The West Australian* (Perth), 23 June 1952, p 1.
38  A/Capt RV Wheatley, letter to A/R Adm HA Showers, 1 August 1952, 'HMAS *Koala* – report of proceedings – June 1952', AWM: AWM78, 189/2.
39  Young, 'HMAS *Koala*, report of proceedings, June 1952', p 3, para 17.
40  Young, 'HMAS *Koala*, report of proceedings, June 1952', p 3, para 20.
41  Lt Cdr LN Morison, 'HMAS *Karangi* – report of proceedings – July 1952', AWM: AWM78, 183/3, p 2.
42  A/Capt FB Morris, letter to the secretary of the Naval Board, 6 August 1952, 'HMAS *Karangi* – report of proceedings – July 1952', AWM: AWM78, 183/3.
43  Lt CF Young, 'HMAS *Koala* – report of proceedings – July 1952', AWM: AWM78, 189/2, p 2, para 10.
44  Lt CF Young, 'HMAS *Koala* – report of proceedings – August 1952', AWM: AWM78, 189/2, p 3.

## 8. VOYAGE OF THE SPECIAL SQUADRON

 1  Gowing & Arnold, *Independence and Deterrence: Vol 2*, p 483.
 2  Cathcart, *Test of Greatness*, p 160.
 3  Gowing & Arnold, op. cit., p 486.
 4  JJ McEnhill, 'Story of Operation Hurricane', NAA:A6455, RC603, p 2.
 5  Ibid.
 6  Torlesse, 'Operation Hurricane – report by the Naval Commander', appendix J.
 7  *Report of the Royal Commission into British Nuclear Tests in Australia: Vol. 1*, pp 26–27.
 8  Cathcart, op. cit., p 194.
 9  Gowing & Arnold, op. cit., p 483.
10  McEnhill, op. cit., p 7.
11  Gowing & Arnold, op. cit., p 486.
12  McEnhill, op. cit., p 10.
13  McEnhill, op. cit., p 22.
14  Ibid.
15  McEnhill, op. cit., p 25.
16  McEnhill, op. cit., p 23.
17  Ibid.

18 'Atom chief pays a secret visit', *The West Australian* (Perth), 2 August 1952, p 3.
19 Symonds, *A History of British Atomic Tests in Australia*, p 70.
20 Air Cdre WL Hely, 'Department of Air – Operation Hurricane – report by Air Officer Commanding Western Area, RAAF', NAA: A6456, R021/001 PART 37, pt I, p 6, para 28.
21 Symonds, op. cit., p 42; *Report of the Royal Commission into British Nuclear Tests in Australia: Vol 1*, p 130.
22 'Campania sailor in court', *The Mirror* (Perth), 2 August 1952, p 2.
23 'Fines for men from atom ship', *The West Australian* (Perth), 2 August 1952, p 6.
24 Bird, *Operation Hurricane*, p 62.

### 9. THE BUILD-UP
1 Gowing & Arnold, *Independence and Deterrence: Vol 2*, p 488.
2 Hely, 'Department of Air – Operation Hurricane (letter from WL Hely, Air Commodore, Air Officer Commanding Western Area to Headquarters Eastern Area describing the work of detachments from No 86 Wing, No 82 Wing and No 5 Airfield Construction Squadron)', p 1.
3 McEnhill, 'Story of Operation Hurricane', p 30.
4 Lt Cdr P Draisey, Royal Commission statement, NAA: A6455, RC709, pp 1–2.
5 Frank L Hill, 'Notes on the natural history of the Monte Bello Islands', *Proceedings of the Linnean Society of London*, vol 165, no 2, June 1955, pp 113–24.
6 Gowing & Arnold, op. cit., p 490.
7 McEnhill, op. cit., p 54.
8 Ibid.
9 Cathcart, *Test of Greatness*, pp 231–32.
10 Cathcart, op. cit., p 231.
11 McEnhill, op. cit., p 45.
12 Gowing & Arnold, op. cit., p 491. The exact wording of Commander Bromley's famous quip varies from account to account.
13 'Doubts about ban on Montebello Islands', *Daily News* (Perth), 2 August 1952, p 1.
14 'Australia Station Intelligence Summary no 6', PDF, Naval Intelligence Division, Navy Office, Melbourne, September 1952, p 19: https://www.Navy.gov.au/media-room/publications/australia-station-intelligence-summaries-1952-1957, accessed 30 January 2019.
15 Walker, *Maralinga*, p 21.
16 'Mystery death', *The Examiner* (Launceston), 12 September 1952, p 1.
17 CTF4, telegram to RNO Onslow, 10 September 1952, 'HMAS *Hawkesbury* – report of proceedings – September 1952', AWM: AWM78, 137/3.
18 Henry J Flack, death certificate, (Marine) Ashburton District, 1/1953, WA Department of Justice, Births Deaths and Marriages.
19 Office of AA&QMG, Western Command, Perth, letter to OC Western Command Transit Camp, Onslow, 2 August 1952, NAA: K1214, 14/2/04; Maj F Haupt, signal to OC Western Command Transit Camp, 4 September 1952, NAA: K1214, 14/2/04.
20 Brian Emmott, interview with the author, 23 August 2019.
21 RC Grace, flight logs, September 1952, personal papers.

22 'Department of Air – Headquarters Western Area – operation instruction no 8/52 –Operation Hurricane', NAA: A6456, R021/001 PART 15, appendix A, p 3.

23 DH Peirson, 'AWRE – report T113/54 – Operation Hurricane – results of aerial radiological survey over the Australian coastline between Onslow and Broome', NAA: A6455, RC306, sect 1.

24 'In the Legislative Assembly', *The West Australian* (Perth), 28 June 1912, p 8.

25 'Medical post vacancy', *The West Australian* (Perth), 16 September 1950, p 8; *Report of the Royal Commission into British Nuclear Tests in Australia: Vol 1*, p 119.

26 Gp Capt GC Hartnell, 'Department of Air – report on reconnaissance to Western Area', NAA: A6456, R021/001 PART 7, para 20.

27 KK Wilson, Royal Commission testimony, NAA: A6448, 2, p 323.

28 HJ Gale, Royal Commission testimony, NAA: A6448, 10, p 5265.

29 HJ Gale, Royal Commission statement, NAA: A6449, 1, p 5.

30 RS Webster, Royal Commission statement NAA: A6450, 5, p 2.

31 R Turner, Royal Commission statement, NAA: A6450, 5, p 2.

32 Gale, Royal Commission statement, p 4.

33 Coulter, *By Deadline to Headline*, p 111.

34 Jim Macartney, telegram to RG Menzies, 10 July 1952, NAA: A1209, 1957/5486.

35 RG Menzies, telegram to Jim Macartney, 13 July 1952, NAA: A1209, 1957/5486.

36 Richie Bright, 'A most unusual post office', in Ricardo Crameri (ed), *Dot Dash to Dot Com – A North-West Odyssey*, RPL Crameri, North Perth, 2002, p 146.

37 Coulter, op. cit., p 112.

38 Margot Lang, 'Exclusive: how WA journalists outfoxed Brits to cover nuclear blast', The Starfish, 22 September 2020: http://www.thestarfish.com.au/2020/09/22/exclusive-how-wa-journalists-outfoxed-brits-to-cover-nuclear-blast/, accessed 27 November 2020.

39 Coulter, op. cit., p 117.

40 'Onslow beats the atom gun with mystery "bomb"', *Daily News* (Perth), 24 September 1952, p 1.

41 'Mystery "bomb" has gone off', *Daily News* (Perth), 27 September 1952.

42 McEnhill, op. cit., p 57. McEnhill states that R–1 was delayed by 24 hours from 18 September to 19 September, but neglects to change the date in the timeline he provides on p 49. Probably as a result, most sources state that the rehearsal began on Thursday 18 September.

43 Cathcart, op. cit., p 211.

44 Cathcart, op. cit., p 233.

## 10. D-DAY

1 Norman Milne, 'The elusive Dr Penney', *The Western Mail* (Perth), 16 July 1953, p 5.

2 Ibid.

3 Ibid.

4 '"Operation Spoofer" was security hoax', *The West Australian* (Perth), 17 November 1952, p 2.

5 EW Titterton, 'Atomic bombs – an expert sums them up', *The Sunday Herald* (Sydney), 21 September 1952, p 2.

6 EW Titterton, Royal Commission testimony, NAA: A6448, 14, p 7619.

7 *Report of the Royal Commission into British Nuclear Tests in Australia: Vol 2*, p 458.

8 G Davey, letter to AD McKnight, 27 August 1952, NAA: A6456, R096/006.

9 Symonds, *A History of British Atomic Tests in Australia*, p 59.

10 Martin, *Robert Menzies: A Life; Vol 2*, p 225.

11 *Report of the Royal Commission into British Nuclear Tests in Australia: Vol 2*, p 457.

12 McEnhill, 'Story of Operation Hurricane', p 59.

13 Cathcart, *Test of Greatness*, p 242.

14 'News and notes: thirst at Onslow', *The West Australian* (Perth), 29 September 1952, p 2.

15 Capt HJ Buchanan, 'HMAS *Sydney* – report of proceedings – September 1952', AWM: AWM78, 329/6, para 4.

16 James G Dorrian, *Storming St Nazaire: The Dock Busting Raid of 1942*, 3rd ed, Pen & Sword Military, Barnsley, 2012.

17 Cathcart, op. cit., p 241.

18 Lt Cdr WG Wright, 'HMAS *Culgoa* – report of proceedings – September 1952', AWM: AWM78, 95/3, p 1.

19 Cathcart, op. cit., p 244.

20 Cathcart, op. cit., p 245.

21 Torlesse, 'Operation Hurricane – report by the Naval Commander', ch 13, para 11.

22 Cathcart, op. cit., p 247.

23 McEnhill, op. cit., p 64.

24 Ibid.

25 Cathcart, op. cit., p. 248.

26 Ibid.

27 Ronald Stark (dir), *Operation Hurricane*, documentary, Ministry of Supply Film Unit, 1952, IWM: https://www.iwm.org.uk/collections/item/object/1060022141, accessed 8 March 2021.

28 McEnhill, op. cit., p 65.

29 Bird, *Operation Hurricane*, p 76.

30 Stark (dir), op. cit.

31 Ibid.

32 Ibid.

## 11. DOUBLE DAYLIGHT

1 'AWRE – report T1/54 – Operation Hurricane director's report – scientific data obtained at Operation Hurricane', NAA: A6454, Z5A, pp 4–5.

2 McEnhill, 'Story of Operation Hurricane', p 66.

3 HG Carter, Royal Commission statement, NAA: A6449, 1, p 108.

4 'Penney's graphic account of bomb', *The Mirror* (Perth), 8 November 1952, p 12.

5 Bird, *Operation Hurricane*, p 77.

6 'Peter George Fletcher (oral history)'.

7 'Penney's graphic account of bomb'.

8  'Peter George Fletcher (oral history)'. Fletcher later became president of the British Nuclear Test Veterans Association and was awarded an MBE in 1999. He died in 2007 at the age of 75.
9  Cathcart, *Test of Greatness*, p 257.
10  Cathcart, op. cit., p 259.
11  Lt Cdr RJ Scrivenor, 'HMAS *Hawkesbury* – report of proceedings – October 1952', para 4.
12  VJ Douglas, Royal Commission statement, NAA: A6450, 1, p 3.
13  The Royal Commission report states that both ships were in the Lowendals along with MRL 252 at H-Hour (*Vol 1*, pp 123–24), but this does not appear to be accurate. Although neither ship's log is available, other ships' logs reveal that the *Koala* left the Montebellos for North Sandy Island on the afternoon of 2 October and was still there the following afternoon. We also know that MWL 251 was at or near North Sandy Island just after midnight on 3 October and was still there later that day. Meanwhile, MRL 252 was in Onslow two hours after the blast and could not possibly have been in the Lowendals at H-Hour. There are a number of other problems with this part of the Royal Commission report, which also misidentifies HMS *Narvik* as HMS *Alert* (a frigate which did not take part in Hurricane but participated in Operation Mosaic four years later) and places HMAS *Limicola* in Onslow when she had left port three days earlier and was being towed into Carnarvon by HMAS *Mildura*.
14  MC Westwood, Royal Commission statement, NAA: A6450, 5, p 1.
15  R Adm JA Eaton, 'Flag Officer Commanding HMA Fleet – report of proceedings – October 1952', AWM: AWM78, 394/2, p 1, para 4.
16  Lt Cdr AI Chapman, 'HMAS *Macquarie* – report of proceedings – October 1952', AWM: AMW78, 213/2, p 3, sect B, para 2.
17  Tom Godfrey (dir), 'Britain explodes atom-bomb', video, *The Daily Telegraph* (Sydney), 25 April 2017: https://www.dailytelegraph.com.au/news/nsw/grim-legacy-for-aussie-veterans-who-witnessed-british-nuclear-testing/news-story/94733ff2c246f4ef6a63953d5a780416, accessed 25 March 2021.
18  You can see a couple of Mike's photos in Tom Godfrey's video 'Britain explodes atom-bomb'.
19  Kelly Burke, 'Grim legacy for Aussie veterans who witnessed British nuclear testing', *The Daily Telegraph* (Sydney), 25 April 2017: https://www.dailytelegraph.com.au/news/nsw/grim-legacy-for-aussie-veterans-who-witnessed-british-nuclear-testing/news-story/94733ff2c246f4ef6a63953d5a780416, accessed 25 March 2021.
20  Lt Cdr J Ferguson, 'HMAS *Mildura* – report of proceedings – November 1951', AWM: AWM78, 221/1, p 1, para 3; Ferguson, 'HMAS *Mildura* – report of proceedings – March 1952', p 2, para 12. Ferguson gives the game away in March 1952 by saying: 'A naval technical party was despatched to bring forward heavy plant and refrigerating machinery, inhibited by this ship last November.'
21  Torlesse, 'Operation Hurricane – report by the Naval Commander', ch 13, paras 10–11; Eaton, 'Flag Officer Commanding Her Majesty's Australian Fleet – report of proceedings – October 1952', p 1, para 3; Cdr JS Mesley, 'HMAS *Tobruk* – report of proceedings – October 1952', AWM: AWM78, 343/2, p 1, para 5; Lt Cdr CT Thompson, 'HMAS *Murchison* – report of proceedings – October 1952', AWM: AWM78, 228/3, p 1, sect 2.

22 'HMAS *Murchison* – ship's log – October 1952', NAA: A6456, R056/004 PART 10, p 10; Mesley, op. cit., p 1, para 5.

23 Capt SH Beattie, 'HMAS *Shoalhaven* – report of proceedings – October 1952', AWM: AWM78, 131/3, p 1, sect 2.

24 WB Plewright, interview with the author, 15 January 2020.

25 WB Plewright, Royal Commission statement, NAA: A6455, RC482, p 1, para 6.

26 Coulter, *By Deadline to Headline*, p 118.

27 Coulter, op. cit., p 119.

28 Thompson, 'HMAS *Murchison* – report of proceedings – October 1952', p 1, sect 3.

29 Cliff Ross & Gwyn Ross, scrapbook, PDF: https://encore.slwa.wa.gov.au/iii/encore/record/C__Rb3108745, accessed 1 April 2021.

30 Ross & Ross, op. cit.

31 Coulter, op. cit., p 123.

32 Richard Murray, column, *The Sunday Times* (Perth), 5 October 1952, p 31.

33 'Atomic history', editorial, *The West Australian* (Perth), 4 October 1952, p 2.

34 'Blast hailed as a return to power', *Daily News* (Perth), 4 October 1952, p 1.

35 Ibid.

36 'Kitchen of a station is shaken', *The West Australian* (Perth), 4 October 1952, p 7.

37 'Pilot sees atomic cloud for 3½ hr', *Daily News* (Perth), 4 October 1952, p 6.

**12. THE AFTERMATH**

1 Symonds, *A History of British Atomic Tests in Australia*, p 36.

2 Ibid.

3 Symonds, op. cit., p 46.

4 Tynan, *Atomic Thunder*, p 131.

5 'Fliers dangle tin can in deadly atom tub', *Argus* (Melbourne), 17 December 1952, p 1 (reported speech). According to the reporter, Stanley and Lambert took their sample from a 3-foot-square tub on the deck of a landing craft anchored 600 yards from Ground Zero. Neither the Hurricane Trial Orders nor any other documents so far uncovered mention this landing craft, which may have been an invention designed to make the trial sound less dangerous than it really was. According to the measurements of the blast provided in the scientific report, any landing craft in that position would have been blown out of the water.

6 Walkling, 'Operation Hurricane – report of the RH Division – Team RH1 – general direction and the control of re-entry', sect 8.

7 'Operation Hurricane – trial orders – HTO 275 – movements and safety of ships in phase III', appendix C to team RH1 report, NAA: A6455, RC250, para 14.

8 DJ Savage, 'Operation Hurricane – report of the RH Division – Team RH7 – contamination sampling', NAA: A6455, RC250, para 3.4.5.

9 Walkling, 'Operation Hurricane – report of the RH Division – Team RH1 – general direction and the control of re-entry', sect 9.3.3.

10 AD Thomas, Royal Commission testimony, NAA: A6448, 15, p 8693.

11 Thomas, Royal Commission statement, p 5.

12 McEnhill, 'Story of Operation Hurricane', p 69.

13  CA Luxford, 'Operation Hurricane – report of the RH Division – Team RH6 – decontamination', NAA: A6455, RC250, sect 3.10.2.
14  Luxford, 'Operation Hurricane – report of the RH Division – Team RH6 – decontamination', sect 3.10.2.
15  Walkling, 'Operation Hurricane – report of the RH Division – Team RH1 – general direction and the control of re-entry', sect 8.
16  Cathcart, *Test of Greatness*, p 264.
17  Gp Capt GC Hartnell, 'Operation Hurricane – brief report – No 82 (B) Wing RAAF Detachment, Broome', NAA: A6456, R021/001 PART 40, p 5.
18  Hartnell, 'Operation Hurricane – brief report – No 82 (B) Wing RAAF Detachment, Broome', p 5.
19  Hartnell, 'Operation Hurricane – brief report – No 82 (B) Wing RAAF Detachment, Broome', p 5.
20  ED McHardie, Royal Commission statement, NAA: A6450, 3, p 1.
21  McHardie, Royal Commission statement, p 2.
22  R Turner, Royal Commission statement, p 2.
23  WR Bovill, Royal Commission statement NAA: A6450, 1, p 2.
24  Gale, Royal Commission statement, p 6.
25  CI Bird, Royal Commission statement, NAA: A6450, 1, pp 3–4.
26  Hartnell, 'Operation Hurricane – brief report – No 82 (B) Wing RAAF Detachment, Broome', p 6.
27  OL Jones, Royal Commission statement, NAA: A6450, 2, pp 1–2.
28  Symonds, *History of the British Atomic Tests in Australia*, p 113.
29  WA Turner, Royal Commission statement, NAA: A6450, 5, p 2.
30  HWH Puxty, Royal Commission statement, NAA: A6450, 4, p 4, para 20.
31  BD Stein, Royal Commission statement, NAA: A6450, 4, p 3.
32  AVM EA Daley, 'Radiological health during Operation "Hurricane" (Monte Bello Islands Oct/Nov 1952) and Operation "Totem" (Emu Claypan SA Oct/Nov 1953', cover letter, NAA: A6456, R021/001 PART 79.
33  Symonds, op. cit., p 221.
34  Bird, Royal Commission statement, p 5. Bird recalled this happening after Operation Hurricane in 1952, but all the evidence indicates that it did not take place until after Operation Mosaic in 1953.
35  Bird, Royal Commission statement, p 8.
36  'Ex-RAAF man could still win compensation claim: ruling about cancer', *The Canberra Times*, 21 May 1988, p 10.
37  HQ No 3 Aircraft Depot, letter to HQ Maintenance Command RAAF, 29 June 1954, NAA: A6456, R026/001.
38  KAN Freeman, Royal Commission statement, NAA: A6450, 2, pp 3–5.
39  'Air Board Orders A125/1954', attachment 3 to AD Thomas's Royal Commission statement, NAA: A6455, RC553, pp 16–17, appendix D and appendix E.
40  Raph, Royal Commission statement, p 4.
41  Wg Cdr RH Gray, 'Department of Air – Operation Hurricane – [letter from Wing Commander 86 (T) Wing to Headquarters Eastern Area in Penrith explaining the reasons for sending No 86 (T) Wing aircraft to Operation Hurricane]', NAA: A6456, R021/001 PART 42, appendix A, p 3.
42  DH Peirson, Royal Commission statement, NAA: A6449, 2, par 23.
43  Peirson, Royal Commission statement, par 13.

44 DH Peirson, Royal Commission testimony, NAA: A6448, 11, p 5565.
45 RC Grace, letter to Department of Health, 1982, private papers. Writing 30 years later, Grace recalled the altitude as 12,000 feet.
46 Grace, letter to Department of Health, 1982.
47 RC Grace, letter to Department of Veterans' Affairs, 1986, private papers.
48 Grace, letter to Department of Veterans' Affairs, 1986.
49 Peirson, Royal Commission statement, par 21.
50 DH Peirson, 'Report T113/54 – Operation Hurricane group reports (part 52) – results of aerial radiological survey over the Australian coastline between Onslow and Broome', NAA: A6455, RC306, sect 5.
51 Peirson, Royal Commission testimony, p 5580.
52 Peirson, Royal Commission testimony, p 5579. Peirson actually expressed his estimate in roentgen equivalent man (rem), a unit of effective dose that superseded the use of roentgen.
53 It seems that the US Air Force was also secretly involved in the air-sampling programme. On Monday 6 October, a B-29 Superfortress made an emergency landing at Darwin, where it was immediately put under armed guard. An RAAF spokesman claimed that the B-29 had been on 'a routine weather flight' when one of its engines failed near the Coral Sea, but it subsequently emerged that the aircraft had been flying over the Timor Sea – suspiciously close to the Montebello Islands. Two days later, another B-29 landed for refuelling at Whenuapai Airfield in Auckland, New Zealand. This aircraft was notable for two reasons: the giant blonde nude painted on its nose and the filter canisters bolted under its wings and fuselage. According to the crew, the B-29 was on a 'long range training flight'. Both aircraft were based in Guam. In 1953, the Australian Government announced that the US Air Force would participate in Operation Totem in South Australia. Only then did a government spokesperson acknowledge that American aircraft had played a role in Operation Hurricane. See: Norman Milne, 'US aircraft probably learnt some of our Monte Bello atomic secrets', *The Western Mail* (Perth), 9 July 1953, pp 3–6; Geoffrey Johns, 'Is Britain giving away some of her atomic secrets?' *The Western Mail* (Perth), 1 October 1953, p 11.
54 *Report of the Royal Commission into British Nuclear Tests in Australia: Vol 1*, p 117.
55 Peirson, 'Report T113/54', sect 6.
56 Peirson, Royal Commission Testimony, p 5599.
57 Luxford, 'Operation Hurricane – report of the RH Division – Team RH6 – decontamination', sect 3.8.1.
58 T Wilson, Royal Commission statement, NAA: A6455, RC470, pp 3–5.
59 Walkling, op. cit.
60 'Notes of meeting of Dr Solandt, Chairman Canadian Defence Research Board, and Professor Martin, Defence Scientific Adviser, with the Defence Committee on 9th October 1952', NAA: A5954, 7/11, p 2 (reported speech).
61 Cathcart, op. cit., p 270.
62 Tynan, op. cit., p 71.
63 'AWRE – scientific data obtained at Operation Hurricane – top secret section of director's report', NAA: A6456, R018/001, sect 7.8.3.

64 'Notes of meeting of Dr Solandt, Chairman Canadian Defence Research Board, and Professor Martin, Defence Scientific Adviser, with the Defence Committee on 9th October 1952', pp 1–2.

65 McEnhill, op. cit., p 71.

66 'Atom data sealed down until Churchill speaks', *The West Australian* (Perth), 17 October 1952, p 3 (reported speech).

67 'Man who saw atom blast arrives with a spear', *The West Australian* (Perth), 8 October 1952, p 3.

68 '"Beautiful" work says Titterton', *The West Australian* (Perth), 20 October 1952, p 4.

69 'Monte Bello bomb greatest blast yet', *Barrier Miner* (Broken Hill), 24 October 1952, p 1.

70 'Fish, birds found alive in atom blast area', *The Telegraph* (Brisbane), 11 October 1952, p 2.

71 Douglas, Royal Commission statement, p 5.

72 S Fletcher, Royal Commission statement, NAA: A6449, 1, pp 3–4.

73 M Pollard, Royal Commission statement, NAA: A6450, 4, p 2. In his statement, Pollard misidentified the *Tracker* as the *Narvik*.

74 'Ship was 12 miles from atom blast', *The Sydney Morning Herald*, 9 October 1952, p 3.

75 'Substance of communication dated 18th October 1952 from High Commissioner for the United Kingdom, Canberra', NAA: A6456, R021/001 PART 36.

76 'Statement by Mr Churchill in House of Commons of Monte Bello atomic test', 23 October 1952, NAA: A6456, R021/001 PART 36.

77 'Penney's graphic account of bomb'.

78 Walkling, op. cit.

79 RA Kendall, 'Operation Hurricane – report of the RH Division – Team RH Miscellaneous 5 – contamination of ships', NAA: A6455, RC250, paras 2–6.

80 S Swainston, statement to the Royal Commission, NAA: A6449, 2, p 1.

81 Swainston, statement to the Royal Commision, p 2.

82 McEnhill, op. cit., p 72.

83 Luxford, 'Operation Hurricane – report of the RH Division – Team RH6 – decontamination', sect 5.5.

84 GE Mabbutt, Royal Commission statement, NAA: A6449, 2 pp 4–5.

85 S Taudevin, Royal Commission statement, NAA: A6450, 5, p 2.

86 WE Smith, Royal Commission statement, NAA: 6455, RC486 pp 2–3. Smith believed that the mooring gear in question was the stockpile of spare mooring cable, but Brennan and others believed it was a small boat mooring. In all likelihood it was a contaminated six-boat trot mooring, which, according to the *Karangi*'s November 1953 report of proceedings, was swamped by the *Koala* in 1952 'owing to contamination' and subsequently recovered by the *Karangi* (AWM: AWM78, 183/3).

87 *Report of the Royal Commission into British Nuclear Tests in Australia: Vol 1*, pp 126–27. There is considerable controversy over the ultimate fate of the landing craft. According to various accounts given by witnesses during the Royal Commission, the LCA was either: taken on board by the *Tracker*; dumped by the *Koala*; or carried back to Fremantle on the forecastle of the *Koala*. All official reports and ships' logs with any relevance are either missing

or suspiciously vague. McEnhill mentions that the landing craft was raised but says nothing more of the matter, implying that it was successfully salvaged (NAA: A6455, RC603, p 72), while the reports of Team RH1 (Health Control) and Team RH6 (Decontamination) ignore the event entirely (NAA: A6455, RC250). The *Tracker*'s log is slightly more helpful, revealing that the *Koala* secured alongside late on 30 October and slipped early in the hours of 31 October, only to return several hours later for the decontamination of the crew (NAA: A13069, SL 70). It does not mention that the landing craft was brought on board. On the balance of evidence, it seems likely that the *Koala* dumped the LCA in the intervening period; it is also possible that the *Tracker* dumped it in deep water, along with 40 drums of radioactive waste, when she left the islands later that day. Although multiple members of the *Koala*'s company insisted that the boom defence vessel carried the LCA back to Fremantle, it seems unlikely that Thomas, who was in charge of decontaminating the ship, would have missed a radioactive landing craft sitting on the forecastle. Perhaps the men were thinking of another landing craft, such as the dreaded ALC 40.

88  Smith, statement to the Royal Commission, p 3.
89  Thomas, Royal Commission statement, p 9.
90  LR Brennan, Royal Commission statement, NAA: A6455, RC692, p 2.
91  Thomas, Royal Commission statement, p 10.
92  Lt Cdr AR Taudevin, 'HMAS *Karangi* – report of proceedings – November 1953', AWM: AWM78, 183/3, p 3, para 16.
93  Taudevin, op. cit., p 4, para 28.
94  Taudevin, op. cit., pp 2–3, para 13.
95  '(2185) Alexander, Donald (Lieutenant Commander)', audio recording, AWM: https://www.awm.gov.au/collection/C1220899, accessed 3 December 2021. The 'Royal Navy lieutenant commander' was almost certainly British-born RAN officer Lieutenant AA Andrews, Head of the Atomic Biological and Chemical Defence School at HMAS *Penguin* in Sydney, who joined the *Karangi* to oversee the survey.
96  S Taudevin, Royal Commission statement, p 2.

## 13. STANDARD OPERATING PROCEDURE

1  The JSTU was also referred to as the Tri-Services Training Unit and the Inter-Service Training Unit.
2  AA Andrews, Royal Commission testimony, NAA: A6448, 4, p 1332.
3  During the Royal Commission, EK Peck, ex-RAAF, testified that the JSTU did not receive any training on board the *Hawkesbury* because the ship was 'hit by a cyclone' (NAA: A6450, 4, p 15). On the other hand, GI Jenkinson, ex-RAE, testified that the lectures took place as planned, but suggested that the airmen may have missed them as they were frequently confined to their quarters with seasickness (NAA: A6448, 15, p 8555).
4  JSTU training report, attachment A to GI Jenkinson's Royal Commission statement, NAA: A6455, RC548, p 1.
5  JSTU training report, p 2.
6  Keith Peck, who was born on 30 September 1922, had a confusing habit of lying about his age. According to his daughter, Sheryl Sutherland, Peck attempted to enlist in the 15th Light Horse Regiment in Grafton at the age of 16, telling the Army that he was 17, but was knocked back when the Army

found out he was lying. In 1942, he enlisted in the AIF, and for some reason
his service records still list his birthdate as 1921 (his first name, Edisley,
is also misspelt as Edsley). Many years later, in 1984, Peck told the Royal
Commission that he was actually born in 1927. The reason for that is equally
colourful. According to Sheryl: 'He met a younger woman in the early 70's, so
told her he was 5 years younger than he was! I think she eventually found out!'
What a character!

7 EK Peck, Royal Commission statement, NAA: A6450, 4, p 2, para 8.
8 GI Jenkinson, Royal Commission testimony, NAA: A6448, 15, p 8531.
9 Jenkinson, Royal Commission testimony, p 8555.
10 Andrews, Royal Commission testimony, p 1321a.
11 Peck, Royal Commission statement, p 8, para 28.
12 Peck, Royal Commission statement, p 3, para 11.
13 Jenkinson, Royal Commission statement, p 2, para 7.
14 Andrews, Royal Commission testimony, p 1338.
15 MD Jellie, Royal Commission statement, NAA: A6450, 2, p 2.
16 Peck, Royal Commission statement, p 7, para 24.
17 Andrews, Royal Commission testimony, p 1322.
18 Jenkinson, Royal Commission testimony, p 8551.
19 Jellie, Royal Commission statement, p 3.
20 Jenkinson, Royal Commission testimony, p 8531.
21 JSTU training report, p 2.
22 Sqn Ldr AD Thomas, letter to Air Cdre Hely, 14 November 1952, NAA:
A6455, RC553.
23 During the Royal Commission, AA Andrews testified that Keith Peck was
sent home early for disciplinary reasons, but LD Monaghan, who reported
the incident in question, was positive that it was Nicholls who was sent home.
Squadron Leader Thomas's letter to Air Commodore Hely supports Monaghan's
recollection. Andrews, it appears, just got the two airmen mixed up.
24 'O24212 Flt Lt EK Peck – service particulars supplied by Department of
Defence', attachment to Peck statement, p 29.
25 Sqn Ldr AD Thomas, 'Radiological health during Operation "Hurricane"
(Monte Bello Islands Oct/Nov 1952) and Operation "Totem" (Emu Claypan
SA Oct/Nov 1953', report, NAA: A6456, R021/001 PART 79.
26 South East Island health control centre, signal to HMAS Hawkesbury, 28
November 1952, attachment C to Jenkinson statement.
27 EK Peck, Royal Commission testimony, NAA: A6448, 3, pp 855–57.
28 Lt Cdr RJ Scrivenor, 'HMAS Hawkesbury – report of proceedings –
November 1952', AWM: AWM78, 137/3, p 2, para 6.
29 Attachments D and I to Jenkinson statement.
30 Jenkinson, Royal Commission testimony, p 8547.
31 Ian Frazer, 'Top Queenslander plants trees, celebrates diggers' victories',
Townsville Bulletin, 21 May 2015: https://www.townsvillebulletin.com.au/
lifestyle/history/top-queenslander-plants-trees-celebrates-diggers-victories/
news-story/1075afae2d3548d78807545a0b700405, accessed 29 September
2021.
32 Douglas, Royal Commission statement, p 6.
33 Cmdre R Rhoades, 'Alleged exposure to radioactive material from Jeep used at
Monte Bello', 8 August 1960, NAA: A6456, R098/021.

34 Douglas, Royal Commission statement, p 5.
35 GW Smith, Royal Commission statement, NAA: A6455, RC490, p 1, para 6.
36 GW Smith, Royal Commission statement, p 2, paras 8–9.
37 Capt WN Saxby, quoted in A/Capt FB Morris, letter to Secretary, Naval Board, 9 October 1953, NAA: A6456, R174/022.
38 Cdre R Rhoades, letter to Medical Superintendent, Repatriation General Hospital, Hollywood, NAA: A6456, R098/021.
39 N Cunningham, unpublished AExSASA manuscript.
40 A/Capt FB Morris, letter to Secretary, Naval Board, 18 December 1953, NAA: A6456, R174/022.
41 A/Capt FB Morris, letter to Secretary, Naval Board, 3 June 1954, NAA: A6456, R174/022.
42 Steve Grant, 'Radioactive Leeuwin Land Rover "a pub tale": claim', *Fremantle Herald*, 27 November 2015: https://heraldonlinejournal.com/2015/11/27/radioactive-leeuwin-land-rover-a-pub-tale-claim/, accessed 8 December 2021.
43 'Factsheet: sale of Leeuwin Barracks, Western Australia', PDF, Australian Government, Department of Defence: https://www.defence.gov.au/about/locations-property/property-disposals, accessed 28 March 2023.
44 BACTEC, 'WAU10010 Subsurface Investigation – Leeuwin Barracks, Fremantle, Western Australia', report to Directorate of Environmental Remediation Programs Infrastructure Division, Defence Support & Reform Group, 2015, p 3.
45 GHD, '0703 Leeuwin Barracks Detailed Site Investigation', report to Department of Defence, 2018, p 28.
46 Douglas, Royal Commission statement, p 6.
47 VJ Douglas, RAN service records, NAA: A6770, DOUGLAS V J.

**EPILOGUE**

1 AS Brown, Secretary, Australian Prime Minister's Department, letter to B Cockram, Deputy UK High Commissioner, 3 September 1953, NAA: A6456, R124/019; A/Capt FB Morris, letter to General Officer Commanding, Western Command, 21 May 1953, NAA: K1214, 14/2/04.
2 'AWRE – scientific data obtained at Operation Hurricane – top secret section of director's report', sect 7.8.5; Arnold & Smith, *Britain, Australia and the Bomb*, p 109.
3 *Report of the Royal Commission into British Nuclear Tests in Australia: Vol 1*, p 140.
4 Symonds, *A History of British Atomic Tests in Australia*, p 251.
5 Tynan, *Atomic Thunder*, p 101.
6 Arnold & Smith, *Britain, Australia and the Bomb*, pp 109–10.
7 Arnold & Smith, op. cit., pp 114–15.
8 Arnold & Smith, op. cit., p 119.
9 Cdre HC Martell, 'Operation Mosaic – Monte Bello atomic tests – 1956 – report by the Operational Commander', NAA: A6455, RC233, p 97.
10 *Report of the Royal Commission into British Nuclear Tests in Australia: Vol 1*, pp 247–48.
11 R Potter, AC Purdie, 'AWRE – report T23/57 – Operation Mosaic – air blast measurements', NAA: A6455, RC241.

12 Lord Penney, Royal Commission testimony, NAA: A6448, 9, p 4302.
13 Penney, Royal Commission testimony, p 4304.
14 Zeb Leonard, 'Tampering with history: varied understanding of Operation Mosaic', *Journal of Australian Studies*, vol 38, no 2, 2014, pp 205–19; Dieter Michel, 'Villains, victims and heroes: contested memory and the British nuclear tests in Australia,' *Journal of Australian Studies*, vol 27, no 80, 2003, 221–28.
15 'Atom cloud may have gone inland', *The West Australian* (Perth), 21 June 1956 (early edition), p 1.
16 Walker, *Maralinga*, p 101.
17 Arnold & Smith, op. cit., p 128.
18 'Fadden says bomb cloud drifted to sea', *The West Australian* (Perth), 26 June 1956, p 2 (reported speech).
19 *Report of the Royal Commission into British Nuclear Tests in Australia: Vol 2*, p 560.
20 JR Quantrill, interview with the author, 27 January 2021.
21 *Report of the Royal Commission into British Nuclear Tests in Australia: Vol 2*, p 592.
22 Nic Maclellan, *Grappling with the Bomb: Britain's Pacific H-bomb Tests*, ANU Press, Acton, 2017, p 1.
23 Sue Rabbitt Roff, 'How Menzies begged Macmillan for the bomb', Meanjin blog, 2 December 2019: https://meanjin.com.au/blog/how-menzies-begged-macmillan-for-the-bomb/, accessed 2 August 2022.
24 Y Lester, Royal Commission statement, NAA: A6455, AB11, pp 5–6.
25 L Lennon, Royal Commission statement, NAA: A6455, AB12, p 5.
26 Lennon, Royal Commission statement, p 6.
27 A Lander, Royal Commission statement, NAA: A6455, AB10, pp 3–4.
28 *Report of the Royal Commission into British Nuclear Tests in Australia: Vol 2*, p 596.
29 *Report of the Royal Commission into British Nuclear Tests in Australia: Vol 1*, pp 181–82.
30 *Report of the Royal Commission into British Nuclear Tests in Australia: Vol 1*, p 321.
31 *Report of the Royal Commission into British Nuclear Tests in Australia: Vol 1*, p 321.
32 ER Drake Seager, Royal Commission statement, NAA: A6449, 1, p 4, para 11.
33 Drake Seager, Royal Commission statement, p 6, para 17.
34 *Report of the Royal Commission into British Nuclear Tests in Australia: Conclusions and Recommendations*, Australian Government Printing Service, Canberra, 1985, p 15.
35 *Report of the Royal Commission into British Nuclear Tests in Australia: Conclusions and Recommendations*, p 16.
36 Tynan, *Atomic Thunder*, p 301.
37 Tynan, op. cit., p 301.
38 Walker, *Maralinga*, p 257.
39 Cathcart, *Test of Greatness*, p 231.
40 https://www.gov.uk/government/publications/nuclear-weapons-test-participants-study/nuclear-weapons-test-participants-study-information-sheet, accessed 24 August 2022.

41  Richard Gun et al, *Australian participants in British nuclear tests in Australia Volume 2: Mortality and cancer incidence*, Department of Veterans' Affairs, Commonwealth of Australia, 2006, p vi.
42  Susie Boniface, 'The damned: chapter 6; the nightmare', *The Daily Mirror* (London), 15 November 2018: https://damned.mirror.co.uk/chapter6.html, accessed 19 August 2022.
43  Joe Buchanunn, 'Study finds no evidence of genetic legacy in children of UK's nuclear test veterans', Brunel University London, 5 July 2022: https://www.brunel.ac.uk/news-and-events/news/articles/Study-finds-no-evidence-of-genetic-legacy-in-children-of-Uks-nuclear-test-veterans, accessed 13 January 2023; Joe Buchanunn, '"Exposure worry" study reveals nature of psychological impact on British nuclear test veterans', Brunel University London, 24 November 2021: https://www.brunel.ac.uk/news-and-events/news/articles/Exposure-worry-study-reveals-nature-of-psychological-impact-on-British-nuclear-test-veterans, accessed 13 January 2023.
44  AJ Marlow, unpublished AExSASA manuscript.
45  David Weber & Emily Piesse, 'Budget 2017: Veterans exposed to nuclear bomb tests welcome Government decision to grant Gold Card access', ABC News, 7 May 2017: https://www.abc.net.au/news/story-streams/federal-budget-2017/2017-05-07/federal-budget-2017-veterans-welcome-gold-card-decision/8504884, accessed 30 August 2022.
46  Susie Boniface, 'Exclusive: Nuclear veterans finally win a medal, and tell Rishi Sunak: "We need more"', *The Daily Mirror* (London), 21 November 2022: https://www.mirror.co.uk/news/politics/nuclear-veterans-finally-win-medal-28550571, accessed 19 December 2022.

# SELECT BIBLIOGRAPHY

A note on sources: most of my primary sources come from the National Archives of Australia (NAA), the Australian War Memorial (AWM) and the National Library of Australia's (NLA) Trove database. Other records were sourced from the UK National Archives (TNA), the UK Imperial War Museums (IWM), the State Records Office of Western Australia (SROWA) and several other smaller archives. The Australian Ex Services Atomic Survivors Association (AExSASA) also provided access to an unpublished manuscript containing the recollections of the association's members.

Three particularly valuable NAA series stem from the 1984–85 Royal Commission into British Nuclear Tests in Australia: series A6448, 'Transcripts of proceedings' (i.e. verbal testimony delivered during the Royal Commission); series A6449, 'Statements received from United Kingdom witnesses' (i.e. written statements made in the UK); and series A6450, 'Statements received from Australian witnesses' (i.e. written statements made in Australia). Numerous individual statements missing from these collections can be found in series A6455, 'Exhibits tendered before the Commission'. All relevant files are listed below.

NATIONAL ARCHIVES OF AUSTRALIA

Exhibits tendered before the Royal Commission into British nuclear tests in Australia during the 1950s and 1960s – alpha-numeric series, NAA: A6455

Original agency records transferred to the Royal Commission into British nuclear tests in Australia during the 1950s and 1960s – 'R' series, NAA: A6456

Royal Commission into British nuclear tests in Australia during the 1950s and 1960s – statements received from Australian witnesses, NAA: A6450

Royal Commission into British nuclear tests in Australia during the 1950s and 1960s – statements received from United Kingdom witnesses, NAA: A6449

Royal Commission into British nuclear tests in Australia during the 1950s and 1960s – transcripts of proceedings, NAA: A6448

'Z series' – [British] Atomic Weapons Research Establishment reports
– single number series with Z or ZB prefix, NAA: A6454

AUSTRALIAN WAR MEMORIAL

Air Commodore Percival (Nobby) Lings interviewed by Ken Llewellyn
about his career in the Royal Australian Air Force (RAAF), audio
recording, AWM: https://www.awm.gov.au/collection/C282960,
accessed 5 May 2020

Alexander, Donald (Lieutenant Commander), audio recording,
AWM: https://www.awm.gov.au/collection/C1220899, accessed
3 December 2021

Reports of proceedings – HMA ships and establishments, AWM:
AWM78

OTHER PRIMARY SOURCES

Admiralty, *Manual of Seamanship: Volume III; BR 67 (3/51)*, Her
Majesty's Stationery Office, London, 1954

'Australia Station Intelligence Summary no 6', PDF, Naval Intelligence
Division, Navy Office, Melbourne, September 1952: https://
www.Navy.gov.au/media-room/publications/australia-station-
intelligence-summaries-1952-1957, accessed 30 January 2019

Australian Ex Services Atomic Survivors Association, unpublished
AExSASA manuscript

BACTEC, 'WAU10010 Subsurface Investigation – Leeuwin
Barracks, Fremantle, Western Australia', report to Directorate of
Environmental Remediation Programs Infrastructure Division,
Defence Support & Reform Group, 2015

Bird, Peter, *Operation Hurricane*, 2nd ed, Square One, Worcester, 1989

Carter, Michael, et al, *Australian participants in British nuclear
tests in Australia, Volume 1: Dosimetry*, Department of Veterans'
Affairs, Canberra, 2006

Coulter, Jack, *By Deadline to Headline*, Access Press, Northbridge,
1997

'Factsheet: sale of Leeuwin Barracks, Western Australia', PDF,
Australian Government, Department of Defence: https://www.
defence.gov.au/about/locations-property/property-disposals,
accessed 28 March 2023

Flack, Henry J, death certificate, (Marine) Ashburton District, 1/1953,
WA Department of Justice, Births Deaths and Marriages

GHD, '0703 Leeuwin Barracks Detailed Site Investigation', report to
  Department of Defence, 2018

Grace, RC, flight logs, 1942–1953, personal papers

Grace, RC, letter to Department of Health, 1982, personal papers

Grace, RC, letter to Department of Veterans' Affairs, 1986, personal
  papers

Gun, Richard, et al, *Australian participants in British nuclear tests in
  Australia, Volume 2: mortality and cancer incidence*, Department
  of Veterans' Affairs, Commonwealth of Australia, 2006

Hamilton, Ian, 'Cocos Drowning', RAAF Airfield Construction
  Squadrons Association homepage: http://raafacs.homestead.com/
  COCOSDROWNING.html, accessed 15 October 2018

Hill, Frank L, 'Notes on the natural history of the Monte Bello
  Islands', *Proceedings of the Linnean Society of London*, vol 165,
  no 2, June 1955, pp 113–24

Hordern, Marsden, *A Merciful Journey: Recollections of a World War
  II Patrol Boat Man*, The Miegunyah Press, Carlton, 2005

Malik, John S, 'The yields of the Hiroshima and Nagasaki nuclear
  explosions', PDF, Los Alamos National Laboratory, Report No LA-
  08819, September 1985: https://lanl-primo.hosted.exlibrisgroup.
  com/permalink/f/17admmo/01LANL_ALMA2186922310003761,
  accessed 14 March 2023

'Memorandum on the atomic bomb by the Prime Minister', 28 August
  1945, TNA: CAB 130/3

'Operation Epicure – report on reconnaissance of Monte Bello
  Islands', TNA: DEFE 16/412

Peter George Fletcher (oral history), audio recording, IWM: https://
  www.iwm.org.uk/collections/item/object/80010940, accessed
  27 June 2019

*Report of the Royal Commission into British Nuclear Tests in
  Australia: Conclusions and Recommendations*, Australian
  Government Printing Service, Canberra, 1985

*Report of the Royal Commission into British Nuclear Tests in
  Australia: Volume 1*, Australian Government Printing Service,
  Canberra, 1985

*Report of the Royal Commission into British Nuclear Tests in
  Australia: Volume 2*, Australian Government Printing Service,
  Canberra, 1985

Stanbury, Myra, 'A survey of sites associated with early pearling activities in the Monte Bello Islands, Western Australia (draft)', PDF, Department of Maritime Archaeology WA, report no 35, January 1986: http://museum.wa.gov.au/maritime-archaeology-db/maritime-reports/survey-sites-associated-early-pearling-activities-monte-bello-islands-western-austr, accessed Tuesday 7 April 2020

'SS *Dorrigo* – masters reports and voyage instructions – 1/1/50 – 31/12/53', SROWA: AU WA S1721 – cons5253 396 [v2], p 2

Stokes, J Lort, *Discoveries in Australia: Volume II*, T&W Boone, London, 1846

Veth, Peter, 'The Aboriginal occupation of the Montebello Islands, Northwest Australia', *Australian Aboriginal Studies*, no 2, 1993, pp 39–50

Veth, Peter, et al, 'Early human occupation of a maritime desert, Barrow Island, North-West Australia', *Quaternary Science Reviews*, vol 168, 15 July 2017, pp 19–29

AUTHOR INTERVIEWS
Brent, Lyn, 10 October 2019
Cunningham, Norm, 28 September 2022
Emmott, Brian, 23 August 2019
Flowers, Denis, 3 September 2018
Heavens, Eric, 2 July 2020
Goodwin, Maxine, 14 December 2019
Marlow, Jim, 3 September 2018, 11 July 2019
Plewright, Bill, 15 January 2020
Quantrill, John, 27 January 2021
Ward, Milton, 3 February 2023

NEWSPAPERS
*The Advertiser* (Adelaide)
*The Age* (Melbourne)
*Argus* (Melbourne)
*Barrier Miner* (Broken Hill)
*The Canberra Times*
*The Courier-Mail* (Brisbane)
*The Daily Mirror* (London)
*Daily News* (Perth)
*The Daily Telegraph* (Sydney)

*The Examiner* (Launceston)
*Fremantle Herald*
*Lithgow Mercury*
*Maryborough Chronicle*
*The Mercury* (Hobart)
*The Mirror* (Perth)
*The Starfish*
*The Sunday Herald* (Sydney)
*The Sunday Times* (Perth)
*The Sydney Morning Herald*
*The Telegraph* (Brisbane)
*The Times* (London)
*Townsville Bulletin*
*The West Australian* (Perth)
*The Western Mail* (Perth)

## SECONDARY SOURCES

Arnold, Lorna & Smith, Mark, *Britain, Australia and the Bomb: The Nuclear Tests and Their Aftermath*, 2nd ed, Palgrave Macmillan, London, 2006

Bramston, Troy, *Robert Menzies: The Art of Politics*, Scribe, Melbourne, 2019

Bright, Richie, 'A most unusual post office', in Ricardo Crameri (ed), *Dot Dash to Dot Com – A North-West Odyssey*, RPL Crameri, North Perth, 2002, p 146

Buchanunn, Joe, ' "Exposure worry" study reveals nature of psychological impact on British nuclear test veterans', Brunel University London, 24 November 2021: https://www.brunel.ac.uk/news-and-events/news/articles/Exposure-worry-study-reveals-nature-of-psychological-impact-on-British-nuclear-test-veterans, accessed 13 January 2023

Buchanunn, Joe, 'Study finds no evidence of genetic legacy in children of UK's nuclear test veterans', Brunel University London, 5 July 2022: https://www.brunel.ac.uk/news-and-events/news/articles/Study-finds-no-evidence-of-genetic-legacy-in-children-of-Uks-nuclear-test-veterans, accessed 13 January 2023

Cameron, Debbie, 'A Pearl fisher from Cheetham Hill – the Big Friday Find', Archives Plus, 21 February 2014: https://

manchesterarchiveplus.wordpress.com/2014/02/21/a-pearl-fisher-from-cheetham-hill-the-big-friday-find/, accessed 22 April 2020

Cathcart, Brian, *Test of Greatness: Britain's Struggle for the Atomic Bomb*, John Murray, London, 1994

Dorrian, James G, *Storming St Nazaire: The Dock Busting Raid of 1942*, 3rd ed, Pen & Sword Military, Barnsley, 2012

Drewe, Robert, *Montebello: A Memoir*, Hamish Hamilton, Melbourne, 2012

Godfrey, Tom (dir), 'Britain explodes atom-bomb', video, *The Daily Telegraph* (Sydney), 25 April 2017: https://www.dailytelegraph.com.au/news/nsw/grim-legacy-for-aussie-veterans-who-witnessed-british-nuclear-testing/news-story/94733ff2c246f4ef6a63953d5a780416, accessed 25 March 2021

Gowing, Margaret & Arnold, Lorna, *Independence and Deterrence: Britain and Atomic Energy 1945–1952; Volume 1; Policy Making*, Macmillan, London, 1974

Gowing, Margaret & Arnold, Lorna, *Independence and Deterrence: Britain and Atomic Energy 1945–1952; Volume 2; Policy Execution*, Macmillan, London, 1974

Greville, PJ, *The Royal Australian Engineers, 1945 to 1972: Paving the Way*, Corps Committee of the Royal Australian Engineers, Moorebank, 2002

Horner, David, *The Spy Catchers: The Official History of ASIO; 1949–1963; Volume 1*, Allen & Unwin, Crows Nest, 2014

Leonard, Zeb, 'Tampering with history: varied understanding of Operation Mosaic', *Journal of Australian Studies*, vol 38, no 2, 2014, pp 205–19

Maclellan, Nic, *Grappling with the Bomb: Britain's Pacific H-bomb Tests*, ANU Press, Acton, 2017

Martin, AW, *Robert Menzies: A Life; Volume 2; 1944–1978*, Melbourne University Press, Carlton South, 1999

Michel, Dieter, 'Villains, victim and heroes: contested memory and the British nuclear tests in Australia,' *Journal of Australian Studies*, vol 27, no 80, 2003, 221–28

Morton, Peter, *Fire Across the Desert: Woomera and the Anglo-Australian Joint Project, 1946–1980*, Defence Science and Technology, Canberra, 1989

Roff, Sue Rabbitt, 'How Menzies begged Macmillan for the bomb', Meanjin blog, 2 December 2019: https://meanjin.com.au/blog/how-menzies-begged-macmillan-for-the-bomb/, accessed 2 August 2022

Ross, Cliff & Ross, Gwyn, scrapbook, PDF: https://encore.slwa.wa.gov.au/iii/encore/record/C__Rb3108745, accessed 1 April 2021

Stephens, Alan, *Going Solo: The Royal Australian Air Force, 1946–1971*, Australian Government Publishing Service, Canberra, 1995

Stark, Ronald (dir), *Operation Hurricane*, documentary, Ministry of Supply Film Unit, 1952, IWM: https://www.iwm.org.uk/collections/item/object/1060022141, accessed 8 March 2021

Symonds, JL, *A History of British Atomic Tests in Australia*, Australian Government Printing Service, Canberra, 1985

Tynan, Elizabeth, *Atomic Thunder: The Maralinga Story*, NewSouth, Sydney, 2016

Walker, Frank, *Maralinga: the chilling exposé of our secret nuclear shame and betrayal of our troops and country*, 2nd ed, Hachette Australia, Sydney, 2016

Wilson, David, *Always First: The RAAF Airfield Construction Squadrons 1942–1974*, Air Power Studies Centre, Fairbairn, 1998

Winterton, George, 'The significance of the Communist Party case', *Melbourne University Law Review*, vol 18, 1992, p 640

# INDEX

Pearce, Noah 48
Peck, Flying Officer Keith 263, 265, 267, 270–1
Peierls, Rudolf 2, 170
Peirson, Doug 151, 152, 236–40, 297
Penney, Adele 10
Penney, William
  after test 212, 219, 222, 237, 242–8
  background 9–17, 41, 56, 63
  Operation Hurricane 99, 113, 116, 117, 167–77, 190, 195–6
  Operation Mosaic 286–9, 301
  Royal Commission 297
Peters, Leading Seaman TK 265
Phillipps, Lieutenant Colonel Max 32, 38, 81, 95, 98
Phillpot, Henry 175
Pioch, Lieutenant Ray 92, 146
pipeline for water 102–7
plague of flies 140–1
Plewright, Able Seaman Bill 201–2, 311, 312
Pollard, Maurice 246
Pom Pom incident 299–300
press coverage
  Australian 64, 74, 79–83, 93–9, 125, 157–64, 204–8, 290, 296
  British 98–102, 157, 208–9
  D-Day 204–10
  D-Notices 157–8
  Operation Hurricane 79–83, 93–102, 127, 157–64, 204–10, 244, 248
  Operation Mosaic 290
  reporters going to Montebellos 93–9, 157
Pridgeon, Percy 125, 142
protective clothing 215, 220, 227, 232, 234, 241, 264, 267
Pugh, Surgeon Lieutenant PG 'Doc' 145

Q
Quantrill, Major John 292, 312
Quebec Agreement 3, 6, 8, 12
Queen Elizabeth II 63, 76, 245, 295, 310
Quennell, Joan 10

R
RAAF Amberley 152, 232, 233, 276
RAAF Pearce 54, 149, 268
radiation 62–5, 85–6, 119–21, 128–9, 194, 211–80
  Aboriginal people, risk to 65, 100, 101, 171, 281, 296
  AERE guidelines 85–6
  air-sampling programme 84–6, 128, 153, 156, 224–6
  contamination 213–59
  dose levels 212–17, 229–31, 241, 249, 268, 271
  effects 194, 200–2
  fallout on mainland 236–40, 281, 288
  falsification of records 200
  follow-up survey 252, 257–9, 281–2
  isodose maps 216, 265, 266, 269

JSTU training in theory 261–4
  measurement 137–8, 156–7, 212
  protection against 215, 220, 227, 232, 234, 241, 264, 267
  re-entry sorties 211–35, 240–8
  servicemen exposed to 213–80, 292, 296, 300–2, 305–11
  sickness from 200, 213, 232, 238, 250, 253, 270, 280, 285, 296
radioactive Land Rover 274–8
radioactive waste 234–5, 253, 284, 296
radioactive water collection 144
Radioactivity Measurement Division 137
Radiochemical Division 141, 144, 154
Radiological Hazard Division 106, 137, 141, 172, 216, 218, 241, 274
Radiological Survey Division 151–2, 155, 236
Raph, Corporal Rex 106, 235
Red Beard 283, 284
re-entry sorties 211–35, 240–8
rehabilitation of test sites 303–4
  UK Government contribution to cost 304
road and landing construction 65–72, 89, 132
Rodgers, JE 206
Rodgers, Myrtle 206
Rodgers, Ted 161, 204, 205
Rodoreda, Loy 72
Rooney, Bill 163
Roosevelt, Franklin D 2, 3, 7
Ross, Cliff 163, 207
Ross, Gwyn 207
Rowan, Leading Aircraftman Michael xv, xviii
Rowe, Mike 199–200
Rowlands, Wing Commander John 117, 165, 166, 187
Royal Air Force (RAF) 85, 117
  No 10 Squadron vii
  No 49 Squadron 283
  No 617 Squadron 205
Royal Australian Air Force (RAAF) 84, 95, 99, 128–9, 132, 149–51
  contaminated aircraft 223–35, 238
  monitoring and air sampling 84–6, 128–9, 153, 156, 224–6
  No 1 (Bomber) Squadron 18
  No 2 Airfield Construction Squadron (2ACS) xii, 77
  No 3 Aircraft Depot (3AD) Decontamination Centre 233
  No 5 Airfield Construction Squadron (5ACS) 51, 65–72, 88, 89, 105, 132
  No 10 (General Reconnaissance) Squadron 129, 239
  No 11 (General Reconnaissance) Squadron 129
  No 38 (Transport) Squadron 18
  No 71 (General Reconnaissance/Bomber) Wing 84
  No 77 (Fighter) Squadron 19
  No 82 (Bomber) Wing 129, 153, 156, 175, 223, 224, 228, 231